JOURNEY
North Coast
500
Mike MacEacheran & Neil Wilson

JOHN O'GROATS
P95
P99
THURSO
P86
WICK
P82
HELMSDALE
BRIDGE
ORTHERN SCOTLAND

PASSING
PLACE

P130
DURNESS
P115
TONGUE
PASSING PLACE
APOOL
P68
DORNOCH
P48
CROMARTY
P49
DINGWALL
START
THE SINGLETON
P32
INVERNESS
END

The road awaits. Five hundred miles of rugged coastline, pristine beaches, majestic mountains and storied castles, the North Coast 500 is an adventure like no other. Whether you commit to the whole route or sample just a section, it promises a breathtaking odyssey through the untamed beauty of Scotland's northern Highlands. From the rollercoaster ride down the Berriedale Braes to the white-knuckle hairpins of the Bealach na Ba, let the road inspire you, and the journey linger long in your memory.

P155
LOCHINVER
P174
P191
POOLEWE
P192
GAIRLOCH
P208
SHIELDAIG
P224
ACHNASHEEN
P220
APPLECROSS
P223
LOCHCARRON

Contents

Plan Your Trip

Go to p30 for the full route map

The Drive

TOMMY LEE WALKER/SHUTTERSTOCK

Stoer Head Lighthouse (p154)

Toolkit

INSIGHT ESSAYS

TITLE PAGE: TOMMY LEE WALKER/SHUTTERSTOCK

My North Coast 500

Mike MacEacheran @mike.maceacheran

I've been discovering new adventures on what is now called the North Coast 500 for four decades. One of my first memories is hiking the steep shoulders of Ben Hope with my dad, aged 12, and being overwhelmed by the scale of the spectacle from the summit; having grown up near Glasgow, it felt like a very different version of the Scotland I was used to. Tongue's hills, Durness' beaches and the Flow Country are eternal highlights – there is always new joy to be found in a region that for many Scots is a blank space at the top of the map.

Mike is an award-winning writer based in Edinburgh. He is a destination expert on Scotland for National Geographic, The Times, The Guardian *and the BBC, and has worked on dozens of guidebooks, including several editions of Lonely Planet* Scotland. *He covered the eastern half of the NC500.*

Duncansby Stacks (p94)

THE WORLD TRAVELLER/SHUTTERSTOCK

MY BEST VIEWS

Duncansby Stacks
Swiftly ignored when rushing by on the road, but impossible to ignore from the vertiginous clifftop overlooking the raging North Sea. p94

RSPB Forsinard Flows
Looming above black ponds and moss-ringed peatlands, the Flows Lookout Tower offers a snapshot of unrivalled wilderness. p110

Kyle of Tongue
Mountains, moorland, a moshing sea and a moody castle. p115

REMIZOV/SHUTTERSTOCK

Suilven (p164)

Neil Wilson @neil3965.bsky.social

I first toured the north of Scotland in my teens, decades before the North Coast 500 was a thing. A passion for mountaineering drew me to the hills of Torridon and Applecross, and field trips as a geology student introduced me to Assynt. I've been back countless times to explore the crags of Wester Ross, roam Coigach's summits and fly fish for trout in Sutherland's lonely hill lochs. Following the route of the NC500 ties all these memories together and whets the appetite for more adventures.

Neil is a freelance writer based in Perthshire. He has worked on more than 100 guidebooks over more than 35 years, including 12 editions of Lonely Planet Scotland. *He covered the western half of the NC500.*

MY BEST HILLS

Suilven

OK, it's everyone's favourite, but with good reason – shapely, impressive and hard to get to, but well worth the effort. p164

Stac Pollaidh

Small but perfectly formed, this peak looks impressive from every direction, but is an easy half-day hike. p168

An Teallach

The colossus of Wester Ross is everything a mountain should be – beautiful, challenging and atmospheric. p184

Dave Broom
@davewasabi

I have been writing about whisky for 40 years. This is a route I have travelled for much of my life, from early days of hiking, climbing and sailing in the west coast and then, through work, exploring the whiskies of the east coast as well as landscape, myth, history, music, language, writing and drams. All of Scotland is here. My tips: read Neil M Gunn; drink in the Dornoch Castle Hotel.

Dave wrote the 'Whisky's Forgotten Coast' essay (p72).

Laurie Goodlad
@shetlandwithlaurie

It's hard to pick a favourite spot, but I love Wester Ross, especially the Bealach na Ba track into Applecross. Sutherland and Caithness have fascinated me since reading *The Silver Darlings*, with their rugged coastlines and fishing towns like Helmsdale being must-sees. I'm a travel writer based in Shetland and wrote *Shetland: Your Essential Travel Guide*.

Laurie wrote the 'Ullapool's Silver Darlings' essay (p178).

Professor Gordon Noble
@northernpicts

I'm a Professor of Archaeology at the University of Aberdeen. I've done lots of smaller segments of the NC500 while working on Pictish and prehistoric sites across the Highlands. My pick of places to visit are Groam House Museum and the Tarbat Discovery Centre, where you can see some magnificent Pictish carved stones and learn about the early history of Scotland.

Gordon wrote 'The 'Painted People' – Pictish history and iconography' essay (p50).

Milly Revill Hayward
@theflowcountry

I grew up in the Highlands and was lucky enough to travel to many places along the NC500 before I knew anything of the now-popular route. Whilst the vast inland landscape of the Flow Country holds a special place in my heart, the drive over to the stunning Applecross Peninsula via the Bealach na Ba pass takes my top spot on the route. I'm based on the northeast coast and work for RSPB Scotland at Forsinard Flows National Nature Reserve.

Milly wrote 'The Flow Country' essay (p118).

Robert Ormerod
@robert_ormerod

I was born in Scotland and I love the chance to head out and experience the sheer beauty of the Scottish landscape. I have a real love of lighthouses and visiting Stoer on one of the most stunning winter days was a real treat. I've worked for National Geographic, Lonely Planet, *Travel + Leisure, The New York Times, The Wall Street Journal, The Financial Times, The Sunday Times Magazine* and *The Guardian*.

Robert photographed the 'Northern Light' essay (p134).

James Gulliver Hancock
@gulliverhancock

I'm a well-travelled illustrator. In my trips across the globe, I've completed many iconic journeys and I love to move around and work from unique places. I've always loved making maps and diagrams and cutaways and now working on these projects for Lonely Planet is an absolute joy. My How Things Work series spans a wide range of subjects, from space stations to trains.

James drew the illustrated map at the start of this book.

Lookout tower, RSPB Forsinard Flows National Nature Reserve (p110)

SHZPHOTO/SHUTTERSTOCK

Hiking the Hills

Northern Scotland's wild, dramatic scenery has made hillwalking one of the most popular pastimes for visitors travelling the North Coast 500.

Munros, Corbetts and Grahams

It would be impossible to tour the NC500 without your eye being drawn to the shapely peaks that adorn almost every view. There are all sorts of hills along the route – from small to huge, easy to challenging.

At the end of the 19th century an enthusiastic Victorian mountaineer, Sir Hugh Munro, published a list of Scottish mountains measuring over 3000ft (914m) in height. He couldn't have realised that his name would one day be used to describe every Scottish peak over that magical 3000ft mark. Many keen hillwalkers today set themselves the target of reaching the summit of (or 'bagging') all 282 Munros.

Since Munro's day, making lists of hills and then ticking them off has become a hugely popular activity. Once you've bagged all the Munros you can move on to the Corbetts, which are hills between 2500ft and 3000ft (762m and 914m) with a drop of at least 500ft on all sides, and the Grahams, defined as hills between 600m and 762m with a drop of 150m. There are 37 Munros, 43 Corbetts and 38 Grahams along the route of the NC500. If ticking lists appeals to you, there are also Donalds and Marilyns to obsess over.

When to go

The best time of year for hillwalking is usually May to September, although snow can fall on the highest summits even in midsummer. Winter on the higher hills is for experienced mountaineers only, requiring the use of ice axe and crampons.

You should avoid areas where you might disrupt or disturb lambing (generally mid-April to the end of May) or deer stalking (1 July to

An Teallach (p184)

FROM LEFT: NEW AFRICA/SHUTTERSTOCK, MAGNUS BJERMO/SHUTTERSTOCK

15 February, but the peak period is August to October). You can get up-to-date information on deer stalking in various areas through the Heading for the Scottish Hills *(outdooraccess-scotland.scot)* service.

The Right to Roam

Access to the countryside has been a thorny issue in Scotland for many years. In Victorian times, belligerent landowners attempted to prevent walkers from using well-established trails. Moves to counter this led to successful legislation for walkers and the formation of what later became the Scottish Rights of Way & Access Society *(scotways.com)*.

In January 2003, the Scottish parliament formalised access to the countryside and passed the Land Reform (Scotland) Bill, creating statutory rights of access to land in Scotland for the first time (popularly known as 'the right to roam'). Basically, the Scottish Outdoor Access Code *(outdooraccess-scotland.scot)* states that everyone has the right to be on most land and inland waters, providing they act responsibly.

As far as wild camping goes, this means that you can pitch a tent almost anywhere that doesn't cause inconvenience to others or damage to property, as long as you stay no longer than two or three nights in any one spot, take all litter away with you, and keep well away from houses and roads.

IGORXIII/SHUTTERSTOCK

MOUNTAIN SAFETY

Essential hillwalking gear you should take with you includes good waterproofs, spare warm clothing, adequate food and drink, map and compass, mobile phone (but don't rely on it), first-aid kit, head torch and whistle (for emergencies). Check the weather forecast before you go, and let someone know your planned route and when you expect to be back. Don't be afraid to turn back if it gets too difficult.

SCOTTISH MOUNTAINS ON THE PAGE

***North-West Highlands*, SMC**

Published by the Scottish Mountaineering Club, this is the definitive hillwalker's guide, including route descriptions, maps and photographs.

***Scotland's Mountain Landscapes*, Colin K Ballantyne**

One for geology nerds, an exploration of Scottish mountains in terms of the underlying rocks and how glaciation, river erosion and giant landslides have shaped them.

***One Man's Legacy*, Mike Dixon**

Fascinating biography of Tom Patey (1932–70), an Ullapool GP who was one of the best Scottish mountaineers of his generation.

HIGHLIGHTS

❶ Ben Loyal, Tongue (p116)

Rising above the head of the Kyle of Tongue, Ben Loyal's distinctive profile gave it the nickname 'Queen of Scottish Mountains'. The highest point is known as An Caisteal (The Castle) for its fortress-like appearance.

❷ Ben Hope, Eriboll (p125)

Ben Hope, rising to 927m, holds the title of Scotland's most northerly Munro. The summit enjoys sweeping views that stretch to Dunnet Head, the Orkney Islands and south to Ben Stack and the distant hills of Assynt.

❸ Suilven, Assynt (p164)

One of Scotland's most distinctive mountains, rising in dramatic isolation inland from Lochinver. Its unmistakable silhouette – shaped like a domed pillar when seen from the coast – makes it a true icon of the North Coast 500.

FROM LEFT: JOAN VENDRELL/SHUTTERSTOCK, ANDREW YOUNG/SHUTTERSTOCK, PECOLD/SHUTTERSTOCK

FROM LEFT: ANGUS ALEXANDER CHISHOLM/SHUTTERSTOCK, SCOTLAND'S SCENERY/SHUTTERSTOCK, SIMON TURNER/ALAMY

❹ Stac Pollaidh, Coigach (p168)

Stac Pollaidh's accessibility makes it a popular choice. A well-maintained path wraps around the mountain, offering stunning views over the surrounding lochs and the neighbouring peaks of Suilven and Cùl Mòr.

❺ An Teallach, Dundonnell (p184)

The giant of Wester Ross offers two Munro summits reached relatively easily from Dundonnell. However, the full traverse of its ridges is one of the finest mountain expeditions in the country, combining technical scrambling with exhilarating exposure.

❻ Coire Mhic Fhearchair, Torridon (p207)

Located on the northern side of Beinn Eighe, this is one of the most breathtaking natural features in Scotland, with towering cliffs reflected in a tranquil lochan. Experienced hillwalkers can continue to the summit of Beinn Eighe.

Castles & Clans

The many castles that punctuate the Highland landscape are the legacy of a violent past, and remain as status symbols for wealthy landowners.

Castles

Scotland is home to more than 1000 castles, ranging from meagre 12th-century ruins to mag-nificent Victorian mansions. They all began with one purpose: to serve as fortified homes for the landowning aristocracy. The appearance of the tower house in the 14th century marks the beginning of the development of the castle as a residence. Clan feuds and cattle raiders meant that local lairds built stone towers in which to live, like those at Castle Sinclair Girnigoe (p92) and Ardvreck Castle (p116).

But as society became more settled and peaceful in the late 18th and early 19th centuries, defensive features gave way to ostentatious displays of wealth and status. The Scottish baronial style of architecture, characterised by a profusion of pointy turrets, crenellations and stepped gables, became all the rage, a trend epitomised by the Victorian splendour of Dunrobin Castle (p79).

You'll notice that almost all of the castles along the NC500 are on the east side; in the west, from Durness south to Applecross, Ardvreck Castle stands alone. This was because the northwest was far removed from the main cause of castle building further south and east – English invasions – and because there was little in the way of productive farmland to keep a castle's occupants supplied with food and drink.

Clans

The history of the Highlands from the 12th to the 16th centuries was volatile and violent. Robert the Bruce's famous struggle to win the Scottish crown involved not only fighting the English, but also contending with his rivals in the Highlands. Even after Bruce had defeated

Dunrobin Castle (p79)

FROM LEFT: STEPHEN ROBERTSON/SHUTTERSTOCK, GIMAS/SHUTTERSTOCK

the English at Bannockburn in 1314 and guaranteed Scottish independence, the wrangling for power between (and amongst) the Highland clans and the Scottish crown raged on for several centuries.

The clan system (from the Gaelic *clann*, meaning 'children') began to emerge in the 12th century, when extended family groups living within a region came together for protection against Viking and Norman invaders and from other family groups – the scarcity of resources in the Highlands meant there was constant competition for land and livestock, and the fighting between rival clans was often ferocious.

The clan was led by a chief who was granted his position through the ancient system of tanistry, in which the heir to the chief was nominated from a pool of eligible candidates whose great-grandfathers had been chiefs before them. This ensured that a chief never died without a potential heir, but resulted in many bloody feuds and murders instigated by those who felt their claim to the title had been denied.

The main clans in the north of Scotland were the Sinclairs of Caithness, the Sutherlands to their south, and the Mackays, Macleods and Mackenzies to the west. The most notorious feud was between the Mackays and the Sutherlands, which lasted from the 14th to the 17th century. You can see Mackay and Sutherland memorabilia at Strathnaver Museum (p113) and Dunrobin Castle (p79) respectively.

ISLANDSTOCK/ALAMY

CLAN TARTANS

The original Highland dress was not the kilt but the plaid – a long length of tartan cloth wrapped around the body and over the shoulder. The wearing of Highland dress was banned after the Jacobite rebellions but revived under royal patronage in the following century. By then, however, many of the old *setts* (tartan patterns) had been forgotten – lots of the clan tartans marketed today are actually Victorian creations.

MAJOR CLAN BATTLES

Battle of Druim na coub (1433)
A classic dispute involving betrayal and revenge, fough between Sutherlands and Mackays in the shadow of Ben Loyal.

Battle of Clachnaharry (1454)
A battle between the Clan Munro and Clan Mackintosh fought on the western outskirts of Inverness.

Battle of Altimarlach (1680)
A stone cross marks the last clan battle in Scotland, fought between Clan Campbell and Clan Sinclair, two miles northwest of Wick.

HIGHLIGHTS

1 Inverness Castle (p34)

The redeveloped Victorian castle that dominates Inverness city centre houses colourful installations and interactive experiences about Highland history and Gaelic culture.

2 Dunrobin Castle (p79)

This classic fairytale fortress, adorned with towers and turrets, was once the seat of the 1st Duke of Sutherland, notorious for his part in some of the cruellest episodes of the Highland Clearances.

3 Castle Sinclair Girnigoe (p92)

Three miles northeast of Wick is this magnificently located clifftop ruin, just a short walk from a car park with interpretative signboards along the way.

FROM LEFT: NATALIA PAKLINA/SHUTTERSTOCK, JOSE MIGUEL SANCHEZ/SHUTTERSTOCK, NATHALIE TURGEON/SHUTTERSTOCK

4 Castle of Mey (p96)

Famously the holiday home of Elizabeth Bowes-Lyon, the mother of Queen Elizabeth II, who restored the semi-derelict castle to its present glory in the 1950s.

5 Castle Varrich (p116)

An atmospheric ruin perched on a crag overlooking the Kyle of Tongue, it was once the seat of Clan Mackay and makes for a pleasant ramble from the nearby village of Tongue.

6 Ardvreck Castle (p163)

A former stronghold of Clan MacLeod, built in 1597 on a rocky point overlooking Loch Assynt; the mountain views from beneath its ruined walls are enchanting.

FROM LEFT: FRANCESCO BONINO/SHUTTERSTOCK, WAYLEEBIRD/SHUTTERSTOCK, AUMPHOTOGRAPHY/SHUTTERSTOCK

Taste of the Highlands

Seafood, especially shellfish, is the standout food experience on the North Coast 500; washed down with with locally produced whiskies and beers.

Sustainable seafood

The north of Scotland is blessed with an abundance of marine life and produces some of the world's finest seafood, renowned for its exceptional quality. A journey around the NC500 provides ample opportunities to sample this bounty, with many restaurants serving shellfish that was landed no more than a few miles away.

FROM LEFT: DANIEL ALFORD/LONELY PLANET, ZEEKING/SHUTTERSTOCK

BEST SEAFOOD MEALS

Captain's Galley, Scrabster (p97)
Caithness' finest freshly landed seafood and sustainable whitefish.

Shorehouse, Tarbet (p148)
Crab and langoustines landed straight from the restaurant's own creel boat.

Crofter's Kitchen, Scourie (p148)
Outdoor kitchen serving garlic crab claws and hand-dived scallops with chorizo.

Seafood Shack, Ullapool (p163)
Finger-licking langoustines in garlic butter, served food-truck style.

Shieldaig Bar & Coastal Kitchen, Shieldaig (p202)
Local seafood with a sea view; grab an outdoor table for lunch.

Left: Seafood Shack (p163)
Right: Creels, Wick (p86)

Sustainability is key in this pristine environment. The most sustainable forms of fishing include creel fishing for lobster, crab and langoustine. These are the small boats (less than 10m) that you'll see all around the NC500, usually crewed by just one or two people, which go to sea for only a day at a time to lay 'creels' – small lobster pots made of netting with a funnel-shaped entrance that the target species can crawl into, but can't get out of. The creels are baited with fish and lie on the sea bed for a day or so before being retrieved. The catch is then sorted by hand so that the fisher can return any shellfish that are too small, or are carrying eggs.

On menus look out for mentions of 'creel-caught' crab, lobster and langoustines, and choose scallops that are described as 'hand-dived' or 'diver caught' – the alternative is dredging for scallops, a method that causes severe damage to the seabed.

Whisky

Scotch whisky (always spelled without an 'e' – 'whiskey' is Irish or American) is Scotland's best-known product and biggest export. The spirit has been distilled here since at least the 15th century. Speyside and Islay are the most famous whisky-producing regions, but there are some famous distilleries dotted along the

BYVALET/SHUTTERSTOCK

east side of the NC500, as well as a handful of new arrivals.

Famous names like Glenmorangie (p66), Balblair (p66) and Old Pulteney (p67) have been around since the first half of the 19th century, but a renewed interest in scotch whisky has seen lots of new distilleries open up in the last decade or so. Names to look out for on the NC500 include Dunnet Bay (p99), Wolfburn (p100) and 8 Doors (p67).

Distillery tours usually last from 60 to 90 minutes, and include a look at the various stages of the whisky-making process – malting and mashing of the barley, fermentation, distillation, and the maturing of the whisky in casks – followed by a tasting session where you get to compare two or three different varieties.

Beer

The last decade has seen a huge rise in the number of specialist brewers and micro-breweries springing up in the north of Scotland. They take pride in using only natural ingredients, and many try to revive ancient recipes, such as heather- and seaweed-flavoured ales. When choosing what to drink with a seafood dinner we usually reach for the white wine, but an increasing number of foodies are pairing shellfish with a crisp, tart, citrussy beer like an IPA – ones to look out for include Spider Monkey (Black Isle Brewing Co.; p41), Whiteout (Cromarty Brewing Company) and Merry Men (John O'Groats Brewery; p67).

HOW TO PEEL A LANGOUSTINE

Langoustines are usually served in the shell, which can be challenging if you've never peeled one before. First, twist the head off, then point the open end of the tail down at your plate and squeeze the sides of the shell together till you hear it crack. Finally turn the tail belly up and use your thumbs to pull the sides of the shell apart until you can extract the meat in a single piece.

DISTILLERY TOURS

Glenmorangie, Tain (p66)
Produces a fine light malt subjected to a number of different cask finishes. The classic tour ends with a two-dram tasting.

Old Pulteney, Wick (p67)
Learn how a coastal location and marine climate influence the character of the whisky. The tour includes two drams and a free tasting glass.

8 Doors, John O'Groats (p67)
If you're short of time, this distillery offers four-dram tastings without a tour, and 45-minute express tours.

Old Pulteney (p67)

FROM LEFT: RVILLALON/SHUTTERSTOCK, GILL KENNETT/ALAMY

THE PULTENEY DISTILLERY Co Ltd
2005
1233
2005
1234
PULTENEY WICK
1074
1073
1072
2013
1104

Crofting Culture

Crofting plays an important role in many aspects of life along the North Coast 500, from close-knit communities to patterns of land use.

Crofting History

Up until the 19th century the most common form of farming settlement in the Highlands and Islands was the *baile*, a township consisting of a dozen or so families who farmed the land granted to them by the local chieftain in return for military service and a portion of the harvest. The arable land was divided into strips called *rigs*, which were allocated to different families by annual ballot so that each took turns at getting the poorer soils; this system was known as *runrig*. The families worked the land communally and their cattle shared the grazing land.

During the mass upheaval of the Highland Clearances, those who chose not to emigrate or move to the cities were forced to eke a living from narrow plots of marginal agricultural land, often close to the coast. This was a form of smallholding that became known as crofting. The small patch of land was not enough to produce a living on its own, and had to be supplemented by other work such as fishing and kelp gathering.

The economic depression of the late 19th century meant that many crofters couldn't pay their rent, but the people resisted eviction, creating instead their own political movement, the Crofters Party. Several of their demands were met by the government in the Crofters Holdings Act of 1886, including security of tenure and fair rents. But it wasn't until 1976 that crofters won the right to purchase their own land and become owner-occupiers. Today in the Highlands and Islands there are around 20,000 crofts averaging 5 hectares in area, supporting a crofting population of around 33,000 people.

CROFTING HERITAGE MUSEUMS

Strathnaver Museum (p113)
Contains a reconstructed croft house complete with communal box bed and roof timbers made from a 19th-century shipwreck.

Ullapool Museum (p174)
The collection here allows you to explore what life was like in a small crofting community, from everyday household objects to farming tools.

Gairloch Museum (p192)
All sorts of interesting displays on life in the Highlands, including locally built fishing boats and a faithful recreation of a crofter's cottage.

FROM LEFT: MARKFERGUSON2/ALAMY, PHOTOMASTER/ SHUTTERSTOCK

DE LUAN/ALAMY

Left: Ruins of Sutherland township
Right: Nineteenth-century crofter's cottage

Crofting Communities Today

It was crofting that created the scattered settlements that are characteristic of the northwest Highlands, with long narrow strips of arable land and unfenced common grazing on the hill above (one of the reasons for sheep wandering onto the unfenced roads). Generations of crofters worked together to carry out essential activities such as building and repairing fences, cutting peat and moving livestock, fostering a strong culture of community and shared purpose that remains evident. Even today a croft is not enough on its own to provide a living, and most crofters have second and third jobs, either in tourism, fishing or community services such as postal delivery, taxi driving, ferry personnel and retail.

Gaelic Language

Scottish Gaelic (*Gàidhlig* – pronounced 'gah-lick' in Scotland) is known by about 69,000 people in Scotland, mainly in the northwest Highlands, Skye and the Outer Hebrides, though only 3500 class it as their main language. Gaelic culture flourished until after the Battle of Culloden in 1746 when the use of Gaelic was discouraged in favour of English. Since the 1970s there have been efforts to prevent the language dying out, notably through offering Gaelic-medium education, and increasing its visibility through the use of bilingual road signs, as you'll see all along the NC500.

THE CAS-CHROM

Crofting land was often poor and stony with thin soil, so that a normal horse-drawn plough could not be used. The *cas-chrom* (Gaelic for 'crooked foot') was used instead, breaking up the ground using human labour. The soil would be heaped into ridges (called 'lazy beds') to increase its thickness and mixed with seaweed for fertiliser before being planted with potatoes or oats. You can see these hand ploughs in any crofting museum.

ESSENTIAL READING

***Set Adrift Upon the World*, James Hunter**
An evocative account of the Sutherland Clearances by historian and former director of the Scottish Crofting Federation.

Between Mountain and Sea: Poems from Assynt
Anthology of poetry by Norman MacCaig inspired by his close association with Assynt in Sutherland.

***The Poor Had No Lawyers*, Andy Wightman**
A penetrating and fascinating analysis of who owns the land in Scotland, and how they got it.

Bilingual road sign

FROM LEFT: WORLD IMAGE ARCHIVE/ALAMY, STEPHEN FINN/SHUTTERSTOCK

A 87

Caol Loch Aillse ¼

Kyle of Lochalsh

Am Ploc 6

Plockton

Baile Mac Ara 4

Balmacara

(A 82)

An Gearasdan 76

Fort William

(A 887)

Inbhir Nis 82

Inverness

A Photographer's Playground

For most of its length the North Coast 500 follows the fringes of northern Scotland, taking in some of the finest coastal scenery in the country.

The Coast

The route winds past photogenic sandy beaches with turquoise waters that wouldn't look out of place in the Caribbean, layered sandstone crags crowned with crumbling castles, lofty sea stacks crammed with nesting seabirds, and the highest vertical sea cliffs in Britain.

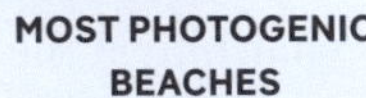

FROM LEFT: DUNCAN ANDISON/SHUTTERSTOCK, GREENTHUMBSHOTS/SHUTTERSTOCK

MOST PHOTOGENIC BEACHES

Torrisdale Bay, Bettyhill (p112)
Hike to the headland at either end of this surf spot for a view along its golden sands.

Durness Beach, Durness (p129)
Popular family beach with a campsite above it; in winter, you can have it all to yourself.

Sandwood Bay, Kinlochbervie (p145)
It's worth the 4-mile hike to enjoy one of the most perfect beaches on the Scottish coast.

Achnahaird Bay, Coigach (p168)
Drifts, dunes and emerald waters with a mindblowing backdrop of the Coigach hills.

Left: Achnahaird Bay, Coigach (p168)
Right: Nesting seabirds, Whaligoe Steps (p87)

The character of the coastline changes as you circle the NC500. The east coast is mainly low-lying and sandy, with the long narrow inlets of the Cromarty and Dornoch Firths giving way to an almost straight coastline from Golspie to Wick. North of Helmsdale the sandy strands of Golspie (p80) and Brora (p81) give way to spectacular cliffs carved into the stratified Caithness sandstone. The rocks here are riven by narrow chasms known as 'geos' (pronounced gyoh, from Old Norse *gjá* meaning 'inlet') and eroded into natural arches and sea stacks, most famously the Duncansby Stacks (p94).

The north coast from Thurso to Cape Wrath is exposed to the full force of the Atlantic and has been sculpted into rocky headlands bejewelled with small sandy coves, the storm-washed sea cliffs rising to a dizzying 195m at Clo Mor near Cape Wrath (p146). The west coast, sheltered by the Outer Hebrides and dissected by glacier-gouged fjords, is more varied still, with pink and grey crags of tortured gneiss and languid curves of golden beaches, sprinkled with uninhabited islands and watched over by the stark silhouettes of mountain sentinels.

Photography tips

Plan ahead Time your photographic efforts to coincide with the 'golden hour', just before sunset or just after sunrise, when the low sun casts atmospheric shadows, lights up the clouds from below, and lends a magical golden glow to your images.

POUL BRIX/SHUTTERSTOCK

Tell a story Use the road as a feature in your photos, leading the eye into the picture and recording the stages of your journey. There are many spots along the way where this works well, notably at Moine House (p124), Kylesku Bridge (p153) and the Bealach na Ba (p222).

Make the weather a feature, not a problem Scotland's weather is notoriously unpredictable, so don't be deterred if the sun doesn't shine. Many memorable images are made in unpromising conditions, when dark clouds can add drama to a mountain scene or shafts of sunlight pierce the clouds in the wake of a shower (see 'Northern Light' essay p134).

Get away from the road Often the best angle can be found a short walk from a parking area; look for a slight rise or rocky knoll that will provide a better vantage point, or find a cottage, croft or bothy to lend interest to the foreground.

Include an activity Booking a guided kayak trip or mountain walk will get you into some stunning locations not otherwise accessible. The local guides are often keen photographers themselves, able to take you to the best spots.

Watch the night skies Northern Scotland is one of the best places in Europe for stargazing and astrophotography. There are official Dark Sky Discovery Sites at Leitir Easaidh (p162), Glen Canisp (near Lochinver, p155) and Castlehill at the south end of Dunnet Beach (p99).

PHOTOGRAPHING THE BEALACH NA BA

The road across the Bealach na Ba (p222) is one of the most iconic locations on the NC500. The best vantage point is above the first hairpin on the way down (no parking; leave your car at the top and walk down). Here you get a panoramic view of the steepest part of the road, with all three hairpin bends in view. Use a wide-angle lens, or take an overlapping image and stitch them together.

ESSENTIAL READING

***Scotland's Finest Landscapes*, Colin Prior**
Absolutely gorgeous images from all over Scotland by one of the country's finest landscape photographers.

***Wild Light: Scotland's Mountain Landscape*, Craig Aitchison**
The result of a seven-year project to capture the best of Scottish landscapes using panoramic format.

***Lonely Planet's Guide to Travel Photography*, Richard I'Anson**
Advice, information and instructions on how to take amazing travel photographs using the latest digital cameras.

Bealach na Ba (p222)

6 Ways to do the North Coast 500

The North Coast 500 is a 516-mile loop that starts and ends in Inverness, but there are as many approaches to the route as there are travellers. These are some ways you can build the trip of a lifetime.

1 The Classic

Time *8 days*

Best for *A balanced trip with enough time to get stuck in*

This itinerary heads anticlockwise, the most popular direction, saving the stunning west coast till last. The timeframe means you'll have fairly short driving days, covering around 65 miles per day, with the opportunity for plenty of stops to enjoy the NC500's beaches, villages, lochs and mountains.

Possible overnights Dornoch, John O'Groats, Kyle of Tongue, Durness, Clachtoll, Ullapool, Gairloch, Shieldaig

ALEX TREADWAY/GETTY IMAGES

2 The Short Trip

Time *4 days*

Best for *The time-poor who still want a proper NC500 experience*

This is about the fastest you can do the NC500 without it being a pointless exercise. You won't be able to linger at every stop, and days on the road will be long (120 miles plus). But you'll get to see those fabulous landscapes unfurl from your windscreen and visit the sights that impress the most, and be back home after a thrill-packed long weekend.

Possible overnights Lybster, Bettyhill, Ullapool, Applecross

3 On a Bike

Time *9 days*

Best for *Outdoor lovers with thighs of steel*

This 40- to 65-mile-a-day itinerary is probably the shortest worthwhile cycling option. The A9 from Inverness north to Wick and Thurso is a busy trunk road, so consider leaving the main NC500 at Evanton and heading cross-country on minor roads via Lairg and Strathnaver to Bettyhill on the north coast. This misses out John O'Groats, but includes the wild and desolate landscapes around Loch Naver.

Possible overnights Lairg, Bettyhill, Durness, Achmelvich, Ullapool, Gairloch, Shieldaig, Lochcarron

MOUNTAINTREKS/SHUTTERSTOCK

Go to p229 for essential trip tips

4 Sustainably

Time *2 weeks*

Best for *Environmentally aware travellers*

With careful planning it is possible to do most of the NC500 on public transport, at least in summer – some bus services reduce to just a few per day, or in some instances once a week, in winter. Currently the only gap is between Scourie and Inchnadamph; one possibility would be to do either the northern or southern half of the route. It's no problem driving the NC500 in an electric vehicle; the biggest gap between charging points is no more than 40 miles.

5 In Winter

Time *12 days*

Best for *Lovers of slow travel*

Again, a bit of planning is needed, but a winter tour is perfectly feasible and has the big advantage that you'll have the route almost to yourself. There are enough hotels, hostels and campsites that remain open all year; the main drawback is shorter hours of daylight and the possibility of snow and ice creating hazardous driving conditions (the Bealach na Ba is often closed by snow). The secret is to take your time and be flexible.

WHEN TO GO

Jun–Aug

The busiest time – popular accommodation books out six months in advance – but the days are long and the sun may shine. July and August can be plagued by midges (tiny biting bugs).

Sep–Nov

September can still be warm, while October and November are colder but quieter, and rich with autumn colour.

Dec–Feb

The quietest spell, but some businesses are still open. There can be wild weather, but also cold clear days. Snow may close passes or rule out hill walks unless you've got an ice axe and crampons.

Mar–May

Variable conditions; the road is quieter than in summer. May is one of the best months to tackle the route.

6 In Reverse

Time *As long as you like*

Best for *Contrarians and traffic dodgers*

Most drivers tackle the NC500 anticlockwise but some folk love doing things differently. The traffic can be lighter, and if you time it right you can be heading out of Durness as dawn breaks over the Kyle of Tongue. And while the east coast is arguably less scenic for a final leg, it is an easier ride if tempers are fraying at the trip's end.

Possible overnights Shieldaig, Gairloch, Ullapool, Lochinver, Durness, Wick, Tain

The Drive

A stage-by-stage, mile-by-mile account of the route. Your journey begins here.

Durness to Lochinver, p140

Lewis

The Minch

Lochinver

Lochinver to Ullapool, p158

Ullapool to Gairloch, p180

Ullapool

The Little Minch

Gairloch

Gairloch to Shieldaig, p196

Shieldaig

Skye

Shieldaig to Inverness, p216

Thurso to Tongue, p104
Durness
Thurso
Tongue
Wick to Thurso, p88
Wick
Tongue to Durness, p120
SCOTLAND
Dornoch to Wick, p74
North Sea
Dornoch
Cromarty Bridge to Dornoch, p56
Cromarty
Bridge
Inverness to Cromarty Bridge, p36
Inverness
START/
END

CITY GUIDE

Inverness

Inverness is not just the start and end point of the North Coast 500. With a lovely riverside setting and a slew of historical attractions, the 'capital of the Highlands' is well worth a day or two of your time in its own right.

WORDS BY **MIKE MACEACHERAN**

Arriving

By air **Inverness Airport** is at Dalcross, 10 miles northeast of the city, off the A96 towards Aberdeen. There are direct scheduled flights from Amsterdam, Belfast, Bristol, London and Manchester. Stagecoach **bus 11/11A** *(£6.50, 30 minutes, every 30 minutes)* runs from the airport to Inverness bus station.

By rail There are at least 10 trains a day from London to Inverness, most requiring a change at **Edinburgh** *(8-9 hours)*. The ***Caledonian Sleeper*** *(sleeper.scot)* provides an overnight service from London to Inverness. Inverness train station is right in the city centre.

By road Inverness is easily reached via the A9, about three hours from either Edinburgh or Glasgow, and 9½ hours from London.

For more information on Arriving, see p230.

HOW MUCH FOR A...

pint of IPA
£4

bowl of cullen skink
£7–8

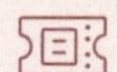

Culloden Battlefield & Museum entry
£14

Tourist Information
Available from **Inverness iCentre** *(visitscotland.com; 9.30am-5pm Mon-Sat)*, on High St

Getting Around

Easily navigable and a joy to explore by foot, most of Inverness's main attractions are dotted along the River Ness and a short stroll from the adjacent bus and train stations. To visit **Culloden Battlefield** (p34), four miles east, take **bus 27** *(hourly, 22 minutes)*. Bus timetables are available at *stagecoachbus.com*.

Campervan hire There are several campervan and motorhome rental locations in and around the city that cater specifically to visitors wanting to drive the North Coast 500.

Driving Inverness is a bit of a traffic bottleneck. During weekday rush hours (and even on weekends) there are often long tailbacks from the traffic lights on the A9 at the Longman Roundabout (the first roundabout south of the Kessock Bridge). Congestion will affect you whether you're heading for the official start of the North Coast 500, along the A862 to Beauly, or across the Kessock Bridge towards the Black Isle. Up-to-date road information is available on *traffic.gov.scot* and the A9 Traffic Info public Facebook group.

Parking Parking in the city centre can be problematic, especially at weekends. Head for the multistorey car parks at Eastgate shopping centre and on Rose St. There is metered (pay by phone or contactless bank card) on-street parking on Culduthel Rd, about 10 minutes' walk south of the castle, and free on-street parking on Bught Rd, near the Ness Islands, a 30-minute walk south of the castle.

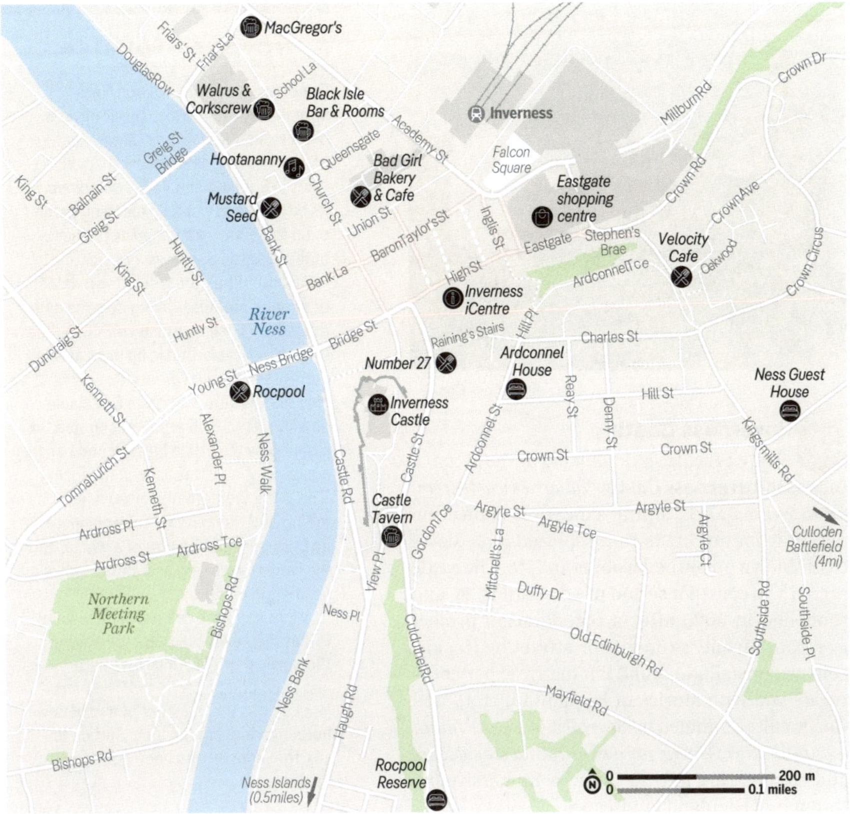

A DAY IN INVERNESS

Kick off your day with breakfast at **Bad Girl Bakery & Cafe** (p35) in the Victorian Market, or **Velocity Cafe** (p35) on Crown Avenue, then wander along **High St** and up to **Inverness Castle** (p34) for a tour of the city's main attraction. If you have time, take a one-hour walking tour of the centre.

Catch a bus out to **Culloden Battlefield** (p34) for a tour of the museum and a guided walk around the site of the battle (allow three to four hours including the bus journey). Alternatively, stay in town and explore the rest of the city with a walk along the river to the **Ness Islands** and back.

Book a table for dinner at the **Mustard Seed** (p35), or try the Scottish seafood at **Rocpool**. (p35). Head to the **Black Isle Bar** (p35) to sample locally brewed beers, then on to **Hootananny** (p35) for live traditional music.

LOWSUN/SHUTTERSTOCK

Inverness Castle

Inverness Castle

The city centre is dominated by the baronial turrets of **Inverness Castle** *(invernesscastle.scot; adult/child £15/8)*, a pink-sandstone confection dating from the 1840s that replaced a medieval castle blown up by the Jacobites in 1746. The castle served as a courthouse and prison until 2020, and reopened in 2025 after a regeneration project to create the city's top visitor attraction. Inside, colourful installations and interactive experiences regale you with stories of Highland history and Gaelic culture, guided by the spirit of a *seanchaidh (shan-uh-khee; Gaelic for a traditional storyteller)* and culminating in a spectacular immersive fly-through of Highland landscapes.

MONSTER TOURISM

Deep, dark and narrow, Loch Ness stretches for 23 miles to the southwest of Inverness. It's Britain's largest body of fresh water, holding more than all the lakes in England and Wales combined. Its bitterly cold waters – reaching depths of up to 330m – are famously the home of the elusive Loch Ness monster.

Highland folklore is filled with tales of strange creatures living in lochs and rivers (see Loch na Beiste, p187), but the origins of Nessie-mania lie in an article published in the *Inverness Courier* on 2 May 1933, entitled 'Strange Spectacle on Loch Ness'. The article recounted the sighting by Mrs Aldie Mackay and her husband of a disturbance in the loch: 'There the creature disported itself, rolling and plunging for fully a minute, its body resembling that of a whale, and the water cascading and churning like a simmering cauldron.'

What you have to bear in mind here is that the newly built A82 road along the north shore of Loch Ness had just been completed in 1933, and Mrs Mackay was the manager of a roadside hotel overlooking the loch. Suffice to say, the monster has been good for business.

RPHSTOCK/SHUTTERSTOCK

Culloden Battlefield

The last pitched battle ever fought on British soil took place on the eastern edge of Inverness in 1746. The Battle of Culloden saw the crushing of Bonnie Prince Charlie and his dream of a restored Stuart monarchy. The National Trust for Scotland's **Culloden Visitor Centre** *(nts.org.uk; adult/child £16/11.50)* has everything you need to know about the battle, including the lead-up and the aftermath, with perspectives from both sides. After a look around the museum, join a 45-minute guided tour (included in the admission price) of the battlefield where 1500 Jacobites were slaughtered by government forces in less than an hour.

Memorial cairn, Culloden battlefield

Where to Stay

You can find a good range of hotels from budget to boutique on Church St and along the riverbank in the city centre. If you want to stay close to the centre but away from noisy nightlife, there's a concentration of B&Bs and guest houses around Ardconnel St (south of High St, and separated from it by a flight of stairs), and across the river on Kenneth St, Greig St and Fairfield Rd. There are campsites on the southwestern edge of town at Bught Park and Torvean.

BEST PLACES TO STAY

Rocpool Reserve ££ Boutique chic meets the Highlands in this sophisticated little hotel. *rocpool.com*

Ardconnel House ££ This Victorian guesthouse is quiet and comfortable yet close to the city centre. *ardconnel-inverness.co.uk*

Ness Guest House ££ Friendly owners and a handy location five minute's walk east of the city centre. *thenessguesthouse.com*

Black Isle Bar & Rooms £ Rooms with private bathrooms upstairs from the Black Isle Bar. *blackislebrewery.com/accommodation*

Food Festival

The two-week **Inverness and Loch Ness Food and Drink Festival** *(visit inversesslochness.com)* takes place in late February/early March to showcase the city's culinary credentials with a series of events and special deals at local eateries. It includes the popular Taste of Inverness event where you get to meet local food producers and restaurateurs and sample the fruits (and vegetables) of their endeavours.

HAGGIS & CULLEN SKINK

Haggis – Scotland's national dish (pictured below left) – is often ridiculed because of its ingredients, which admittedly don't sound promising – the finely chopped lungs, heart and liver of a sheep, mixed with oatmeal and onion and stuffed into a sheep's stomach bag. However, it actually tastes surprisingly good. Haggis is usually served with champit tatties and bashed neeps *(mashed potatoes and turnips)*, with a generous dollop of butter and a good sprinkling of black pepper. Try it at the **Castle Tavern** *(castletavern.pub; food served noon-8.30pm)*.

Another Scots speciality, supposedly invented at the fishing village of Cullen on the coast of the Moray Firth, 50 miles east of Inverness, is **cullen skink** (pictured below right). This hearty and warming soup is made with smoked haddock, potato, onion and milk or cream; to sample some in Inverness head to **Number 27** *(number27 inverness.co.uk; noon-10pm)* or **MacGregor's** *(macgregorsbars.com; 5-9pm Mon-Thu, 2-9pm Fri-Sun)*.

FROM LEFT: PHILIP KINSEY/SHUTTERSTOCK, RICHARD GRIFFIN/SHUTTERSTOCK

BEST PLACES TO EAT & DRINK

Mustard Seed ££ Bustling restaurant with a Mediterranean vibe. *noon-2.30pm & 5-9.15pm*

Bad Girl Bakery & Cafe £ Brilliant breakfast and lunch spot in the Victorian Market. *9am-6pm Mon-Sat, 10am-5pm Sun*

Black Isle Bar & Rooms ££ Serves own-label organic craft beers and wood-fired pizzas. *1pm-1am*

Walrus and Corkscrew ££ Relax over a bottle of wine and a platter of local cheese. *1-10pm Sun-Thu, to midnight Fri & Sat*

Inverness

Buckle up for the road trip of a lifetime: there's no letting up once you leave Inverness and this stage is as relaxing as the NC500 gets. It's largely the domain of fisherfolk and farmers and, while the road around the Black Isle dives into forests and through grain fields, it largely hugs the coast, where dolphin-watching safaris abound – take binoculars. Alternatively, the route from Beauly to Dingwall further inland follows the road less travelled.

Mike MacEacheran

Cromarty Bridge

THIS LEG

- Inverness
- Kessock Bridge
- Munlochy
- Fortrose
- Chanonry Point
- Rosemarkie
- Cromarty
- Udale Bay
- Cromarty Bridge

Driving Notes

The route north towards the Cromarty Firth follows the A9, but is at its most memorable when diverting east along the A832 and continuing around the Black Isle coast. Don't be fooled: this isn't an island, but a misnamed peninsula, with your road winding past pretty towns, beaches and dolphin-stocked bays.

Breaking Up Your Journey

Cromarty, with its cluster of red sandstone houses and bobbing boats, is the Black Isle at its prettiest and a fine place to overnight, with a lovely coffee shop, cinema, bakery and pizzeria. Fortrose is another option earlier on the route, with a better range of services and a standout pub, while Strathpeffer is the best option for a Victorian-era Highland hotel.

Mike's Tips

BEST MEAL Seafood and wood-fired pizza at **Sutor Creek** (p41), Cromarty.

FAVOURITE VIEW Gaze at steep cliffs and beaches from **McFarquhar'sBed** (p45).

ESSENTIAL STOP Go dolphin watching at **Chanonry Point** (p42), or join a wildlife safari trip in **Cromarty** (p45).

ROAD-TRIP TIP Driving in a campervan or motorhome? Stock up on beers for the nights ahead at organic **Black Isle Brewing Co.** (p40) near Munlochy.

River Sgitheach

END

Cromarty Bridge, p48
Dolphin- and seal-watching on the road north

Dingwall

Strathpeffer

Discover Dingwall & Strathpeffer, p49
Two towns, two different experiences, from tales of Vikings and Macbeth to stories about Scotland's first (and last) spa town.

Black Isle Brewing Co., p41
Award-winning organic craft brewery

Beauly Firth

0 5 km
0 2.5 miles

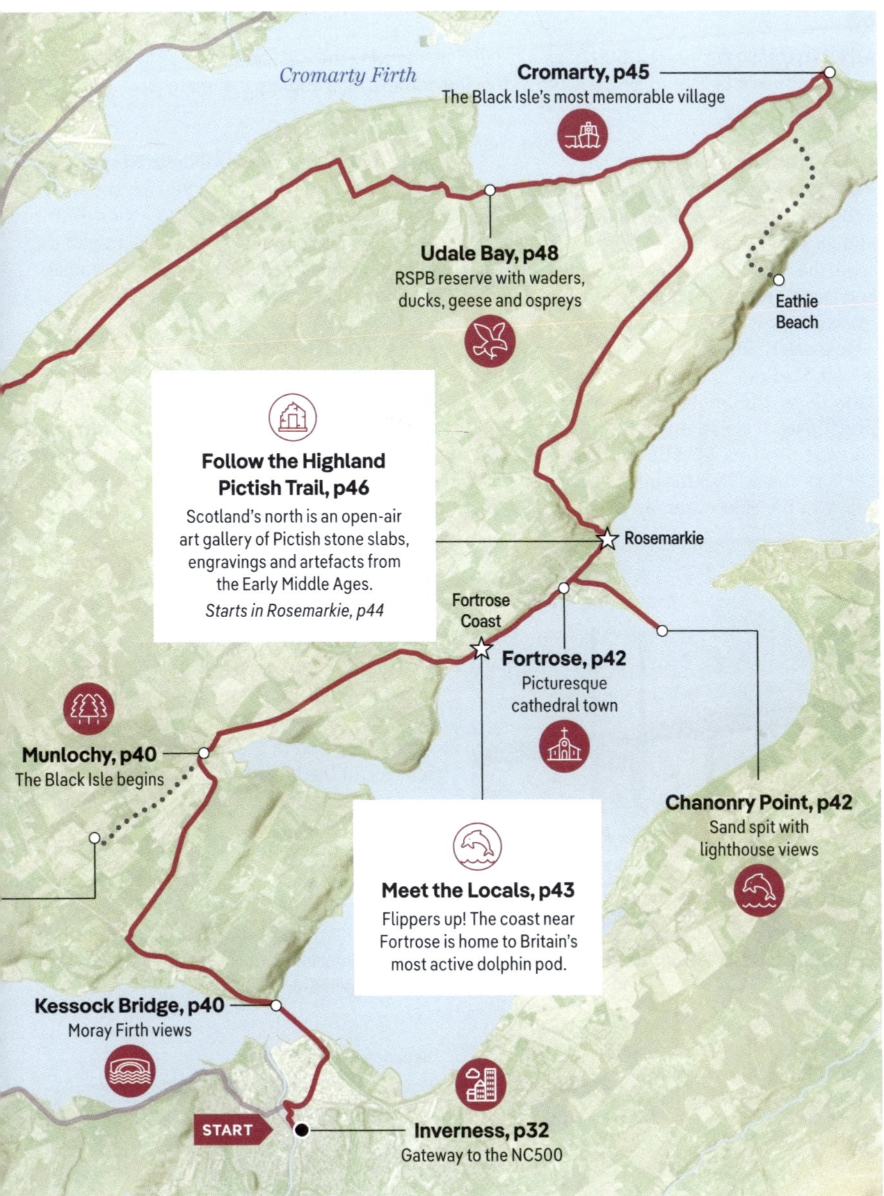

Cromarty Firth
Cromarty, p45
The Black Isle's most memorable village
Udale Bay, p48
RSPB reserve with waders, ducks, geese and ospreys
Eathie Beach
Follow the Highland Pictish Trail, p46
Scotland's north is an open-air art gallery of Pictish stone slabs, engravings and artefacts from the Early Middle Ages.
Starts in Rosemarkie, p44
Rosemarkie
Fortrose Coast
Fortrose, p42
Picturesque cathedral town
Munlochy, p40
The Black Isle begins
Chanonry Point, p42
Sand spit with lighthouse views
Meet the Locals, p43
Flippers up! The coast near Fortrose is home to Britain's most active dolphin pod.
Kessock Bridge, p40
Moray Firth views
START
Inverness, p32
Gateway to the NC500

PREVIOUS STOP The NC500 begins in Inverness, leaving the Highlands' capital in the rear-view mirror, before striking out into a stunning corner of the country that many Scots never reach.

Kessock Bridge

The logic behind your decision to embark upon the NC500 is brought sharply into focus almost immediately after leaving Inverness: soon, the windscreen fills with Highland drama and the A9 roadside becomes less populated – increasingly wild and far-flung.

Kessock Bridge begins beside the city's Caledonian Stadium, home of Inverness Caledonian Thistle on the banks of the Moray Firth – previously, it's also hosted Elton John, Rod Stewart, Andrea Bocelli and Duran Duran. Then it's up-and-over the inlet, as dolphins glide below in the cold water. After half a mile, the cable-stayed bridge leads to **North Kessock** and a car park and bakery overlooking the water. A staircase below takes you to a view of the bridge hanging high above the meeting of the Moray and Beauly Firths. It's especially dramatic around sunset, late in summer.

Kessock Bridge

ANGUS ALEXANDER CHISHOLM/SHUTTERSTOCK

The Road to Fortrose

Turning east off the A9 onto the no-frills B9161, the sense is of striking out into undiscovered territory: the Black Isle is off the main NC500 loop and a place to be visited for its own sake, not simply driven through. That makes it an equally good warm-up for so much of the journey that lies ahead.

At **Munlochy**, the main reason to break your journey is to make a wish, just like the ancient Celts once did. **Clootie Well**, hidden in Black Isle Wood at the end of a steep fir-lined trail, is a traditional shrine to St Boniface and one associated with ancient healing traditions. Here, the dyed-in-the-wool ritual sees a rag or 'cloot' dipped in the well's water, then tied to a tree in the hope that a sickness will fade as the cloth deteriorates over time. Bring a cloth to wish for your own good health, but if doing so make sure it is biodegradable for the environment.

When you're on the A832 and on the road to Avoch – a jumping-off point for dolphin-watching safaris – you'll be on the coast heading towards Fortrose.

Inverness
3 miles
Kessock Bridge
5.5 miles

Black Isle Brewing Co.

DETOUR: Black Isle Brewing Co.

Two miles from the A9, northeast of Arpafeelie

Your first NC500 detour. Regardless of the time of day, it's worth stopping in at **Black Isle Brewery** *(blackislebrewery.com)*, an organic artisan brewery that's one of Britain's best. It's located on an old farm road near Munlochy and operates an admirable sustainable life cycle on its grain-to-glass farm. There's a shop to stock up on the latest craft IPAs, pale ales and stouts, plenty of merchandise to show your love for this nook of the north, plus tours of the brewery and nearby vegetable market garden. Try a glass of Goldfinch, its gluten-free hoppy session ale, or a tropical Halo low-alcohol IPA – at 0.3%, it's the perfect companion for a road trip.

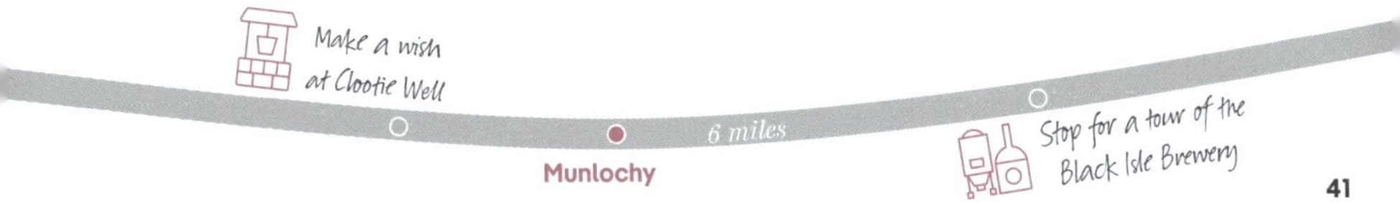

BEST PLACES TO EAT

The Anderson, Fortrose £
Smoked BBQ, cheesesteaks and burgers in this lively hotel, with an extraordinary craft beer and whisky collection. *(theanderson.co.uk; 4-11.30pm; limited opening in winter)*

Sutor Creek, Cromarty ££
Long-loved seafood restaurant serving crab, calamari and fish and chips, plus fab wood-fired pizza. *(sutorcreek.co.uk; noon-8pm Wed-Sun)*

Slaughterhouse Coffee, Cromarty £
Speciality barista-run nook overlooking the slipway, with second-hand books, good music and cakes. *(9am-3pm Thu-Mon)*

Glen Ord Distillery, Muir of Ord £
Atmospheric distillery serving rare drams, cocktails and non-alcoholic drinks, plus hot pies and soup. Cask-to-glass tasting tours are also recommended. *(malts.com/en-gb/distilleries/the-singleton; 10-6pm May-Aug, to 5pm Sept-Apr)*

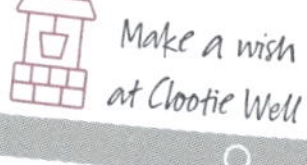

6 miles

Munlochy

Fortrose

The closest the Black Isle has to a metropolis, this busy town is noteworthy for photogenic **Fortrose Cathedral** *(free; open daily)*, a medieval jumble of red-sandstone ruins. There's the vaulted crypt of a 13th-century chapter house and sacristy to potter around, as well as the south aisle and chapel, both dating to 100 years later. In the 17th century, as one story has it, Oliver Cromwell removed most of the cathedral's masonry for his citadel at Inverness.

Elsewhere, Fortrose is worth a wander, not least for dropping into **Bakhoos Bakery**, a sourdough and viennoiserie specialist. Like everything here, you'll find it on the High Street.

Chanonry Point

From Fortrose High Street, it's around 1.5 miles southeast along Chanonry Ness through Fortrose & Rosemarkie Golf Club (the road cuts right between the fairways and greens) to **Chanonry Point**. Only in recent times has it become popular as a destination that makes a virtue of its unusual geography – it takes seconds to walk to both points of the beach-haloed spit of land and, often, there are twitching wildlife enthusiasts waiting to spy pods of northerly bottlenose dolphins. The cetaceans congregate here throughout the year, making the headland one of the best places in the UK to spot them from the mainland. At times, seal and porpoise appear too.

Along the Way We Saw...

BLACK ISLE BREWING CO. The road across the Kessock Bridge towards the Black Isle always fills me with anticipation. This time, my journey happily brought me to the barn doors of Black Isle Brewing Co., home of my favourite Scottish beer (hoppy Goldfinch Session IPA, for the record). It was an opportunity to nose around the brewery farm's five-acre market garden in dappled sunlight, but also to stock up on its seasonal releases, like a New England pale ale and bourbon barrel-aged imperial Scotch ale. I left with my nostrils tingling.

MIKE'S TIP: *Beer-lover nirvana can be found overnight by booking the brewery's handcrafted Shepherd's Hut, overlooking cereal fields murmuring with horses, cattle and sheep.*

Mike MacEacheran

Meet the Locals

With more than 50 miles of dramatic coastline to explore, the Black Isle is a stunning backdrop for a marine-life safari in good company.

HOW TO

Nearest stop: Fortrose

Getting here: From Inverness, the Black Isle is around 30 minutes and 13 miles away. Dolphin-watching trips leave daily from Avoch on the south coast and Cromarty on its northernmost tip. The two villages are 11.4 miles apart, with a trip each way taking 20 minutes.

Cost: adult/child/under-3s £25-37/20/free

'Look over there!' is a common refrain on the Black Isle. There are endless opportunities to see the coast while driving around the peninsula and, no matter how busy or quiet its country roads and seaweed-wrinkled beaches are, you're never really alone.

That's because unscheduled appearances from the area's resident 200-odd bottlenose dolphins is all part of the experience. The cetaceans, one of the most northerly pods in the world, brave the chilly waters year-round, but you don't have to – they can be regularly spotted from land, with **Chanonry Point** and **Kessock Bridge** being enviable locations to spot them in their natural environment.

For a more community-supporting, immersive experience, several operators run daily one- to two-hour tours, weather and tides permitting. Based in Cromarty, **EcoVentures** *(ecoventures.co.uk; from £37)* offers two-hour trips on a speedy, custom-built RIB to scout the seas for the peninsula's resident colony, while **Dolphin Trips Avoch**'s vessel is a 7m *Dory (dolphintripsavoch.co.uk; £25)*. Don't worry if there are no dolphins: you might still spot pilot whales, basking sharks, seals, harbour porpoises and otters.

FROM LEFT: ERIC ISSELEE/SHUTTERSTOCK, CATHERINE BRAID/GETTY IMAGES

Besides the marine life, there are fabulous views across the Moray Firth to **Fort George**, a defence garrison bound to the story of the Jacobite rising of 1745. Built in 1727, it was occupied and blown up by Bonnie Prince Charlie's forces in 1746, then rebuilt as the mightiest artillery fortification in Britain. You'll see far more dramatic lighthouses on the road ahead, but **Chanonry Lighthouse** still looks sublime at dusk.

Rosemarkie

It takes only a few minutes to return along the isthmus and onto the coastal road to neighbouring **Rosemarkie**, but if truth be told you'll be travelling back up to 1700 years. The 17th-century village overlooks a picturesque bay and is a worthwhile stop to visit **Groam House Museum** *(groamhouse.org.uk; donations welcome)*, which houses a terrific collection of Celtic and Pictish art found in the area.

JONATHAN W. COHEN/GETTY IMAGES

Waterfall, RSPB Fairy Glen

Who were the Picts? In a nutshell, the 'Painted Ones' (p50) were ancient tribes who lived in northeastern Scotland from 300 to 900 CE and all that remains of their legacy is place names and – crucially – beautifully carved stones. Inside the museum, you'll find around 15 examples of sculptural art, including the magnificent **Rosemarkie Stone** (p46), and designs similar to those on Celtic-Irish stones. Found around 1250 years ago in Rosemarkie's medieval church, they tell the stories of the power of kings, church and saints.

RSPB Fairy Glen

From here, the A832 tucks inland past **RSPB Fairy Glen**, where there's a steep-sided dell hiding a trail that leads to two magical waterfalls and a rushing stream. Leave your vehicle in the car park at the northern end of Rosemarkie's High Street, then set aside around one hour for the 2.5 mile return trip through broadleaf woodland to the tune of birdsong. The path can be muddy and the steps slippery and uneven, but to spend time here is to see why locals once thought otherworldly sprites used to hide in the shadows. Today, you'll more commonly see grey herons, stalking fish or a buzzard circling overhead.

Rosemarkie to Cromarty

The Black Isle is a covered patchwork of fields and farms and that comes to the fore on the next stretch of single-track road towards Cromarty. Indeed, the 'black' in the name refers not to any dark mystery, but to the rich and frost-free soils, which leave the fields looking pitch-black all winter. Coming off the A832, take the road to **Eathie**, where there are options to

Rosemarkie

9 miles

Stop at Fairy Glen Falls

The B-road via Eathie is a rollercoaster for cyclists

stop for further walks to **Eathie Beach** through pine and spruce forest, and **McFarquhar's Bed**, a natural stone arch surrounded by sea caves and best visited at low tide. Folklore say this was once used by a local smuggler for hiding contraband.

Cromarty

Twenty minutes' drive from Rosemarkie, the pretty port village of Cromarty sits at the tip of the Black Isle overlooking the Cromarty Firth – its name is derived from 'crooked bay' in Gaelic and the claim is it's the best-preserved historic town in the Highlands. Roots were put down here as far back as the mid-12th century and its huddle of traditional fishing and merchants' houses continues to draw visitors. Take a walk along the beach or a boat trip to see the dolphins playing in the firth. This will also be your first sighting of the North Sea oil-drilling rigs, whose towering derricks are silhouetted to the north of the road for this part of the journey.

continued on p48

WILDLIFE ENCOUNTERS

Top spots to meet the Black Isle's most famous residents (from east to west) include:

Ord Hill
Once home to an Iron Age hillfort, this forested mound hides a healthy population of red squirrels and woodland birds. Take binoculars to spot dolphins surfing the seascape below.

Culbokie
Peaceful woods on the north shore home to red squirrels, ducks and herons, with Cromarty Bridge nearby for spotting seals.

***Tip** Look to the skies! A reintroduction programme has successfully resulted in red kites becoming common.*

BERNABE BLANCO/SHUTTERSTOCK

Offshore drilling rigs, Cromarty Firth

7 miles

Cromarty

Cromarty has an enjoyable half-hour walk – park at the ferry slipway

Follow the Highland Pictish Trail

Tumble through time to learn about a lost Highland kingdom of warrior kings, monks and enigmatic art though stone.

HOW TO

Nearest stop: Rosemarkie

Getting here: Rosemarkie is 15 miles northeast of Inverness, follow the A9 and A832.

Strathpeffer is reached along the A835 and is 9 miles form the Cromarty Bridge.

Thurso's North Coast Visitor Centre is 110 miles further along the North Coast 500.

Cost: Free, donations welcome.

More info: *highlandpictishtrail.co.uk*

The Legacy of the Picts

Throughout the NC500, as seen on finely carved stones, hillforts set on towering hills, or in sculpture guarded by museums, the Picts have left their mark. These traditions, religious sites and finely worked jewellery appeal because they are less about what has been left behind and more about the stories they tell and mysteries to still puzzle over.

The Picts, who lived from 300 to 900 CE, are among Europe's most concealed peoples, ruling much of what is now Scotland, but also largely forgotten about in their homeland. The **Highland Pictish Trail** seeks to redress that, with a map, app and online guide to dozens of sites scattered from the Black Isle to Caithness and Sutherland.

Pictish Stones

Among the highlights are their most visible legacy: the **Pictish Stones**. At the **Groam House Museum** in Rosemarkie, the **Rosemarkie Stone** is an elaborately decorated cross covered in inscribed patterns of the sort that archaeologists would start reading, as if looking for clues to reveal a path to a carefully hidden secret. Another to add to your adventure is Strathpeffer's 7th-century **Eagle Stone**; this one is ornamented with a heavily incised bird of prey and connected to a Nostradamus-like figure from local history,

DOUG HOUGHTON SCO/ALAMY

MODERN 'PICTS'

On Film
Films crews came to Wester Ross for *The Eagle* (2011), an epic swords-and-sandals flick about a Roman legionnaire (Channing Tatum) coming to Pictish Scotland.

In Music
Based on the Isle of Eigg, low-fi Scottish musician Johnny Lynch performs under the moniker 'The Pictish Trail'.

For Cyclists
The Pictish Trail is a 466-mile bike-packing route in the east of Scotland traversing the ancient Pictish kingdoms.

Left: Eagle Stone
Below: Johnny Lynch, AKA The Pictish Trail

the Brahan Seer. Also known as 'Dark Kenneth', the seer was gifted with the ability to predict future events. Park at the Highland Museum of Childhood and follow directions to see the stone from there.

Further along the NC500 is the **North Coast Visitor Centre** in Thurso, which has an entire collection of iconic carvings. One highlight is the **Skinnet Stone**: look closely to see its rare depiction of a Romanesque horse-drawn chariot. The Picts have long gone, of course, but driving the NC500 is far better understood with their stories in mind.

ANDY CATLIN/ALAMY

Cromarty is also a place where artists converge. A hub for this is the **Cromarty Community Development Trust**, an old brewery repurposed as an art gallery and venue for concerts and workshops. The village's other highlight is **Hugh Miller's Birthplace Cottage & Museum**, the original thatch-roofed home of a local stonemason who became something of a local celebrity in the 19th-century as a geologist and writer.

Udale Bay

From Cromarty, the road turns west, hugging the north shore of the Black Isle and winding though fields, farms and forests. It's less pocketed with sights than the peninsula's southern coast, but you'll still see beaches, barns and slurry-slicked fields. After 10 miles, peaceful intertidal **Udale Bay** makes an enjoyable stop-off on the drive, particularly during ground-nesting breeding season when flocks of migrating wigeons gather on its mudflats and ospreys fish in the bay. From April to August, the RSPB wetland habitat also thrives with thousands of ducks, geese and waders like lapwings, snipes and redshanks. The view across the bay is a peek at what's to come further north.

Cromarty Bridge

More countryside views roll by as the road leads southwest across the northern flank of the Black Isle, past Culbokie and onto the A9 across **Cromarty Bridge**, where glossy seal heads can be seen popping up in the water below. Turning east, the road finally begins to point north and from here your next must-visit destinations, including Tain, Dornoch and Golspie, are all in easy reach.

Udale Bay

9.5 miles

Cromarty Bridge

Keep an eye out for porpoises and seals

KEV GREGORY/SHUTTERSTOCK

Cromarty Bridge

BEST PLACES TO STAY

Rosemarkie Camping & Caravanning Club £
As close to the Moray Firth beach as you can get, with well-maintained facilities, electric hook-ups and a shop. *(campingandcaravanningclub.co.uk)*

The Allangrange, Munlochy ££
Cosy five-bed hotel close to the Black Isle Brewing Co., with gastropub meals, Sunday roasts and a beer garden. *(theallangrange.co.uk)*

Newhall Mains, Cromarty £££
Luxury two-bed cottages and interior-designed suites on a former farm with its own private airfield. *(newhall-mains.com)*

The Highland Hotel, Strathpeffer ££
Baronial-styled and standing tall since 1882, this Victorian-era retreat specialises in scenic rooms and nods to the past. *(highlandhotel.co.uk)*

Discover Dingwall & Strathpeffer

The Viking- and Victorian-era towns of Dingwall and Strathpeffer make for an interesting detour or overnight from the main NC500 route.

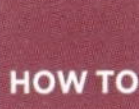

HOW TO

Nearest stop: Cromarty Bridge

Getting here: Dingwall is 5 miles west of Cromarty Bridge along the A682; Strathpeffer is a further 5.5 miles west of Dingwall.

When to go: May to September

More info: *visitwester-ross.com*

Leaving the Black Isle behind, most travellers continue north – but to experience what was once Scotland's spa capital, it's worth heading inland.

After five miles, the A862 passes through market town Dingwall, once a Viking settlement on the frontier of the Norse earls. Dingwall Castle is also believed to be the possible birthplace of Macbeth, who would go on to become the King of Scotland in the 11th century and be made famous by William Shakespeare. Like the tragic plans of Macbeth in the play, the fortification fell into ruin and now no longer exists.

There is more to see in Strathpeffer, five miles to the west. Once a renowned health resort, at its peak during Victorian times, the landed gentry swarmed to its grand hotels, spa houses and pavilions, and the sight was of men in top hats and genteel ladies in petticoats bathing in and drinking the sulphurous waters from the Morrison Well.

Of this history, little remains, but the Strathpeffer Pavilion has been restored into an events venue, while the renovated Pump Room offers a dash through local history.

FROM LEFT: MR SW PHOTO/SHUTTERSTOCK, DENNIS BARNES/GETTY IMAGES

Right: Strathpeffer

INSIGHT

The 'Painted People': Pictish History & Iconography

The Picts rose to become a dominant northern kingdom from 300–900 CE, and left behind iconic carved stones that illuminate Pictish life. Their legacy can be seen at places like Inverness Museum, Groam House Museum, and the Tarbat Discovery Centre – and along the North Coast 500 route.

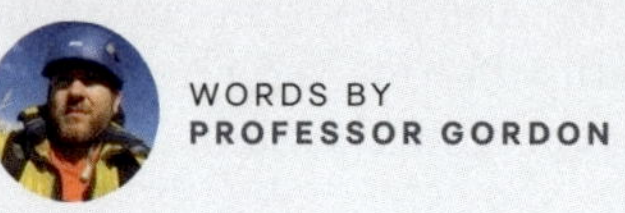

WORDS BY
PROFESSOR GORDON NOBLE

The Troublesome Enigma

The Picts were first mentioned in late Roman sources in 297 CE as a collective name for troublesome, barbaric peoples living north of the Roman frontier. They went on to become the dominant kingdom in northern Britain, forming the precursor to the medieval kingdom of Alba and ultimately of Scotland. The territory of Pictland encompassed the area north of the Firth of Forth and stretched to the Highlands and to the Northern and Western Isles (see map). The Picts have long remained an enigma because of the dearth of historical sources they left behind, but they have left a major legacy to European art and culture in the form of the carved stones that span an era of pagan belief to that of early Christianity.

The Highland area of the North Coast 500 route included the Pictish area of Cat, a region that equated to Caithness and Sutherland, while the area around Inverness was part of the Pictish kingdom of Fortriu. In Adomnán's *Life of St Columba* – written around 700 CE and recounting the life of the founder of the famous Christian monastery of Iona – the early Christian St Columba is said to have met the powerful Pictish king, Bridei, son of Maelchon, at his stronghold somewhere around the Inverness area in the late 6th century. Bridei is described as *regulus* (king) and had

Cattle depicted on the Calf Stone, Tarbat Discovery Centre

hostages from 'Orcades' (the Orkney Isles) in his court.

Archaeological sites of the Pictish period have traditionally been difficult to identify, but there are settlements from this era that can be visited today. Craig Phadrig fort overlooking Inverness may have been the seat of King Bridei. At the fort, excavations in the 1960s revealed imported pottery and clay metalworking moulds for making high-status dress accessories, and hanging bowl vessels dating from the 5th to 7th centuries. In Caithness, unusual Pictish-era longhouse-style buildings, known as 'wags', are still standing in some cases, the most accessible of which is the site of Wag of Forse, located near Latheron, between Wick and Dunbeath.

The Highlands would have formed a rich landscape setting for Pictish society. While our written sources for the Picts tell us little about daily life, *Life of St Columba* includes passages that refer to cattle farming (Calf Stone), catching salmon and hunting boar in the Highlands and Islands of Scotland during the Pictish period. Farming would have dominated the lives of most, with families involved in agricultural tasks such as ploughing, reaping, and feeding and caring for animals. The highest-status sites on mainland Scotland have shown evidence of the finer things in life, with artefacts indicating that wine from the Mediterranean, and foodstuffs and drinking vessels from France were imported.

Pictish Symbols

The truly emblematic icon of the Picts is the symbol tradition – a distinctive group of symbols (p52), both abstract and naturalistic, including striking animal designs and recognisable objects such as mirrors and combs. They are found most commonly carved on stone monuments, with over 200 examples known from eastern and northern Scotland, including

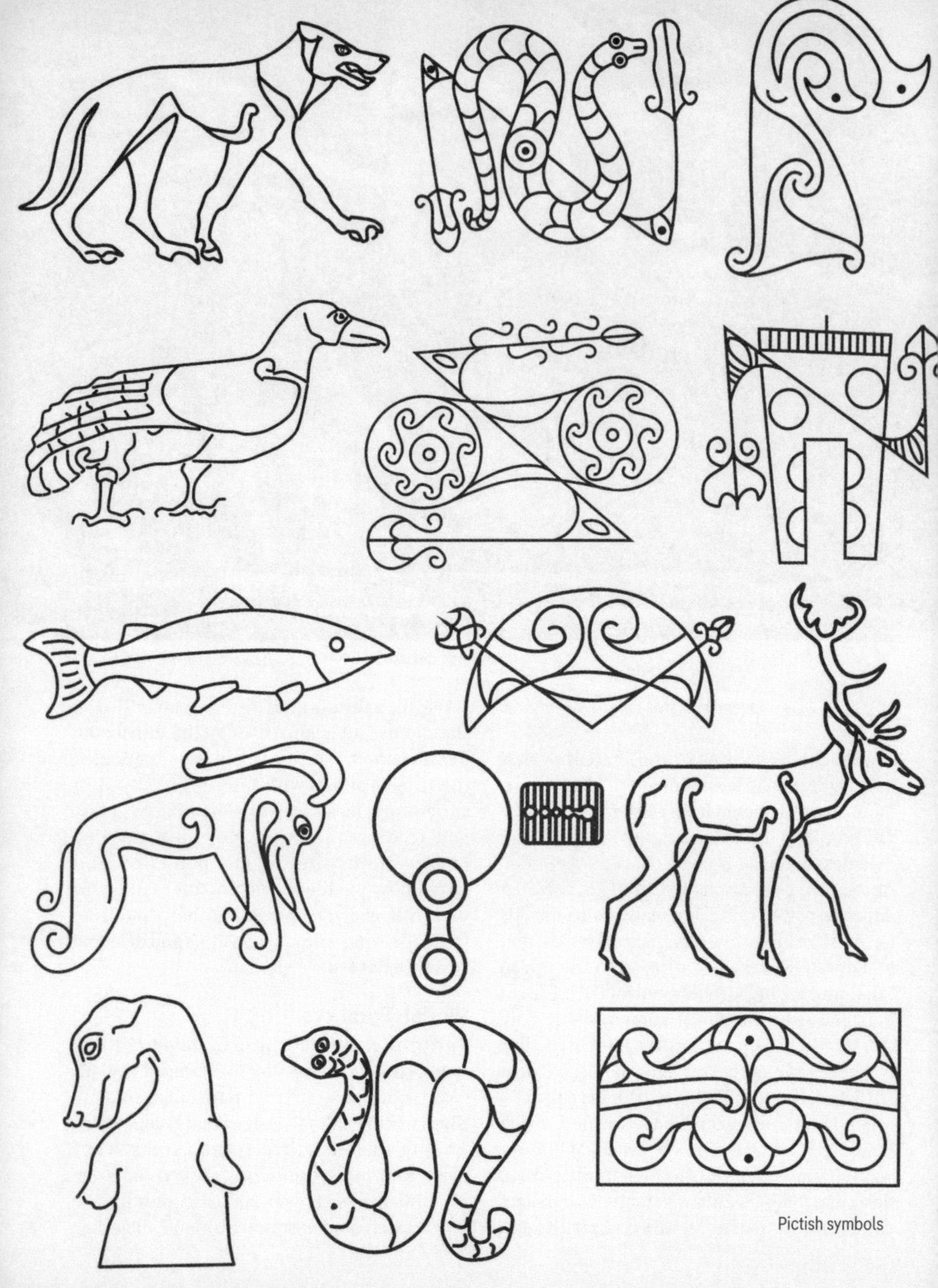

Pictish symbols

from the Inverness area, Ross and Cromarty, Sutherland and Caithness. Approximately two-thirds of the stone carvings in this part of Scotland are incised symbol stones and the other third are Christian cross-slabs that include symbol designs. The symbols also appear on cave walls, metalwork, bone and other objects including high-status silver plaques and chains.

There has been little agreement about the number and range of symbols, but around 30 core symbols have been suggested. No one has fully cracked the code of what these mean – there have been repeated attempts to decipher their meaning since they were 'rediscovered' in the 19th century. Interpretations have included the symbols representing pagan or Christian religious beliefs, indicators of rank or tribal identity, representations of marriage alliances, memorials to the dead, as well as countless less-grounded speculations. Some of the examples found on Christian cross-slabs suggest the symbols 'labelled' people and are most likely to have been conveying names – the common pairing of symbols perhaps representing parts of the names of Pictish individuals. The markings are found in the context of settlements, personal objects and burials – in all cases, they may have been representing identities, e.g. the names of owners or occupants, of significant living or dead members of the community.

> The Picts have long remained an enigma because of the dearth of historical sources they left behind, but they have left a major legacy to European art and culture in the form of their carved stones.

The symbol stones have long been identified as Pictish because their distribution closely matches the extent of the Pictish kingdoms. Recent dating suggests that this form of communication could have origins in the Roman period, with examples from a promontory fort in Aberdeenshire dating from the 3rd or 4th century. This is a period in which the Picts were in contact with the literate culture of Rome through military encounters, trading and perhaps even military service. The Pictish carvings provide incredible detail for some of the aspects of Pictish life, their religious and spiritual outlook, and even what some of them looked like.

Visit the Sites

The foremost place to start exploring the stones and the Picts is at *highlandpictishtrail.co.uk*. The five best spots on the NC500 route to get familiar with the Picts and their carvings are: Inverness Museum, Groam House Museum (p44) on the Black Isle, Tarbat Discovery Centre at Portmahomack, Dunrobin Castle Museum and North Coast Visitor Centre (p46) in Thurso. These sites are all on the east coast of the NC500, but there are examples of Pictish art to be found dotted along or near most stretches of the drive.

Inverness Museum has a collection of ten Pictish stones, and a number of objects from the Pictish era such as fragments of brooches and a wonderful pendant carved in cannel coal from Breakachy near Beauly. The pendant features an elaborate interlaced Christian cross on one side and lightly carved animals on the other – a Pictish cross-slab in miniature. The real highlight of Inverness Museum though is the fabulous Pictish wolf carving from Ardross.

Groam House Museum, like the Tarbat Discovery Centre, requires a short detour from the NC500 route, but the effort is strongly rewarded. In Rosemarkie, the collection of early medieval carved stones at Groam House is likely to be from one of the most important churches of northern Pictland. The stones include the magnificent Rosemarkie cross-slab, boldly decorated on one side with a striking cross with key pattern and vine scroll – like the page of an illuminated manuscript set in stone.

The Tarbat Discovery Centre displays the stupendous finds made during archaeological excavations that ran from the 1990s to 2007 on a hitherto unknown Pictish monastic settlement. Situated in the former church of St Colman's, the exhibits chart the development of the site as an elite Pictish settlement and then a monastic community. The digs uncovered a large church vallum enclosure and a road heading towards the church, where the remains of craftwork were found, including extremely rare evidence for the production of both precious metalwork and vellum for illuminated books made during the life of the monastery. The carved stones are a particular highlight here (e.g. the Dragon

Left: Rosemarkie cross-slab
Below: Dragon Stone

Stone), with hundreds of fragments of stone crosses, composite shrines and architectural fragments found during the excavations.

The magnificent cross-slabs at Nigg and Shandwick on the Tarbat Peninsula (p63) are also well worth visiting, as is the replica of the Hilton of Cadboll stone, just a few miles from Portmahomack. The small museum within the grounds of Dunrobin Castle (p79) is an eccentric delight with a number of striking Pictish monuments on show amongst an eclectic mix of museum objects arranged in the original Victorian 'cabinet of curiosity'-style displays. The most magnificent stone is from nearby Golspie and has an intricately carved Christian cross on one side, and a Pictish figure bearing an axe and a range of Pictish designs including the 'Pictish beast', salmon, and the abstract double-disc and crescent and V-rod symbols on the other side (Golspie Stone).

And finally, the North Coast Visitor Centre in Thurso displays three impressive Pictish stones from the local area, including the Skinnet Stone with a very rare depiction of a Pictish horse-drawn vehicle, two different crosses and a range of Pictish symbols (Skinnet Stone).

Elsewhere on the NC500, you can see a range of Pictish and early Christian monuments. Other highlights include the Farr Stone in the grounds of Strathnaver Museum, the nearby cross-slab at Reay, the cross-slab and the tall symbol stone at Edderton, Sutherland, and the Eagle Stone (p46) at Strathpeffer. On the west coast of the NC500, the symbol stone in the wonderful Gairloch Museum and the cross-slabs on display at the Applecross Heritage Centre are also well worth a visit.

Left: Skinnet Stone
Right: Golspie Stone

Cromarty Bridge

It could be argued this section through Easter Ross is when the NC500 really gets into gear: the coast becomes populated with world-class single-malt whisky distilleries and links golf courses, the landscape unbuttoning itself and beginning to puff up its chest. The result is a swell of hills and pine-forested glens to the west and a succession of bays and windswept beaches, just beyond the roadside and colliding with the roiling North Sea.

Mike MacEacheran

Dornoch

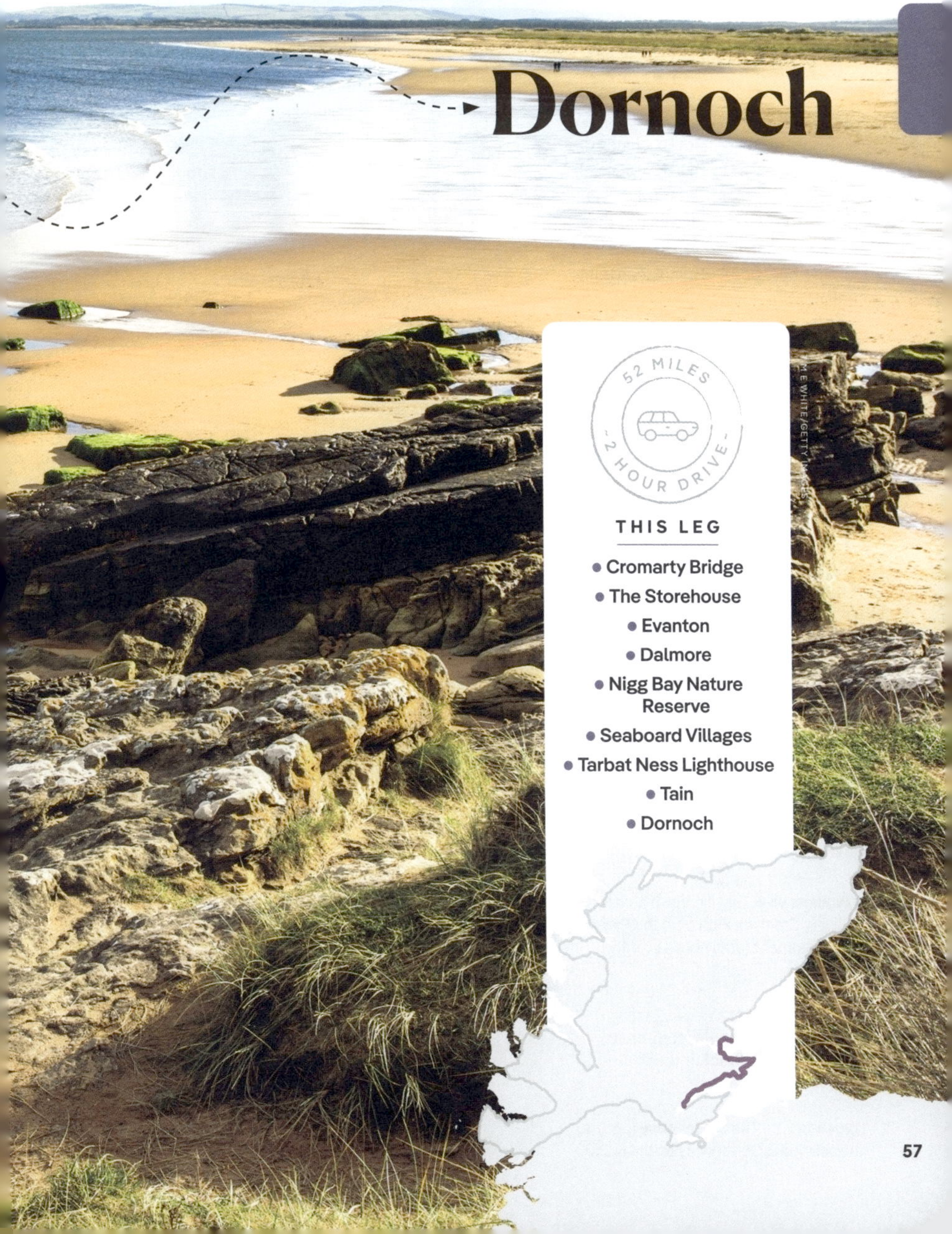

THIS LEG

- Cromarty Bridge
- The Storehouse
- Evanton
- Dalmore
- Nigg Bay Nature Reserve
- Seaboard Villages
- Tarbat Ness Lighthouse
- Tain
- Dornoch

Driving Notes

The road largely sticks to the busy A9, a lifeline in the northern Highlands that runs all the way to Thurso. Like much of the east coast, the surrounding scenery is swimming with beaches and bays, and the quietest roads veer off this backbone, leading deeper into the Easter Ross Peninsula via Nigg, Balintore and Portmahomack.

Breaking Up Your Journey

This is a tranquil place of farms and distilleries, cattle and grain. It may be less dramatic than the west coast but there's beauty here, not least in the food and drink. A stop at The Storehouse at Foulis feels almost compulsory, while there are plenty of services in whisky town Tain and in Dornoch, a large seaside resort packed with hotels, campsites and motorhome parks.

Mike's Tips

BEST HOTEL Golf fan or not, the **Royal Golf Hotel** (p63) in Dornoch is a terrific base for coastal walks, fireside pints and fresh-off-the-boat seafood.

FAVOURITE VIEW Looking down across the silvery Cromarty Firth from the **Fyrish Monument** (p60) above Evanton.

ESSENTIAL STOP Whisky tasting at **Glenmorangie** (p66), or at nearby **Balblair** (p66).

ROAD-TRIP TIP **The Storehouse** (p60) is the best roadside services on the NC500.

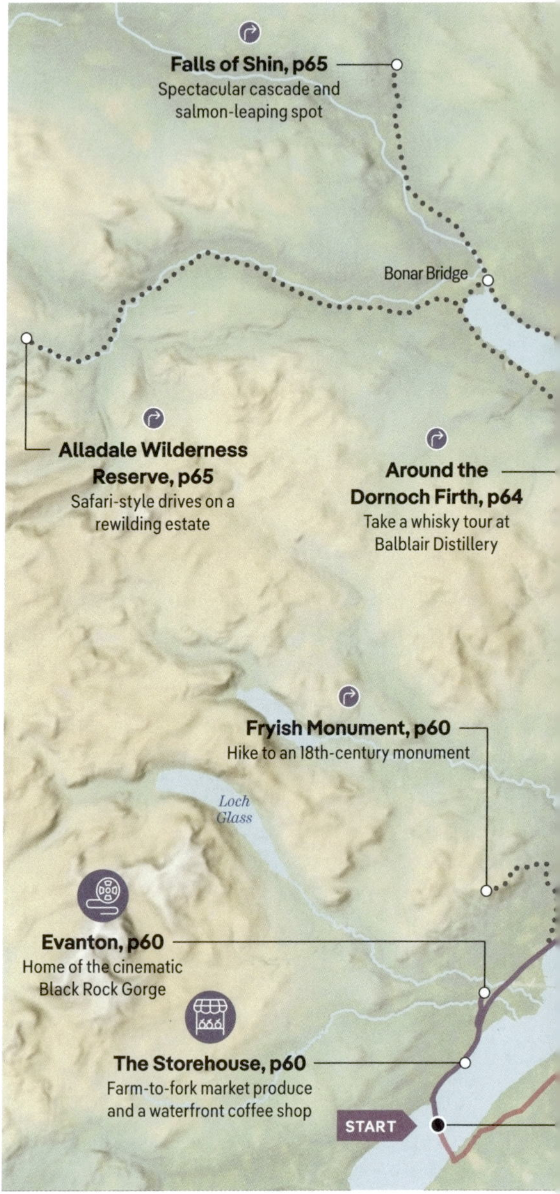

Falls of Shin, p65
Spectacular cascade and salmon-leaping spot

Bonar Bridge

Alladale Wilderness Reserve, p65
Safari-style drives on a rewilding estate

Around the Dornoch Firth, p64
Take a whisky tour at Balblair Distillery

Fryish Monument, p60
Hike to an 18th-century monument

Loch Glass

Evanton, p60
Home of the cinematic Black Rock Gorge

The Storehouse, p60
Farm-to-fork market produce and a waterfront coffee shop

START

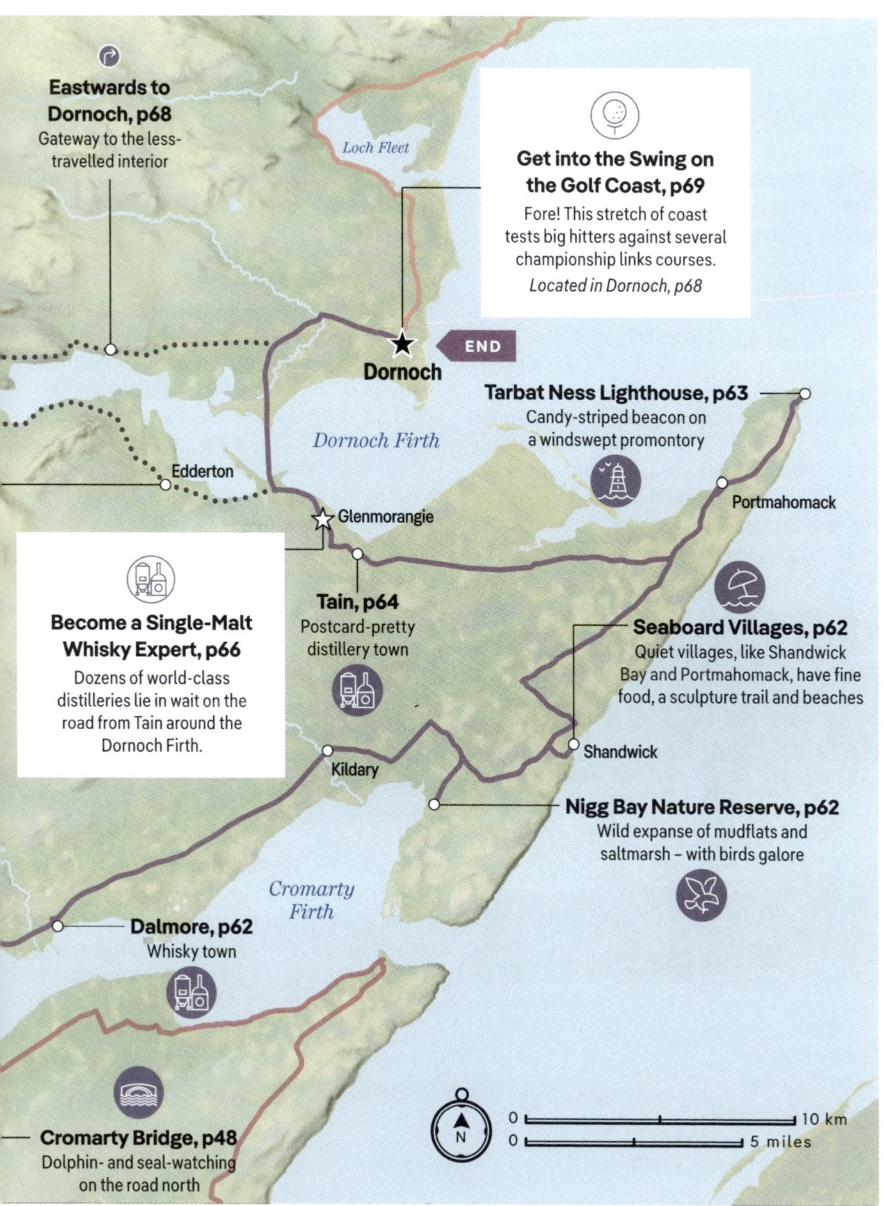
Eastwards to Dornoch, p68
Gateway to the less-travelled interior
Loch Fleet
Get into the Swing on the Golf Coast, p69
Fore! This stretch of coast tests big hitters against several championship links courses.
Located in Dornoch, p68
END
Dornoch
Tarbat Ness Lighthouse, p63
Candy-striped beacon on a windswept promontory
Dornoch Firth
Edderton
Glenmorangie
Portmahomack
Become a Single-Malt Whisky Expert, p66
Dozens of world-class distilleries lie in wait on the road from Tain around the Dornoch Firth.
Tain, p64
Postcard-pretty distillery town
Seaboard Villages, p62
Quiet villages, like Shandwick Bay and Portmahomack, have fine food, a sculpture trail and beaches
Shandwick
Kildary
Nigg Bay Nature Reserve, p62
Wild expanse of mudflats and saltmarsh – with birds galore
Cromarty Firth
Dalmore, p62
Whisky town
Cromarty Bridge, p48
Dolphin- and seal-watching on the road north
N
0
10 km
0
5 miles

PREVIOUS STOP The drive north from Cromarty Bridge is filled with the potential of seeing marine life at play in the Cromarty Firth, with the A9 hugging the inlet's north shore and furrowing through farmland.

The Storehouse at Foulis

At the northern end of **Cromarty Bridge**, the A9 passes through a signposted roundabout that feels like the gateway to the NC500 proper: from here on in, the coastal road is more direct and can be followed, almost religiously, right the way round to Ullapool and beyond.

With that in mind, you'll want to stock up on goodies and snacks and there's no better place than **The Storehouse**, a food hall par excellence inside a restored 18th-century farm depot. There's a superb cafe-restaurant with outdoor seating for lungfuls of North Sea air, but the real highlight for road trippers is the farm shop. Pick up some fine cheeses, jams, chutneys and breads, plus a bottle of whisky or gin and you'll be all set.

JOHN BRACEGIRDLE/ALAMY

Black Rock Gorge

The Road to Alness

After The Storehouse, the first noteworthy stop is **Black Rock Gorge**, a hidden box canyon. In the village of **Evanton** two miles north of Foulis, park on Camden Street, then follow the street up along the tree line, past the Evanton Community Woodlands' log cabin to the signposted gorge. There's a muddy downhill track to get to the bridge over the mile-long gorge, then you're in the midst of the dark contorted canyon, with the rushing Allt Graad (River Glass) far, far below.

It's little wonder the vice-like chasm was chosen as a location in the fourth **Harry Potter** film. Suspend your imagination and you might be able to picture the young wizard on his broomstick being chased by a dragon in *The Goblet of Fire*. To walk the forested loop, it's a 2.5-mile (1½-hour) round trip – though you'll be far quicker if being chased by a Hungarian Horntail or Chinese Fireball.

DETOUR: Fryish Monument

While driving further north towards Alness, one peculiarity sticks out on a hilltop on the western horizon: a striking triple arch structure. This is the **Fyrish Monument**, a stone battlement ruin built on the orders of

Cromarty Bridge

2 miles

The Storehouse

2 miles

Keep an eye out for dolphins north of Cromarty Firth

Fryish Monument

former British army officer Sir Hector Munro, 8th Laird of Novar, who fought in India during the late 18th century. It was built during the Highland Clearances in 1782 and is said to have been constructed purely to keep the locals in work.

The monument – a replica of a similar arched gateway that once stood Chennai, India – can be reached after a gentle **round-trip hike** *(two to 2½ hours; 3.75 miles)*, offering spectacular views from the top. To get there, take the minor B1976 road to **Boath** west of Alness, park at the Novar Estate car park, then follow the signposted Jubilee Path.

If you continue along the B1976 to Dalnvaie, you'll pass by one of the most recent success stories in Scotland: **Ardross Castle**. Its

BEST PLACES TO EAT

The Oystercatcher, Portmahomack ££
Wonderful seafood-focused tasting menus with oysters, scallops and lobster the headliners. *(the-oystercatcher.co.uk; 5-9pm Thu-Sat May-Oct)*

Platform 1864, Tain £
All-rounder for breakfast, lunch, dinner, coffee, cake and cocktails in Tain's former railway station. *(platform1864.com; 10am-10pm Mon-Thu, to midnight Fri & Sat, to 7.30pm Sun)*

Cocoa Mountain, Dornoch £
Award-winning truffles, bars and chocs to stock up on for the drive, plus a signature hot chocolate lathered in cream and melted chocolate swirls. *(cocoamountain.co.uk; 10am-5pm)*

The Golden Gorse, Dornoch £££
Hidden inside the grand Dornoch Station hotel, this is the place for Michelin-worthy meat and seafood, plus Sunday roasts. *(marineandlawn.com/dornochstation/dining-golden-gorse; noon-late)*

6 miles

Evanton

Take a hike to the Fryish Monument

100-acres are the setting for both the wildly popular UK and US versions of *The Traitors* reality TV show – but, sadly, the turreted mansion is only open as a wedding venue or exclusive-use event location.

Into Whisky Country

For road-trippers, **Alness** is a functional service town, with its main lure lying in neighbouring **Dalmore** just over the A9 bypass. The small community is a nexus of whisky production and the **Dalmore Distillery**, overlooking the salt-tanged Cromarty Firth, has been making world-renowned single malts since 1839. The whole operation is even more remarkable when you consider its history; during WWI, the distillery and its large warehouses were repurposed by the US navy to assemble and deploy mines that were laid between Orkney and Norway. In 1920, an accidental mine detonation and subsequent fires destroyed much of the premises. Fast forward to today and, happily, a new visitor centre debutied in 2025.

Nigg Bay Nature Reserve

At the south of this hammer-headed peninsula, five miles east of Kildary, you might find yourself alone in the salt marshes and mudflats of **Nigg Bay Nature Reserve** – that is, apart from October to February, when more than 10,000 ducks and pink-footed geese arrive in the RSPB reserve to overwinter. Visit at high tide when the birds are drawn closer to shore.

Denmark has a world-famous bronze of the *Little Mermaid* overlooking Copenhagen Harbour, but you don't need to go that far to see something similar. A short drive five miles north to Balintore brings you past delightful Shandwick Bay beach to the **Mermaid of the North**. The 3m sculpture is the highlight of the area's low-key **Seaboard Sculpture Trail**.

MARTEN_HOUSE/SHUTTERSTOCK

Dalmore Distillery

Road to the Seaboard Villages

From Dalmore, the A9 north now gives you a couple of options. It's straight ahead for the last six miles to Tain for another lip-smacking date with the distillers and maltmen of Glenmorangie, where newly arrived travellers warm their noses and hearts with drams of floral, citrus-spiced whisky. Otherwise, after eight miles, the B1975 branches off at **Kildary**, leading to **Easter Ross** at its most agrarian. For those wanting to get right off the beaten track, this is the road to opt for, as there are subtle highlights dotted along the Easter Ross coast amongst the so-called **Seaboard Villages**: Hilton of Cadboll, Balintore and Shandwick.

4.5 miles

Nigg Bay Nature Reserve

Tarbat Ness Lighthouse

A half-hour drive along the coast, the small former fishing village of Portmahomack has a lovely setting gazing out from the western edge of **Tarbat Ness** that juts out into the North Sea. There's a beach walk, discovery centre with Pictish stones, splendid seafood restaurant and dinky harbour designed by Scots engineering great Thomas Telford, who masterminded the west coast's Caledonian Canal.

You could drive (or cycle) to the end of the peninsula to see candy-striped **Tarbat Ness Lighthouse**, the tallest on the Scottish mainland at 40m, but a better option is to hike the circular **coastal path** *(90 minutes; 5 miles)*. In summer, look out for huge swells of gannets, kittiwakes and auks.

BEST PLACES TO STAY

Castlecraig Clifftops, Nigg £
Four lovely glamping pods set on a family-run livestock farm overlooking the Cromarty Firth. Minimum three nights. *(castlecraigfarm.com)*

Glenmorangie House, Fearn by Tain £££
Whisky-flavour-inspired rooms (yes, it's a thing) at this deliciously handsome, branded guesthouse with six doubles and three cottages. *(glenmorangie.com)*

Royal Golf Hotel, Dornoch ££
Exactly what's needed after a long day: warm service, cosy rooms, a relaxing bar with crackling fire and a steak-seafood restaurant. *(highlandcoasthotels.com/royal-golf-dornoch)*

Dornoch Castle Hotel, Dornoch ££
A plush old castle, with characterful tower and Elizabethan-style rooms, a la carte restaurant and whisky bar brimming with vintage drams. *(dornochcastlehotel.com)*

Tarbat Ness Lighthouse

MACIEJ OLSZEWSKI/SHUTTERSTOCK

Tarbat Ness Lighthouse

13 miles

12.5 miles

Shandwick

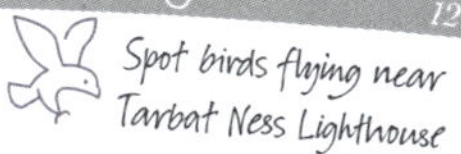

Spot birds flying near Tarbat Ness Lighthouse

Tain

It's a relaxing 10-mile drive to **Tain**, the road slaloming through fields with views of the Dornoch Firth, your roadside companion for the next stretch of the journey. While Tain is Scotland's oldest royal burgh, rising to fame when pilgrims descended to venerate the relics of St Duthac in the Middle Ages, the sandstone town is now a languid place, but there are still a few attractions.

Chief among these is **Tain & District Museum and Clan Ross Centre** *(tainmuseum.org.uk; April to October)*, set in a campus on the grounds of St Duthus Church. Some people come to learn about Tain-tinted heritage (one claim is King James VI of Scotland made multiple pilgrimages to the town), but most stop off to visit the **Glenmorangie Distillery**. Since it was first built on the site of a farm in 1843, it has become one of the world's bestselling single-malt brands.

DETOUR: Around the Dornoch Firth

The fast A9 leads from Tain across the **Dornoch Forth Bridge**, but the 22-mile (30-minute) loop around the low-lying Dornoch Firth is a beautifully scenic, if short, addition to the NC500's eastern section. At Edderton, a road peels off to the right to **Balblair Distillery**, with a worthwhile visitor centre in a former malting building. Even if you're clock-watching, it's worth taking a quick dogleg detour up the B9176 at Easter Fearn to the **Dornoch Forth viewpoint**. From granitic hills frilled in heather moorland in the far distance to oak woodland foregrounding the tidal seascape, this is a snapshot of the wild Highlands at its most gentle.

Along the Way We Met...

PAUL MADEN Sometimes, it feels like a different world up here. Before moving here in 2006, I was a mere chocolate hobbyist with no plan, but it felt so right to make and serve the most delicious fine chocolates surrounded by golden beaches, pristine lochs and incredible mountains. My advice is to take the opportunity to stop and explore, as there are hidden secrets everywhere. And, of course, drive considerately and respect our wonderful nature. Please do follow the countryside code at all times.

Paul is the co-owner of Cocoa Mountain (cocoamountain.co.uk), with chocolate cafes in Dornoch and Durness.

PAUL'S TIP: *I'd encourage people to visit Dornoch for some sophisticated retail therapy, and – definitely – a visit to Cocoa Mountain on Castle Street for a well-deserved mug of hot chocolate!*

The Glenmorangie Distillery is a 30-minute walk from Tain

9.5 miles

Tain

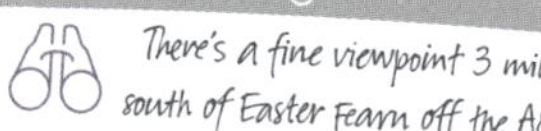

There's a fine viewpoint 3 miles south of Easter Fearn off the A836

DETOUR: The Falls of Shin

From the viewpoint above the inlet, it's a quick return back onto the A836 and over **Bonar Bridge** to the northern shores of the Dornoch Firth. You've now left Easter Ross behind and entered the historic county of Sutherland, an area once ruled by nobles, including the earls of Orkney and Sutherland.

It takes around 20 minutes to drive eastwards from here to the seaside resort town of Dornoch and at least double that to head west to see the thundering **Falls of Shin**, 16 miles along the A837 on the road to Lairg. The cascade is worth the out-and-back trip along the Kyle of Sutherland, not least for views of turreted **Carbisdale Castle**, a privately owned masterpiece of baronial architecture looming next to Culrain train station. As for the falls, it's only a short downhill footpath from the car park to salmon-viewing glory: from June to September, the Atlantic fish spectacularly hurl themselves up the falls on their way upstream to spawn.

DETOUR: Alladale Wilderness Reserve

This rewilding project makes a great addition to a more immersive journey away from the main NC500 route. A self-styled 23,000-acre utopia, with lodges, nature-based activities and wildlife safaris, it's 13 miles (30 minutes) west of Ardgay near Bonar Bridge off the A836, and is at the vanguard of the country's wider environmental movement.

A two-night minimum stay is required, but it's more than worth it for e-biking in the company of wild stags, hiking the Glun Liath ridge, fly-fishing for brown trout and – the highlight – seeking out golden eagles, otters, red deer, red squirrels and black grouse, Scotland's alternative Big Five.

continued on p48

Bonar Bridge

IAIN MASTERTON/ALAMY

Become a Single-Malt Whisky Expert

On the NC500, life seems imbued with whisky, but to really understand it you need to do more than drink it.

HOW TO

Nearest stop: Tain

Getting here: Follow the A9 north of the Black Isle.

The whisky route: Due to geography and population, most distilleries on the NC500 are located between Inverness and Thurso on the east coast.

Health and safety: All distilleries have a range of tours to choose from, including ones without tastings. Scotland has a zero tolerance policy to drink-driving, allowing only 50mg of alcohol per 100ml of blood.

More info: *scotch-whisky.org.uk*

The Story of Scotch

Scotland has the world's greatest number of whisky distilleries, estimated by some to be more than 150, with the popularity of the 'guid auld Scotch drink', as national bard Robert Burns called it, set to push that number closer to 200 in coming years.

The Highlands association with the spirit began as early as the 15th-century when, as way of using up surplus malted barley, monks produced *uisge beatha* (the water of life). Jump a century or so on and, in 1644, the first official taxes on production caused a rise in illicit distilling, and smuggling became standard practice. Ever since legalisation in 1823, the flavour profile has been refined, softer grain whisky has flooded the market and, today, around 43 bottles are shipped worldwide every second.

Whisky Hunting

It stands to reason that a whisky distillery visit should be near the top of your NC500 must-do

list. There are 13 in Easter Ross and Caithness alone (eight offer tours) and, as no two distilleries are the same, each one is an education into the culture of the Highlands itself.

Of the historic brands, **Glenmorangie** in Tain is arguably the best-known label, with the most sophisticated **visitor experience** *(45 minutes, £23)*, while **The Singleton at Glen Ord** *(1¼ hours, £22)* and **Balblair** *(1½ hours, £25)* are both set in handsome locations. Further up the coast, formally mothballed **Brora** has been given a second life by Diageo and has reopened for ultra-exclusive **private tours**

ROBERTHARDING/ALAMY

OTHERS TO DISCOVER

The Dalmore, Alness
A highly anticipated new visitor experience opened in 2025.

8 Doors Distillery, John O'Groats
A newcomer in whisky terms (opened 2022), this micro distillery is another reason to visit the famous landmark.

Wolfburn Distillery, Thurso
Built on the site of a historic distillery, this modern production option lies east of Thurso.

Left: Glenmorangie Distillery
Below: The Anderson, Fortrose

(from £225). One of the oldest warehouses, **Old Pulteney** *(1½ hours, £20)* is located in the heart of Wick and is the most suitable for those who do not want to drive afterwards.

Where to Drink

At around 5pm each day, in pubs and hotels like **The Anderson** in Fortrose (p41), **Mackays Hotel** in Wick (p86) and the **Beinn Bar** inside The Torridon (p209), something miraculous happens when the cork is pulled from a top-shelf bottle. The sun disappears over the horizon, a fire is lit and, by the hour of bedtime, everything is fuzzy and glorious.

FRASER BAND/ALAMY

CLAUDINE VAN MASSENHOVE/SHUTTERSTOCK

Dornoch Cathedral

DETOUR: Eastwards to Dornoch

From Bonar Bridge, the last stretch of this section to Dornoch along the A949 is a straightforward rush through forests, with the **Dornoch Firth** on the right. If you're coming by bike, you might want to play awhile at the **Kyle of Sutherland Trails**, just outside Bonar Bridge and home to two twisting mountain bike circuits that soar though the trees.

Otherwise, its onwards past the sprawling country-sports estate of **Skibo Castle**, an exclusive private members club with a £30,000-plus joining fee. For the abridged backstory, Scots philanthropist Andrew Carnegie came in 1898 and transformed the estate into what he coined 'heaven on earth'. A brief stint on the A9 before going back to the A949 through Camore delivers you to Dornoch: the first must-see town on the NC500's east coast.

Dornoch

The old market town of Dornoch, two miles from the A9, uses time-tested methods to keep its visitors entertained. There's a beautiful beach beyond the dunes, two championship links golf courses looking over the firth, and shops and boutiques with the vintage appeal of the seaside.

Dornoch Cathedral is worth a look, offering weirder history than you might expect; in 1722, the last witch executed in Scotland was boiled alive here in a cauldron of hot tar (by all accounts, she turned her neighbours' daughter into a pony). Across the road on Castle Street is a row of historical buildings, including the **Carnegie Courthouse** (now a restaurant) and the **Old Jail** (oddly, an interiors shop). **Historylinks Museum**, on the street behind, will help you fill out the rest of the town's timeline.

Dornoch

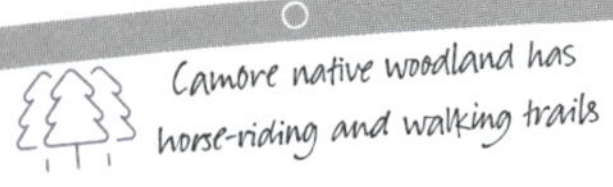
Camore native woodland has horse-riding and walking trails

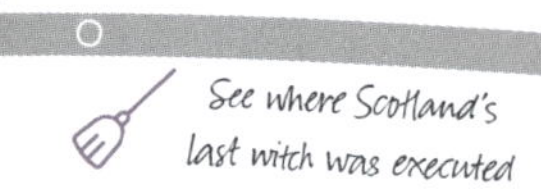
See where Scotland's last witch was executed

Get into the Swing on the Golf Coast

Scotland invented the game of golf as it's known today, and the east coast packs in as much wildlife as it does birdies, eagles and albatrosses.

HOW TO

Nearest stop: Dornoch

Getting here: Turn east off the A9 at Evelix for 3 miles.

Cost: Green fees vary. Bonar Bridge starts from £15; Royal Dornoch costs between £175 and £320 for one round on its Championship Course.

Tip: Twilight tee times are cheaper, as are rounds outside of the peak April to October season.

More info: *scottishgolf.org*

The lion's share of golf courses on the NC500 can be found to the east, with the combination of rolling dunes, sandy coastlands, sea views – and unpredictable weather – creating the ultimate test for golfers. On the waterfront at Dornoch, **Royal Dornoch Golf Club** is the one most often spoken of in reverential tones – regularly, it features highly in best-of-the-world rankings. That's both because of its design and its history, dating back to around 1616 (even before the 18-hole round was created in St Andrews in 1764). Still today, it maintains elements of the original layout and motifs contrived by legendary figure Old Tom Morris, known as 'The Grand Old Man of Golf'.

Local golfers are quick to remind you that the fingerprints of another illustrious course architect – James Braid – are also found along the coast. The five-time winner of the Open Championship was the brains behind Royal Troon, Carnoustie and Gleneagles, as well as the 18 holes at Brora Golf Club, dating to 1891. The quirk on this bucket-list course is that it's not uncommon for sheep to be spotted grazing on the greens. Other wildlife encounters are on tap at **Bonar Bridge Ardgay Golf Club**'s 9 holes, thanks to a location hunkered amid gorse and hills. Time for another? Then set your sights on Thurso and **Reay Golf Club**, the most northerly course on the British mainland and another designed by Braid. Absolutely par-fect.

GO FURTHER

Wick Golf Club
One of the oldest courses on the NC500 opened in 1870.

Durness Golf Club
Brag-worthy newcomer with 9 holes overlooking Balnakeil Bay.

Gairloch Golf Club
The west coast's best: historical link course with Hebridean island views.

CHRISTOPHER BABCOCK/SHUTTERSTOCK

Royal Dornoch Golf Club

Loch Brora
GEORGE MACIVER/ALAMY

Into the Great Outdoors

A journey on the NC500 is often thought of as one to be taken while sitting still. The relationship between the road and wheels of a car, camper van or bike is crucial, but much of the Northern Highlands' most beautiful corners can only be experienced in another way: while on foot.

WORDS BY **MIKE MACEACHERAN**

Leave the Road Behind

On the map, every part of the NC500 rewards the traveller with a dream checklist of outdoor pursuits. The northwest is prime mountaineering, hiking and sea kayaking territory, with paths to follow and islands of pilgrimage to land on, as the Picts, Celts and Vikings once did centuries ago. Then there is the beach-fringed north coast, where surfers ride moshing waves and bird-watchers congregate on clifftops to trespass, momentarily, into stunning seabed cities alive with gannet, guillemot, razorbill and puffin.

There are multiple reasons to get active on the NC500, but it's also true to say that the memorable hills, lochs, forests and firths between Cromarty and Dornoch offer more ways in which to be challenged by the landscape than any other. For on this section of the journey, all-comers of all ages, abilities and interests are taken care of.

Highs & Lows

For spells on the water, there are two island-speckled firths, where canoeists, kayakers and SUPers can paddle to freedom. Based in Brora, Sutherland Adventure Company *(sutherland adventurecompany.com)* offers lessons on Loch Brora, as well as daydream-worthy paddles along the coast to Golspie via Dunrobin Castle – on such an out-and-back journey, the coast feels more alive than it ever could from behind a steering wheel.

Also in the business of mussing up your hair, Lairg-based family tour operator Go Wild Highlands *(gowildhighlands.co.uk)* offers sustainably minded canoe safaris on the Kyle of Sutherland estuary. The clincher is this is part of the wider NC500 route that so few visitors see.

Hiking and mountain biking are the backbone of many adventures along the NC500 and Ben Wyvis, near Garve, is the Everest-in-waiting on this slice of the coast. The 1046m-high peak *(9 miles, 5½ hours return)* offers commanding views of corries, heathland habitats and – on a fine day – an expansive panorama of the magnificent mountains of Torridon and the Fannichs.

Likewise, downhill bikers are best served in nearby Balblair Forest in Bonar Bridge *(forestryandland.gov.scot/visit/balblair)* and on the nerve-wracking Highland Wildcat trails above Golspie *(highlandwildcat.com)*. Of course, the whole area is wonderful for road cyclists, and the Dornoch Firth loop from Tain *(37 miles/3½ hours)* and Loch Buidhe circuit from Dornoch *(31 miles; 3 hours)* are local favourites

Rewild Yourself

Tucked away on a sweeping rewilding estate near Ardgay on the Dornoch Firth, Alladale Wilderness Reserve *(alladale.com)* is the closest travellers can get to the thrill of an African safari. Birdwatching, brown trout fly-fishing, and animal-viewing bike rides in ancient Caledonian forest are commonplace, but it is the wild wellness experiences, including foraging, mindful walking and forest bathing that are the best teachers about the landscape's hidden meanings and signals.

Your rewilding journey might also begin on the coast when learning about the Dornoch Environmental Enhancement Project (aka DEEP), an ambitious, five-year initiative to revive a native European oyster reef and establish a self-sustaining ecosystem of 4 million oysters in the Dornoch Firth. Glenmorangie Distillery *(glenmorangie.com)*, one of the principal backers of the project, is a basecamp to learn more about why rewilding oysters is critical for regenerating the coastal ecosystem and keeping it in balance.

Keep Swinging

Unlike so much of the NC500, Dornoch is also home to imagination-pricking golf courses that anyone with an interest in the sport will have heard about long before they've planned to visit Scotland. The two clubs that will turn a trip into a lifetime's-best are Royal Dornoch *(royal dornoch.com)*, with more than 400 years of history and its dune-knitted links Championship Course, and, to the north, Brora Golf Club (broragolfclub.co.uk). Even if you're not into golf, its worth strolling across the public access fairways at Dornoch to its glorious beach (but only when there's no one in play). The lung-filling views may even be enough for you to hit the practice tee.

In fact, the cluster of courses here, including members-only Skibo Links *(carnegieclub. co.uk)*, Bonar Bridge Ardgay *(bonarbridge ardgaygolfclub.co.uk)* and Golspie Golf Club *(golspiegolfclub.co.uk)*, is greater than elsewhere on the NC500 loop. Plus this slice of coast is engaged in the very writing of Scottish golf history itself.

BARMALINI/SHUTTERSTOCK

INSIGHT

Whisky's Forgotten Coast

There are multiple reasons to head off on the NC500, but it's fair to say that whisky isn't top of most travellers' minds. Most think whisky is Speyside and Islay, not the far northeast coast. Think again.

WORDS BY **DAVE BROOM**

Inextricably Linked

The stretch of the NC500 from Inverness to Castletown is home to 14 distilleries, of which 12 are open to the public: Glen Ord, Glen Wyvis, Teaninich (no tours), Dalmore, Invergordon (no tours), Glenmorangie, Dornoch, Balblair, Clynelish, Brora (prebook only), Old Pulteney, Wolfburn, Eight Doors, and Stannergill. Including one or two on your trip would add another layer to your journey into a place and its culture.

Whisky is inextricably linked to the northeast's story. By the 18th century, it had been an integral part of Highland life for three centuries, its making (and drinking) part of Gaelic culture.

Made from barley ripened in the summer months when the cattle were moved to the high *shielings* (pastures), the harvested grain would be put in a sack, immersed in a burn, then spread out on a barn floor to germinate. It was then dried over a peat fire, ground, mixed with spring water, fermented using the house's sourdough yeast, and distilled in a small copper still.

The process was successful here because of the land. The coastal plain and northern straths were well set for growing barley, while the thick fertile soils of the Black Isle were home to the Ferintosh distilleries of Duncan Forbes who, in the 1690s, was granted exemption from paying duty for his backing of William of Orange's usurping of King James II. By 1784, when its duty-free status was abolished, the four Ferintosh distilleries were producing two-thirds of the (legal) whisky in Scotland. None of them survive.

Moonshining

Farm distilling was effectively banned at the same time, but production continued. Farmers became illicit distillers not out of choice but necessity, as the money made from whisky was the only way to pay the rising rents. By 1816, it was estimated that 300 small stills were in operation in eastern Sutherland, predominantly in Strath Brora and Kildonan.

Moonshining was used as a reason for forced removals, when people were displaced to make way for sheep. Ironically, the Brora distillery was established in 1819 by the Duke of Sutherland to employ some of the people cleared from his wife's land. He was following the example of other landowners, such as 'The Blind Captain' Hugh Munro who built Teaninich in 1816, or Alexander Matheson who, having made his fortune as a partner in the Asia-based trading firm Jardine Matheson controlling exports of opium into China, founded Dalmore in the town of Alness in 1839.

Wick's Old Pulteney distillery was built in 1826 due to the expansion of the town as a major herring port – the boats were manned by cleared farmers. By the 1840s, when over 1000 boats were berthed in its harbour, over 800 gallons of whisky were being consumed in Wick each week. Unsurprisingly, a strong temperance movement emerged and the town imposed Prohibition between 1922 and 1947.

A Journey to Flavour

Whisky, like wine, is about flavour, and though the 150 distilleries in Scotland all follow the same process, each one has a character that is unique – a fingerprint, a twist of DNA. The distilleries along the NC500 take you on a journey of flavour, and you will find one which you like.

Whisky, like wine, is about flavour, and though the 150 distilleries in Scotland all follow the same process, each one has a character that is unique.

The whiskies here tend not to be smoky. Rather, they lead you through a world of different fruits – ginger and citrus in Glen Ord; passion fruit and orange in Glenmor-angie; the apples and green-gage of Balblair; tinned pear and pineapple in Clynelish; and Dalmore's dark raisin, fig and blackcurrant. They feel different too. Teaninich and Old Pulteney are oily – the latter has a briny tang, Glenmorangie is creamy, and Clynelish and Brora are fat and palate-clinging.

This is also a place of creativity. Glenmorangie's Lighthouse experimental distillery is a playground to explore every parameter within Scotch, while in Dornoch's tiny, former fire station next to Dornoch Castle Hotel (itself home to a world-class whisky bar), the Thompson brothers are using old barley strains and a range of different yeast types to create a modern, old-style drink.

It's a perfect encapsulation of the north-east's distilleries. Individual, aware of the past, but always looking forward. Whiskies that are products of people, place and history, but which also speak of the present – and the future.

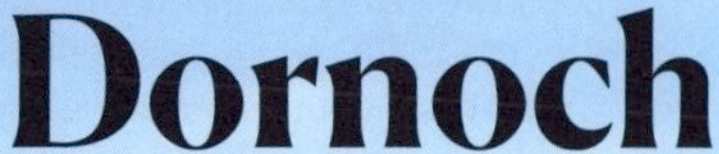

Dornoch

The NC500 is not short on history, but if I was to pick one stage that best represents its head-on collision of Neolithic, Pictish, Viking, Celtic, Clan and – yes, really – gold-rush heritage, then it's this one. There's something particularly poignant about standing at a 5000-year-old chambered cairn at first light, or touring a turreted castle that seems to have dropped out of the pages of a fairy tale. Make the most of it because, as the road continues, such stories are often sidelined by the increasingly dramatic landscapes.

Mike MacEacheran

Wick

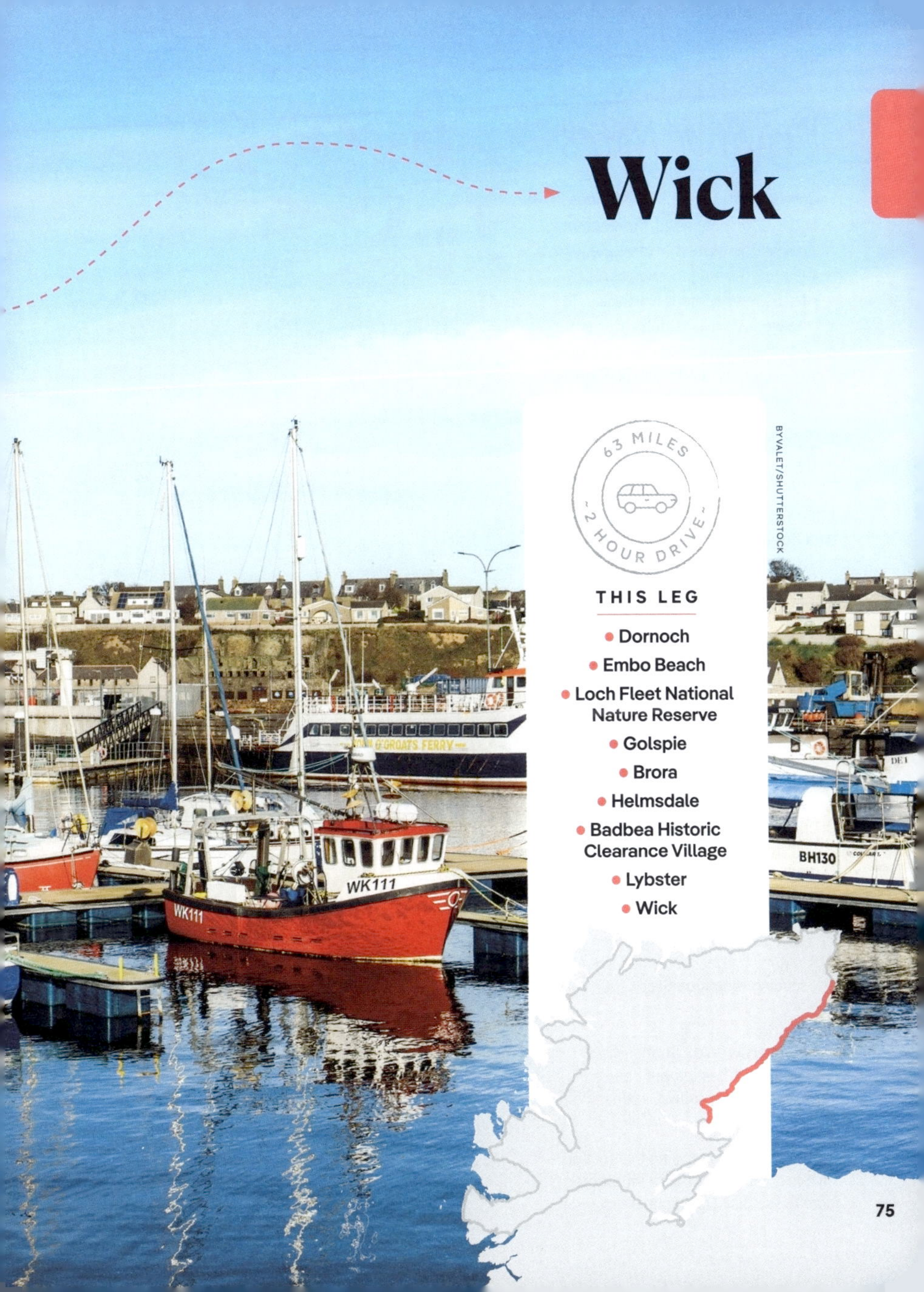

THIS LEG

- Dornoch
- Embo Beach
- Loch Fleet National Nature Reserve
- Golspie
- Brora
- Helmsdale
- Badbea Historic Clearance Village
- Lybster
- Wick

BYVALET/SHUTTERSTOCK

Driving Notes

Compared to so much of Caithness and Sutherland ahead, this section is by far the easiest to navigate. To the east, the land topples abruptly into the tempestuous North Sea. To the west, the roadside verges are crowded with farms and steeply sloped forests. Largely, the feeling is of being squeezed between the two.

Breaking Up Your Journey

Many travellers rush through this section. Don't do it. Brora makes for a fine interlude, with its wave-whipped beaches and tidal harbour, while Norse-settled Helmsdale is a handsome former herring fishing village. Whatever you decide, do not bypass Whaligoe and its knee-juddering steps. The views are worth the calf burn.

Mike's Tips

BEST HOTEL A bagpipe-playing manager, plus a smartly designed pub, restaurant and cosy rooms at Brora's **Royal Marine Hotel** (p86).

FAVOURITE VIEW The hidden natural harbour below the zig-zagging **Whaligoe Steps** (p87).

ESSENTIAL STOP Scotland has hundreds of castles, but none are like majestic **Dunrobin Castle** (p79).

ROAD-TRIP TIP If tackling this section in one day, make an early start: there's more to see than you might at first think.

END

Wick, p86
Largest town on the east coast

Whaligoe Steps

Grey Cairns of Camster

Occumster

Lybster, p83
Historic herring port

Dunbeath

Puzzle over Ancient Stones and Cairns, p84
Caithness is awash with ageless archaeological sites – play Indiana Jones by decoding its riddles

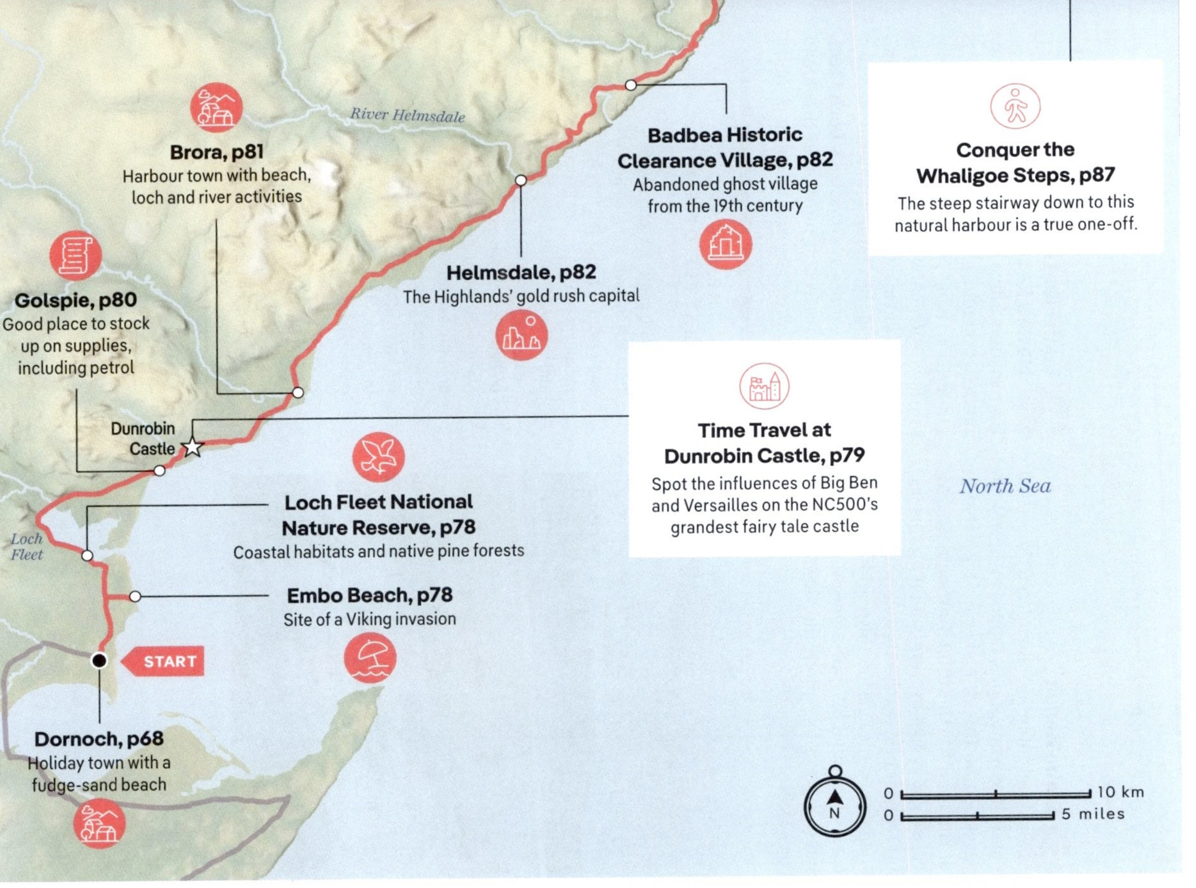

River Helmsdale
Brora, p81
Harbour town with beach, loch and river activities
Golspie, p80
Good place to stock up on supplies, including petrol
Dunrobin Castle
Helmsdale, p82
The Highlands' gold rush capital
Badbea Historic Clearance Village, p82
Abandoned ghost village from the 19th century
Conquer the Whaligoe Steps, p87
The steep stairway down to this natural harbour is a true one-off.
Time Travel at Dunrobin Castle, p79
Spot the influences of Big Ben and Versailles on the NC500's grandest fairy tale castle
Loch Fleet National Nature Reserve, p78
Coastal habitats and native pine forests
Loch Fleet
Embo Beach, p78
Site of a Viking invasion
START
Dornoch, p68
Holiday town with a fudge-sand beach
North Sea
N
0
10 km
0
5 miles

PREVIOUS STOP It can be a wrench to leave Dornoch, but like much of the route so far, there's an interesting coastline ahead – and it bursts with highlights.

Embo Beach

A belt of broad-shouldered dunes and a midriff of white sands, lapped by knee-high waves, **Embo Beach** makes for a great stop on the road north out of Dornoch. The A9 will be your constant companion on this leg, but Embo is best reached by following Station Road out of the seaside town and along the coast for around 3.5 miles. Once there, you'll find rock pools to explore and views across to Loch Fleet.

Loch Fleet National Nature Reserve

The road from Embo leads directly to this happy hunting ground for birds. Among the ospreys and terns arriving from Africa in spring, and wildfowl such as wigeon and greylag geese dropping in during winter, there are bird hides and pinewoods blooming with wildflowers.

The brackish reserve overlooks **Loch Fleet**, with its estuary feeding into the North Sea, and can be visited either from its south or north

LAURENCE LEECH/ALAMY

Embo Beach

THE STRANGE BATTLE OF EMBO

In the 13th century, Viking invaders from Scandinavia tried to raid tiny settlement of Embo, but they hadn't reckoned with the Earl of Sutherland and his loyal fighters.

The story goes that, to seal victory on Embo Beach, the earl felled the plunderers' leader, not with a sword or battle axe, but with the severed leg of a horse. To commemorate the battle, the Earl's Cross was erected south of the beach – find it amid the tangled gorse bushes.

The tomb of the earl's heroic servant Richard de Moravia, who was killed during the incursion, sits inside Dornoch Cathedral.

Embo Beach

Loch Fleet National Nature Reserve

Dornoch

3.4 miles

10.9 miles

1.9 miles

The A839 turns inland towards Lairg and the Flow Country

Time Travel at Dunrobin Castle

Nearly 750 years of history awaits at this classic fairy tale chateau that's more *Beauty and the Beast* than *Brigadoon*: come for the richly-decorated interiors, stay for the falconry displays.

HOW TO

Nearest stop: Golspie

Getting here: From Golspie, Dunrobin Castle is 2 miles further north along the A9. The entrance driveway runs between hardwood trees that magnificently frame the huge house.

Opening times: end of March to end of October

Cost: adult/child £14.50/9

More info: *dunrobincastle.co.uk*

OTHER HIGHLIGHTS

Falconry
Regular displays, included in the ticket price, take place daily on the castle lawn at 11.30am and 2.30pm.

Tea Room
The lures of soups, sandwiches, homemade cakes and ice creams encourage visitors to stay that bit longer.

The most northerly of Scotland's great houses and long family home of the Earls and Dukes of Sutherland, **Dunrobin Castle** links landscape, architectural heritage and storytelling in ways few other castles in the Highlands do. Only 22 of its 189 rooms are on display, but you'll still want to set aside a half-day to tour both the maze-like inside and gardens in bloom.

The castle's fame has grown thanks to the influence of Sir Charles Barry, better known as the brains behind London's Houses of Parliament. He remodelled the castle between 1835 and 1850 – the clock tower hints at a mini Big Ben – and he turned the building from a fortified lair into a swanky baronial house, inspired by Queen Victoria's Balmoral. The cascading gardens riff on the design of those at the Palace of Versailles.

Inside, there are interiors from over the centuries, and artworks and artefacts from the history of Clan Sutherland. Like so many castles, this one too is home to a ghost: legend says the Seamstress Room is frequented by the spirit of an imprisoned girl from the rival Clan Mackay.

GIMAS/SHUTTERSTOCK

Library, Dunrobin Castle

banks. There is no official car park on the south shore, so the opposite side – 11 miles north on the A9, turning off at Golspie – is the best option for access. Both **Balblair Woods** and **Little Ferry Beach** have car parks and walking trails.

Golspie

Being so close to the showstopper that is Dunrobin Castle and Gardens, the village of **Golspie** is a good place to stock up on any essentials, but also worth a longer stay if you fancy stretching your legs.

Ben Bhraggie, a hump of a hill overlooking the town, is a six-mile (four-hour) return yomp along forest tracks and over moorland, and worth it to see the colossal statue marking its summit. This 30m effigy is a controversial tribute to George Granville Leveson-Gower, the first Duke of Sutherland and once the wealthiest man in Britain, who became notorious for his role during the Highland Clearances of the early 19th century. By forcibly evicting thousands of tenant farmers to make way for profitable sheep farms, he inflicted all sorts of woes on the community, with relocation leading to overcrowding, famine and, often, emigration.

In one particularly ghastly case, the roof of a croft was set on fire to prevent the previous tenants returning – with an elderly, bedridden woman still inside. Take a moment and reflect on what was dubbed 'the Devastation of Sutherland'. For bikers, the **Highland Wildcat Trails** are a variety of graded tracks that plummet from the summit to sea level.

Along the Way We Met...

FIONA BARRIE I've lived and worked in Brora for more than 40 years. I love the walks, nature, views, countryside, farms, distillery and peace that the village has. When you go 'up the street' as we say, there is always someone to have a 'blether' and a laugh with.

Fiona is the sous and pastry chef at the Royal Marine Hotel in Brora (royalmarinebrora.com)

FIONA'S TIP: *The 'Old Coffin Road' walk is where you will find it all. Loch Brora, hills, a wonderful seaview and a seat on top of Clyne Kirk hill overlooking Brora. From start to finish, you are surrounded with all that I love about this area.*

Golspie

Dunrobin Castle is hidden in a woodland 1 mile north of Golspie

5.7 miles

Brora

Set aside time for Brora's two broad tidal beaches

11.4 miles

Golspie to Brora

The road north to Brora is the beginning of 'broch country'. These Iron Age-era monuments are scattered along this stretch of the east coast, with **Carn Liath Broch**, three miles from Golspie, being a particularly good example of a drystone roundhouse tower. Then, it's a short five-mile blast of coastal views towards Brora.

Brora

The drystone harbour at **Brora** is still very much a working concern for the town's small fishing fleet, rather than a depository of pleasure boats. Located at the mouth of the River Brora, the quayside is a scenic spot to stroll towards two handsome beaches, which are scythed by the gently frothing estuary and rising tides.

Besides the natural attractions on offer, Brora is a peaceful tourist town, with shops, hotels and cafes to refuel at. Just to the north, **Clynelish Distillery** *(tours from £17, 45 minutes; malts.com)* produces one of the four whiskies that make up the world's most famous blended Scotch: Johnnie Walker.

Carn Liath Broch

CHRIS GRIFFITHS/GETTY IMAGES

BEST PLACES TO EAT

Cocoa Skye, Brora £
Artisan chocolates and waffles, coffee and sandwiches in the heart of the harbour town. *10am-3pm, Mon-Sat, from 11am Sun*

La Mirage Restaurant, Helmsdale £
Fish and chips, seafood platters and prawn cocktails, all served amid kitsch decor. *(lamirage.co.uk; noon-8.45pm)*

Puldagon Farm Shop & Restaurant, Wick £
A local food hero with farm-to-table to the max and Highland beef burgers, made from cattle reared on the farm. *(puldagonfarm.co.uk; 10am-4pm Wed-Sun)*

The Curing Yard, Brora ££
The signature restaurant of the Royal Marine Hotel is a standout for residents and drop-in diners: enjoy seafood, steaks, sharing boards and specials. *(highlandcoasthotels.com/royal-marine-brora; noon-8.30pm)*

On the Gold-Rush Trail in Helmsdale

Undulating coastline ripples all the way north to **Helmsdale**, hidden inside a deep coastal ravine, where you should stop to try your hand at something rarely, if ever, associated with the Highlands of Scotland: gold panning.

Timespan Heritage Centre recounts the backstory of the short-lived, but feverish Kildonan Gold Rush of 1869, but more fun is to play would-be prospector by having a gold-panning session on the Kildonan Burn, 20 minutes inland from the coast. A permit needs to be bought from the **Suisgill Estate** *(adult/under-16s £10/free, Apr-Sept; suisgill.co.uk)*, while a kit comprising a pan, hand sieve and trowel can be hired from the **museum** *(£5; timespan.org.uk)*. In return, should you find any 'gold in them thar hills', you must pledge to share the wealth with the authors of this book.

VINCENT LOWE/ALAMY

Badbea Historic Clearance Village

Into Caithness

From Helmsdale, the A9 races tightly along the coast, above cliffs and farmlands that sweep to the sea and into **Caithness**, the 'headland of the Catt people', an ancient Pitch tribe, and a swathe of country pockmarked by ancient chambered cairns, crofting villages from the Highland Clearances era and deep Norse roots.

Speeding along the road here isn't a good idea: slow down and pay special attention to the roadside deer warnings, as this next section towards Navidale has one of the highest number of recorded red deer/vehicle collisions in the country.

Badbea Historic Clearance Village

Soon after, a viewpoint out to sea arrives only four miles out of Helmsdale, then the next point of interest before Dunbeath is **Badbea Historic Clearance Village**. It's hard to imagine now, but back in the 1790s this was effectively a ramshackle refugee camp for those displaced from surrounding estates.

The ruins and crumbling drystone remains hardly paint the full picture of how bleak life was; a local story tells that children were tethered to posts in bad weather to prevent them from being blown clean off the vertiginous clifftop.

With this context, it makes for a haunting one-mile (30-minute) ramble through the bristling gorse to see both the abandoned settlement and nearby **Ousdale Broch**. These distinctive Iron Age structures are something Caithness specialises in, and this is one of the finest examples on the NC500.

Helmsdale

6.1 miles

Take extra care on this stretch – it's red-deer country

Badbea Historic Clearance Village

9 miles

ROB FORD/ALAMY

Laidhay Croft Museum

The Road to Dunbeath

From Badbea, the A9 roller coasters along clifftops, with hairpin bends and steep gradients, and the vast expanse of the lonely blanket bogs of the Flow Country (p118) to the left of the roadside. Cone-shaped Morven, the highest mountain in pancake-flat Caithness, also broods to the west at 706m.

As you pass **Berriedale**, you will have a fine vantage over the North Sea and gently rolling farmlands – the sense is that this north-easternmost corner of Scotland is an on-the-edge stepping stone and gateway to the sea, the islands of Orkney and Shetland, and the Nordic countries.

Five miles from Berriedale, **Dunbeath** is hidden in a steep glen and is worth a stop to see its dinky harbour. Once teeming with herring boats as the Caithness coast basked in riches from the fishing industry, little remains but a picturesque ice-house and fisherman's bothy.

Just north of here, **Laidhay Croft Museum** *(laidhay.co.uk; summer only)* is a 250-year-old rush-thatched longhouse – imagine a cross between a Viking stronghold and Caithness farmhouse. The building has been turned into a museum chronicling the humble life led by crofters from the mid-1800s to WWII, and there's a jumble of farm tools in the cowshed, plus old cooking cauldrons and rusting pans. Find the museum and its tearoom a little more than one mile beyond Dunbeath.

Lybster to Wick

Just before Lybster is where the road north splits: the A9 veers inland on the more direct route to Thurso, while the NC500 continues northeast for 13 miles on the slower, coast-embracing A99 to Wick.

At this point, the road signs read eight miles to **Lybster**, but your next must-see is around four miles further along the road to Whaligoe.

continued on p86

Puzzle Over Ancient Stones and Cairns

Five thousand years of history sits right by the roadside: few road trips can compete with the NC500's wealth of prehistoric and Neolithic tombs, chambered cairns and stone monuments.

HOW TO

Nearest stop: Lybster

Getting here: For the Grey Cairns of Camster, turn north of the A99 at Occumster and continue for 5 miles.

More info: All the sites are managed by Historic Environment Scotland *(historicenvironment.scot)*, free to enter and open 24hrs every day of the year.

Historic Monuments

There are many stories written in the stones on the NC500. Some of the oldest cairns in Britain lie scattered along the north coast of the Highlands, but Caithness is arguably home to the most impressive.

Hill o'Many Stanes

The first stop off the A99 is the **Hill o'Many Stanes** and it still holds the power to capture the imagination. The sight of more than 200 miniature standing stones erected in a fan shape in more than 22 rows on hillside moorland provokes all sorts of reactions. Bewilderment, surprise, sheer wonder as to why the Neolithic peoples who once lived here 4000 years ago would create this odd stone arrangement (according to academics, it was possibly for gatherings or religious ceremonies). And to think, once there were more than 600 in the same pattern.

Cairn o' Get

Back on the A99, the road delivers you to **Cairn o' Get**, a prehistoric burial cairn a half-mile detour on a B-road northwest of Whaligoe. Parking is beside **Loch Watenan**, a short walk away. The chambered burial cairn once stood 3m high, making it clearly visible across the boggy moorland, but now it's a ramshackle collection of upright stones, with two below-ground chambers. To get into the spirit of things, salute the Norse and Christian gods, Neolithic man and Mother Goddess of Earth, before climbing back into your car.

MARK HICKEN/ALAMY

MORE ROCK STARS

Achavanich Standing Stones
More than 4000 years old, this is an unusual horseshoe-shaped structure of 36 stones near Loch Stemster, six miles north of Lybster.

Hilton of Cadboll Stone
Found in Hilton near Balintore, this is a reconstruction of what many believe is the most magnificent Pictish stone slab. The original is in Edinburgh's National Museum of Scotland.

The Shandwick Stone
Just south of Hilton in the Seaboard Villages, this Pictish slab features hunters and a Pictish beast, and is covered with interlocking spirals.

Left: Hill o'Many Stanes
Below: Grey Cairns of Camster

Grey Cairns of Camster

The **Grey Cairns of Camster** saves the best to last. This pair of haunting Neolithic tombs, reconstructed to shed light on ancient funerary practices, originally dates from between 4000 BCE and 2500 BCE, and are among the country's oldest manmade structures.

For those into their films, crawling into the chambered cairns by the hazy light of a phone or torch is suggestive of an Indiana Jones or Lara Croft adventure. To get here, follow New Clyth Rd off the A99 for five miles.

BEV LEWIS/SHUTTERSTOCK

Lybster, like many Caithness fishing villages, experienced the boom-and-bust of the herring industry – at one time more than 100 fishing boats squeezed into the harbour. This history, plus coffee and cake, is ready to be absorbed at the **Waterlines Heritage Centre**, right next to stacked creel nets on the harbour.

Wick

Not so long ago, you'd be told that your nose would smell **Wick** several miles before you got close to it. This once-booming fishing town, at one time the largest herring port in Europe, retains its status as the northeast's most populated place, and brims with hotels, restaurants, cafes, pubs and services. There are deeply rooted Norse connections here too: the name Wick, derived from Old Norse Vik and meaning 'bay', was given by the Vikings. But for all that, the town really merits only a quick pit stop rather than a longer stay.

The story of its fishy rise and fall is fleshed out at the rambling **Wick Heritage Centre**, with fully furnished rooms crammed with memorabilia of the herring heyday, as well as fishing equipment, rigged-out boats, a kippering kiln, cooperage and working lighthouse.

Passing visitors tend to be drawn more to **Old Wick Castle** from the 12th century. Little more than a ruined four-storey tower, its real attraction is the location: on a chiselled headland, cradled by towering cliffs and best seen in stormy, grey light when the North Sea is roaring. The saga of Wick is also partially retold through whisky at the **Old Pulteney Distillery** tours on Huddart Street.

PETR KLAPKA/SHUTTERSTOCK

Old Wick Castle

BEST PLACES TO STAY

NC500 Pods, Brora £
Clean and comfy glamping cabins with a communal sauna and private hot tubs. *(nc500pods.co.uk)*

Royal Marine Hotel, Brora ££
Waterfront foodie hotel with terrific staff and service, a fab restaurant and a cheerful pub tribute to local hero and famous fishing fly-tyer Megan Boyd. *(highlandcoasthotels.com/royal-marine-brora)*

Golspie Inn, Golspie ££
Historical inn dating to 1808, with individually styled rooms, restaurant and outdoor terrace. *(golspieinn.co.uk)*

Mackays Hotel, Wick ££
Next to Ebenezer Place, the world's shortest street at 2.75m, this family-run stalwart boasts a fine selection of 30 rooms, plus No.1 Bistro for pub grub and steaks. *(mackayshotel.co.uk)*

Conquer the dramatic Whaligoe Steps

Wick

Conquer the Whaligoe Steps

To get a sense of what life was once like on the Caithness coast, a trip up and down the Whaligoe Steps is a whirlwind of wild seafaring history.

HOW TO

Nearest stop: Whaligoe

Getting here: There is a tiny car park at the top of the steps, located down a small residential lane off the A99. A better idea is to leave your vehicle at the Cairn o' Get car park, which is signposted on the opposite side of the road.

Tip: Caution is necessary on the near-vertical steps, particularly on wet days, as the stone stairs are uneven and slippery. Come when it's dry if you can.

Whaligoe Haven is a treasure hidden from the eye, only revealing itself at the very last minute. It's a natural harbour, both remarkable by design and hemmed in by 76m-high cliffs. For that reason, its reputation has been embellished in recent years by those who've descended the zigzagging Whaligoe Steps, as well as those prone to hyperbole. Juxtaposed comments have described it as both a 'stairway to heaven' and a 'stairway to hell'.

What's not disputed is that the staircase was spectacularly cut into a cliff face to the east of Whaligoe in 1792 and once used by the wives of fishermen to carry loaded baskets of herring, salmon and shellfish almost 76m up from the seafront harbour. Colour can be hard to come by on storm-grey days here, but the 337 steps lead down to cliffs nested by yellow-lipped fulmars and bright-beaked terns. Look out for the oily hoods of seals popping up like periscopes.

If you're fit, the walk will take 20 to 30 minutes, otherwise you'll want to set aside at least an hour to explore the steps fully.

Whaligoe Steps

FROM LEFT: GREENS AND BLUES/SHUTTERSTOCK, PHOTOVISIONS/SHUTTERSTOCK

Wick

Caithness really comes into its own on this stage of the NC500. Despite it largely being a treeless, low-lying landscape bossed by farmers, cattle and crops, the coastal road waltzes past castellated clifftops, jagged sea stacks and eerie headlands – all scoured by wind and rain, and atmospheric enough to be the star turn of any visually stunning nature documentary. I love the Duncansby Stacks – it's Scotland's equivalent of Australia's Twelve Apostles.

Mike MacEacheran

Thurso

HUBERT.B/SHUTTERSTOCK

THIS LEG

- Wick
- Castle Sinclair Girnigoe
- Nybster Broch
- Duncansby Head Lighthouse
- John O'Groats Signpost
- Castle of Mey
- Dunnet Head Lighthouse
- Dunnet Bay
- Thurso

Driving Notes

The NC500 doesn't get any more straightforward than this: the A99 motors north from Wick to John O'Groats then, so as not to abruptly tip into the North Sea, wheels left onto the A836 all the way to Thurso, the capital of the northern Highlands. All roads lead around the coast, so it's hard to get lost.

Breaking Up Your Journey

Between Wick and Thurso, there are two obvious places to refuel: John O'Groats, with its overly touristy cafes and stores, and Dunnet, a fine stop with a gin distillery and bracing clifftop walks at the most northerly point of the British mainland. In between, the Castle of Mey has a seasonal tearoom.

Mike's Tips

BEST MEAL Takeaway **Captain's Galley, Scrabster** (p97) fish and chips, landed right on the harbour.

FAVOURITE VIEW All visitors make a point of visiting John O'Groats. More should stop at **Duncansby Stacks** (p94) only two miles away.

ESSENTIAL STOP Join the puffins, kittiwakes, razorbills and guillemots at **RSPB Dunnet Head** (p98).

ROAD-TRIP TIP Don't drive between Duncansby Head and John O'Groats (unless you have to). Take the four-mile round-trip **coastal walk** (p96) for an immersive encounter with land and sea.

35 km to Orkney Isles

RSPB Dunnet Head

Surf's Up at Thurso East, p101
Terific breaks, swells and rollers make this the NC500's top surf spot

END

Thurso East

Thurso, p99
The northernmost town on mainland Britain

Orkney Isles

Norwegian Sea

Sanday

Orkney Isles

Mainland

Stromness

Hoy

North Sea

Main Map

0 20 km
0 10 miles

0 5 km
0 2.5 miles

N

Dunnet Head Lighthouse, p97
The true northernmost point of mainland Britain
Duncansby Head Lighthouse, p92
Classic coastal views and an edge-of-the-world feeling
John O'Groats Signpost, p95
Tourist hub and famous landmark
Duncansby Stacks
Castle of Mey, p96
Royal family stronghold
Hike the Dramatic Duncansby Stacks, p94
This short loop to two scenic sea pinnacles enjoys outstanding views of cliffs, beaches and and wave-eroded rocks
Dunnet Bay, p99
Starting point for walks and surf lessons
Nybster Broch, p92
Iron Age building dating to 200 BCE
Old Keiss Castle
Extend your Trip to the Orkney Isles, p102
This archipelago is an exotic mix of Neolithic, Pictish, Viking and Christian history – it's almost a country in it own right.
North Sea
Ackergill Tower
Castle Sinclair Girnigoe, p92
Toothy ruin overlooking the North Sea
Wick, p86
The largest town on the east coast
START

PREVIOUS STOP Wick is the busiest town on the east coast. Avoid the Highland 'rush hour' by leaving after 9am, then it's an easy drive, tracing the coast's contours all the way to Thurso.

Castle Sinclair Girnigoe

If you're partial to a ruined clifftop castle or two, the first stretch of the A99 north should be high on your list of first stops on this section. Immediately north of Wick, **Castle Sinclair Girnigoe** is a 20-minute drive and your reward is a complex of higgedly-piggedly stone structures that fit the brief of the textbook windswept Scottish castle: it couldn't look more perfect.

From the outside, this heap of ramshackle turrets and staircases appears forsaken and forgotten, however, it was once the ancestral home of the earls of Caithness and the chiefs of Clan Sinclair, historically one of the north's most powerful families. The history of the castle is both one of bloodshed and of feuds – the structure was destroyed in 1680 following a dispute over the family title. Look below, down to Sinclair's Bay (known locally as Reiss Beach), a broad arc of white sand where you can occasionally spot seals.

ESPY3008/GETTY IMAGES

Nybster Broch

Nybster Broch

Around 10 miles on the coastal road north from Wick (doubling back from Castle Sinclair Girnigoe), you'll arrive in Nybster, home to the **Caithness Broch Project** *(thebrochproject.co.uk)* and a centre of study for the stone-built, circular towers that date back more than 2000 years.

No part of Scotland has more impressive brochs than Caithness. The Iron Age roundhouse structures, predominantly used by clan chieftains as forts and residences, are striking examples of prehistoric British architecture, particularly impressive when seen on the coast. These days, there's not much left of **Nybster Broch** – it really needs a drone's-eye view to get a sense of scale. But its rocky headland is atmospheric and there are plenty of nooks and crannies to survey. To find the broch from the A99, look for the Harbour Car Park sign, then follow the path.

Duncansby Head Lighthouse

The golden age of lighthouses is long gone, but accompanied by circling gulls, nesting guillemots and eiders, you can undertake your own journey to see several standout examples

Wick

4.4 miles

Castle Sinclair Girnigoe

Nybster Broch

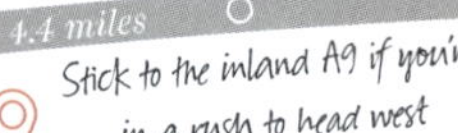

Duncansby Head Lighthouse

CASTLES GALORE

Only a few minutes north of Wick is five-storey **Ackergill Tower**. Over history, it's been a clan seat for the Keiths, who fought frequently with their neighbours, the Sinclairs. More recently, it's been a wedding venue and, now, it's the private residence of a millionaire US philanthropist.

Old Keiss Castle is another nearby ruin of precarious stone that looks like it could fall into the North Sea at any given time. It's closed to visitors, but the view of New Keiss Castle, the ruin's replacement and another private residence, is a reminder that Scotland's history is still very much lived in.

on the NC500. **Duncansby Head Lighthouse**, on the most northeasterly part of the British mainland, is reached after wheeling right off the main A99 and following the clearly signposted farm road for two miles across gentle grassland until it stops abruptly atop a precipitous cliff.

Like many classic 20th-century lighthouses, Duncansby Head was built by the famous Stevenson family of lighthouse engineers, a dynasty that created 97 major beacons across little more than a century of lighting up the Scottish coast (Dunnet Head to the immediate east is another example). There's a car park here and information panels about the chesspiece lighthouse above the 60m-high cliffs. Below, the tidal streams of the ferocious Pentland Firth garnered it the unnerving title 'Hell's Mouth'. On a clear day, uninhabited Stroma and the Orkney Isles beckon across the current.

The roads near Duncansby Stacks are single-track roads used by farm vehicles

EXPERIENCE

Hike to the Dramatic Duncansby Stacks

It's only one mile to these spectacular sea-surrounded monoliths, but this short hike delivers one of the finest views on the NC500

HOW TO

Nearest stop: Duncansby Head Lighthouse

Getting here: Turn right off the A99 at John O'Groats and follow the road to the Duncansby Head car park.

Tip: Wear waterproof shoes or boots, as the trail can often be boggy.

To get from the Duncansby Head car park to the coast's star sea stacks takes only around 20 minutes. But even those in a hurry couldn't deny devoting more time to these sublime rock formations – you'll want to set aside at least an hour.

Turning south, it's a downhill stomp from the 100-year-old lighthouse to the coast and, almost immediately, your pace slows, perhaps to take photos, but more likely because the hypnotic rocks, crashing waves and scent of grass, damp earth and, maybe, fresh rain, is soothing and you remember why you're here: to slow down.

By the time you reach the fenced-off cliff edge, the **Duncansby Stacks** will be unmissable: on a wild weather day, these resemble two vampire teeth dramatically protruding from the foaming white lip of surf below. After stopping to peer down into the narrow **Geo of Sclaites** tidal cleft in the side of the cliff, it's then an uphill 10-minute hike, with the stacks getting darker – more impressive – the closer you get.

Come early or late in the day and you can have the final viewpoint all to yourself.

FROM LEFT: FOREST BADGER/SHUTTERSTOCK, EYESTRAVELLING/SHUTTERSTOCK

Along the Way We Met...

IONA MCLACHLAN Between John O' Groats and Durness is a very special bit of coastline. Some of the best waves in the world roll in here. I've lived around Thurso my whole life and the surf is incredible because it gets both the Atlantic Ocean and North Sea swells – you can always find good waves. The cold is often people's first thought, but with a good wetsuit everyone stays super warm. My favourite spot is Thurso East: this is Scotland's premier right-hand reef break and a world-class barrel on its day.

Iona is a champion surfer and co-owner of North Coast Watersports (northcoastwatersports.com) based in Dunnet.

IONA'S TIP: *Visit Torrisdale Beach. It's often overlooked, but it's my favourite beach in the world.*

John O'Groats

For decades, pilgrims and road trippers have stopped at this tiny end-of-the-road settlement to say they've been to the northernmost point of the British mainland. The thing is, it's not: that's Dunnet Head (p97), 15 miles to the west, even if the gift-shop owners that try to squeeze every penny from tourists at the visitor complex wished it was.

It all began with Jan de Groot, a 15th-century Dutchman who was granted the ferry rights between the harbour and the Orkney Islands by James IV. As legend tells, he charged one 'groat' for the seven-mile ferry crossing, but academics today claim the term derives from the Dutch *de groot*, meaning 'the large'. There is truth in both theories: on the seashore, look for 'Groatie Buckies', cowrie shells once used as currency.

Despite the hype, there's not much to do in **John O'Groats** bar take a photo at the whitewashed signpost, initially installed to mark journey's end. There are cafes, craft and gift shops, a brewery and distillery – and a £3 parking charge.

POMPAEM GOGH/SHUTTERSTOCK

John O'Groats Signpost

6.9 miles

Don't forget to take a photograph

A LONGER WALK

John O'Groats to Duncansby Head

This four-mile round trip takes the more avid hiker from John O'Groats harbour and along the foreshore via Robert's Haven and the Bay of Sannick to Duncansby Head. This is open farming land, with fences and stiles, so make sure to respect grazing animals and keep your distance from the cliff edge as you approach the Ness of Duncansby.

LENKA.FILOVA/SHUTTERSTOCK

Dunnet Head

John O'Groats to Mey

West of John O'Groats, the A99 morphs into the A836 and the flatlands are level enough to see Dunnet Head and sweeping pasturelands busy with tractors, farmhands, haystacks and livestock. Lonely churches and powder-white crofts break the green and brown colour scheme, and you might be tempted to increase your average speed, as there are little roadside diversions between here and **Mey**, six miles west and put on the map by Elizabeth Bowes-Lyon, the late Queen Mother.

The Castle & Gardens of Mey

Despite being so far from Buckingham Palace in London – nearly 700 miles to the south – the turreted **Castle of Mey** maintains an important connection to the British royal family. It became the private holiday home of the late Queen Mother, who bought the estate in 1952 and, now, it remains closed during late July and early August for around 10 days for King Charles III and Queen Camilla's annual visit before they take up residence in Balmoral in the Cairngorms.

The rest of the summer – from 1 May until 30 September – the grounds and house are open to the public. Inside, it's as opulent as you'd expect, albeit homely with plenty of personal touches – the late Queen Mother's sky-blue coat and hat still hang in the hallway. Up the grand staircase, is her former study and rooms decorated with bad-taste toys and gifts. Perhaps surprisingly, parties of 10 can now book expensive dinners and eat at the **King's Table** *(from £595pp)*, offering an unprecedented glimpse into the private life of the British monarchy.

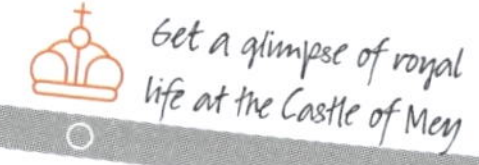

Get a glimpse of royal life at the Castle of Mey

Castle of Mey

8.5 miles

Castle & Gardens of Mey

The B-Road to the End of Britain

From Mey, it's an easy 20 minutes to the most northerly point of the British mainland, **Dunnet Head**, a drive that sets out at a trot, before slowing to a single-track minor road that climbs gently across a moorland peninsula to **Dunnet Head Lighthouse**, built almost 200 years ago by Robert Stevenson, grandfather of *Treasure Island* author Robert Louis Stevenson. On the B855 from Dunnet, the road passes through the northern Highlands in microcosm: there are farms, silvery lochans, a pier nudging up to a panorama of sea stacks, peaty moorland adding a splash of colour and – always – the crashing North Sea. Below the lighthouse is a viewing balcony to watch seabirds soar and dip for fish.

BEST PLACES TO EAT

Stacks Deli, Bakery & Coffee House, John O'Groats £
Fab all-rounder serving home-baked goodies, sausage rolls, cakes and coffee. *(stacksbakery.co.uk; 10am-4pm)*

Olive, Thurso £
Coffee, pizzas and pastas, breakfast and brunch at this community-centred cafe with plenty of designer touches. *(9am-4pm Mon-Sat)*

Capillas Tapas Bar, Scrabster ££
Spanish restaurant inside an old chapel, serving seafood sharers and specials like monkfish and chorizo kebabs. *(5-10pm Thu, noon-midnight Fri & Sat)*

Captain's Galley, Scrabster ££
Caithness' finest freshly landed seafood and sustainable fish; beside the Scrabster Ferry Terminal. *(captainsgalley.co.uk; 5-9pm Thu, noon-3pm & 5-9pm Fri, noon-9pm Sat, 1-7pm Sun)*

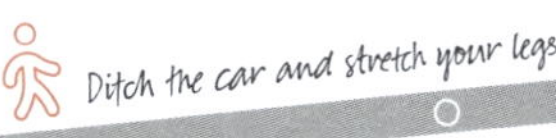

Dunnet Head Lighthouse

5.7 miles

TOBY HOULTON/ALAMY

BEST PLACES TO STAY

Dunnet Bay Caravan Club Campsite, Dunnet Bay £
Plenty of pitches and space for motorhomes a stone's throw from the beach and amid the dunes. Non-members welcome. *(caravanclub.co.uk)*

Braeside Retreats, Thurso ££
Waking up on a family-run farm is the draw of these glamping pods, four miles outside Thurso. *(braesideretreats.co.uk)*

Forss House Hotel, Thurso ££
This creaky Georgian mansion is on a 20-acre country estate with a salmon-stocked river, classy restaurant, whisky bar and elegant rooms. *(forsshousehotel.co.uk))*

The Granary Lodge, Mey £££
Luxurious 10-room B&B on the grounds of the Castle of Mey and overseen by King Charles III. Good enough for royalty, really. *(castleofmey.org.uk)*

RSPB Dunnet Head

This 20-acre seabird city is almost a different country to Wick, where this section of the NC500 starts. Apart from the striking lighthouse and car park, there is nothing at **RSPB Dunnet Head** with the exception of ground-nested grasslands and sea cliffs – oh, and it's a noisy, 360-degree blur of fulmars, razorbills, guillemots, kittiwakes and puffins come the **spring and summer breeding season** *(1 April to 15 August)*. In Orkney, across the water, the puffins are wonderfully nicknamed 'tammie norries'.

For a demanding 12-mile hiking loop around the headland, leave the car in Dunnet village and, by sticking to the coast, follow the sandstone cliffs and you'll largely be alone and

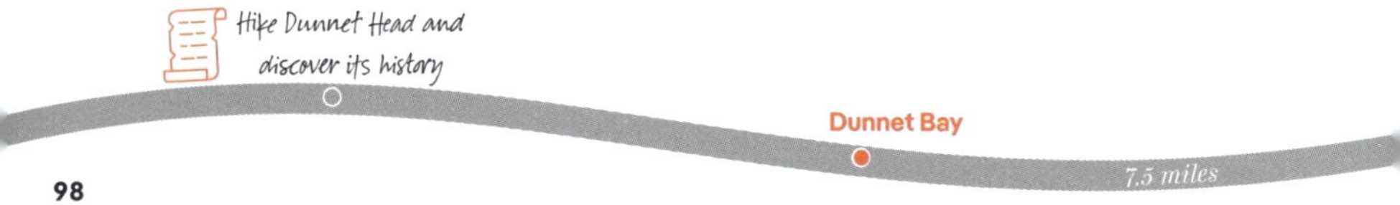

Hike Dunnet Head and discover its history

Dunnet Bay

7.5 miles

Fulmar, RSPB Dunnet Head

left in communion with nature. The journey should take around four to five hours and along the way you'll spy the leftovers of a radar station installed during WWII – for a period, the headland was a Coast Defence station.

Along Dunnet Bay to Thurso

It's a quick drive back to Dunnet and on to the main road west, where you should stop at **Dunnet Bay Distillers**, a spirit house that specialises in foraging local botanicals for its award-winning Rock Rose Gin. Tours and cocktail workshops are worth dropping in for, otherwise pick up a souvenir for a true taste of Caithness (the signature drop has notes of sea buckthorn, juniper and sherbet lemon).

From here, it's a short walk up and over the machair-fringed dunes onto **Dunnet Beach**, a two-mile sweep of sheltered sand for sunbathing, paddling or beachcombing. If it's one of those days when the only colour is in the sea, then, perhaps, surfing should be your calling. A drysuit is essential: this isn't Australia.

Thurso

From Dunnet Bay, it's almost a straight line to **Thurso**, Britain's most northerly mainland town and the closest the NC500 has to a metropolis outside Inverness. The river town takes its name from the Norse god of thunder and strength, with the Vikings naming it 'Torsaa', or Thor's River.

Thurso

The road to Thurso is pancake flat

The wild peatland of the Flow Country is now ahead of you

PECOLD/SHUTTERSTOCK

St Peter's and St Andrew's Church, Thurso

There are plenty of reasons to stop, including hotels, shops, restaurants and a pretty church square, but largely you're here for the unlikely opportunity to try cold-water surfing at **Thurso East** and to drop in to the **North Coast Visitor Centre** *(free; highlifehighland.com)* tucked inside Thurso Town Hall.

Beside tourist information and a cafe, the star turn is the permanent exhibition telling the story of Caithness across some 359 million years of history, from Devonian-era fossils to the Dounreay nuclear plant, located west of the town centre.

For those following the **Pictish Trail**, the Ulbster Stone is carved with more symbols than any other slab found in the Highlands. On the western edge of the town, **Wolfburn Distillery** has tours and tastings within walking distance of the centre.

TOP SURF SPOTS

Head Thurso East
The classic NC500 surf spot, with iconic right-hand barrels.

Brims Ness
A heavy reef break, five miles west of Thurso and beside Brims Castle.

Thurso Beach
A beginner spot at the western edge of the bay.

Dunnet Beach
Good choice for beach for learners and improvers, 15 minutes east of Thurso (p95).

Surf's up at Thurso East

The call to surf is real: where the land meets the sea, the liquid blue swell at Thurso East generates barrelling right-hand waves that break over a kelp-covered reef.

HOW TO

Nearest stop: Thurso

Getting here: Follow the main road through Thurso to the northeast for around 1 mile.

More info: North Coast Watersports *(northcoastwatersports.com)* offers lessons for beginners on Dunnet Beach and equipment hire (surfboards, paddle boards and kayaks), as well as RIB tours and surf retreats.

Once, Thurso Bay was the gateway to a new world for the Vikings, who arrived over the marbled waves carrying raven banners from Scandinavia to Britain's shores. Fast forward to today and the scene at **Thurso East** is still one of conquest, but of a different sort. On a day of light offshore winds and rideable swell, locals swaddled in thick neoprene wetsuits and ink-black hoods can be spotted with surfboards, seeking to heroically ride the waves as their forebears did.

Thurso East isn't Hawaii, but this has become a surfing hot spot in recent years, thanks to the perfect storm of conditions for experienced cold-water riders. Exposed to the Atlantic, the coastline is open to big depressions that leave surfers on the receiving end of huge swells, with north-facing prevailing winds grooming the waves and creating world-class breakers.

Come from September through to May for the most dependably curly conditions (locals say February is best) or, should you prefer to keep your feet on dry land, then drop in for the annual **Scottish National Surfing Championships**, held on Thurso East every late March/early April around Easter.

FROM LEFT: LILKIN/SHUTTERSTOCK, NIGEL MANSFIELD/ALAMY

EXPERIENCE

Extend Your Trip to the Orkney Isles

Scrabster Ferry Terminal, north of Thurso, is a handy jumping-off point for a longer trip across the Pentland Firth to Orkney.

HOW TO

Nearest stop: Scrabster

Getting there: NorthLink Ferries operates regular 1½-hour sailings from Scrabster to Stromness on Mainland (Orkney's main island) at least twice a day. Timings are at 8.45am and 7pm Monday to Friday; noon and 7pm Saturday. Ferries return to the mainland at 6.30am and 4.45pm Monday to Friday; 9am and 4.45pm Saturday.

Cost: £21.35/24.95pp in low/high season; cars/motorhomes from £69/77; bicycles are free.

Bookings: *northlinkferries.co.uk*

Tip: The ferry passes the Old Man of Hoy sea stack – make sure to be on deck when it does.

True North

Scotland's true north lies just across the water. This is an archipelago far closer to Norway than it is to London and which has more in common with Scandinavia than it does Scotland. There's a cathedral rich with the stories of Viking sagas, elemental monuments, Neolithic villages and magical stone circles to puzzle over. That all adds up to plenty of excuses to detour off the NC500 to discover these islands that perfectly marry reality and daydreams.

Heart of Neolithic Orkney

Taking the ferry from **Scrabster** you'll arrive in **Stromness**, Orkney's prettiest harbour. A car or bike is necessary to explore beyond the town and, once on the road, the map ahead leads to the **Heart of Neolithic Orkney**, a succession of UNESCO World Heritage Sites, including a circle of towering standing stones (Stones of Stenness), a Neolithic henge (Ring of Brodgar) and – arguably the high point – a 5000-year-old prehistoric village (Skara Brae). Check the history books and you'll find this ancient settlement of dwellings is older than the Great Pyramids of Giza. Squint a little and imagine tumbling through time.

Norse Tales

Viking history leads to St Magnus Cathedral in the capital **Kirkwall** and it is both a wonderfully ornate red-sandstone pile and Scotland's oldest cathedral. Founded in

BARBARA ASH/SHUTTERSTOCK

PLACES TO STAY

The Ferry Inn, Stromness
Unfussy rooms and hearty pub grub where the boat comes in. *ferryinn.com*

Cantick Head Lighthouse Cottages, Hoy
Far-flung, windswept and isolated, these holiday lets next to a historic lighthouse tower have cliff views, kitchens and a hot tub. *cantickhead.com*

Kirkwall Hotel, Kirkwall
In the thick of things, with well-appointed rooms, a restaurant and a whisky bar run in league with the town's Highland Park distillery. *kirkwallhotel.com*

Left: Stones of Stenness
Below: St Magnus Cathedral, Kirkwall

1137 by Viking Earl Rognvald, it is one of three buildings in the islands bearing the name of Orkney's patron saint (the other two are in Birsay and on the island of Egilsay).

There's far more to discover, of course. The sea stacks of **Hoy** (like the sandstone buttes of Monument Valley dumped into the North Atlantic). The sunken warships of **Scapa Flow**. The Churchill Barriers connecting Mainland to Burray and **South Ronaldsay**. The brochs and chambered cairns of **Rousay**. The peace, wildness and corncrakes of **Papa Westray**. You'll just need more time.

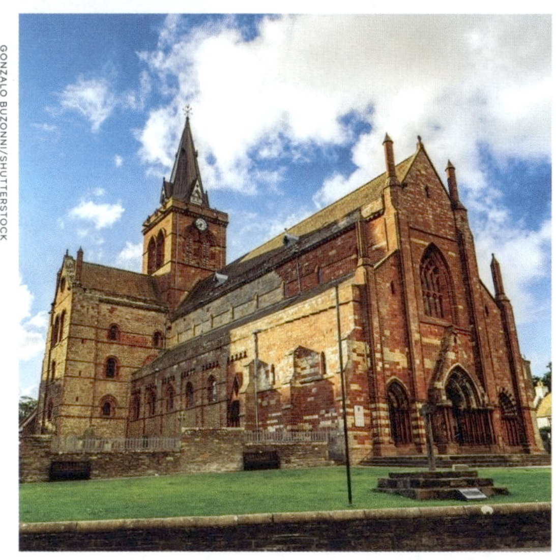

GONZALO BUZONNI/SHUTTERSTOCK

Thurso

Welcome to quintessential Highland country. First impressions are of a stretch of coastal moorland that is desolate and empty. There's so much space here that it's easy to find yourself alone, and the blanket bogs of the Flow Country, the serpentine inlets and thick brow of hills create a meditative landscape that I love. In ever-variegated light, there is a powerful feeling of isolation that becomes addictive – this is the NC500 that many people yearn for long after leaving.

Mike MacEacheran

Tongue

LUCENTIUS/GETTY IMAGES

THIS LEG

- Thurso
- Dounreay
- Melvich Beach
- Strathy Beach
- Bettyhill Viewpoint
- Bettyhill
- Borgie
- Coldbackie Beach
- Tongue
- Castle Varrich

Driving Notes

All eyes are fixed to the west as this section largely sticks to the A836, with the road unspooling cinematically through peatlands and past wild beaches that are big, beautiful...and barely touched.

Breaking Up Your Journey

This is one of the emptiest stretches of the NC500 and options to stop and refuel are few and far between. The small villages of Strathy and Bettyhill have one or two cafes, but the detour to RSPB Forsinard Flows in the midst of the UNESCO-worthy Flow Country is the most rewarding option for a blast of fresh air on your face and slice of cake at Forsinard Lodge's tea room.

BEST MEAL Scrabster haddock and sticky toffee pudding is the dream combo at **Varrich Restaurant** (p109).

FAVOURITE VIEW At the top of the Forsinard Observatory overlooking bog pools and precious peatlands at **Forsinard Flows National Nature Reserve** (p110).

ESSENTIAL STOP Get your swimming gear on and brave a cold-water plunge at **Coldbackie Beach** (p115) or **Torrisdale Bay** (p112).

ROAD-TRIP TIP The **Store Cafe** (p109) in Bettyhill is the closest the NC500 gets to a roadside diner, with long opening hours and pleasing grub.

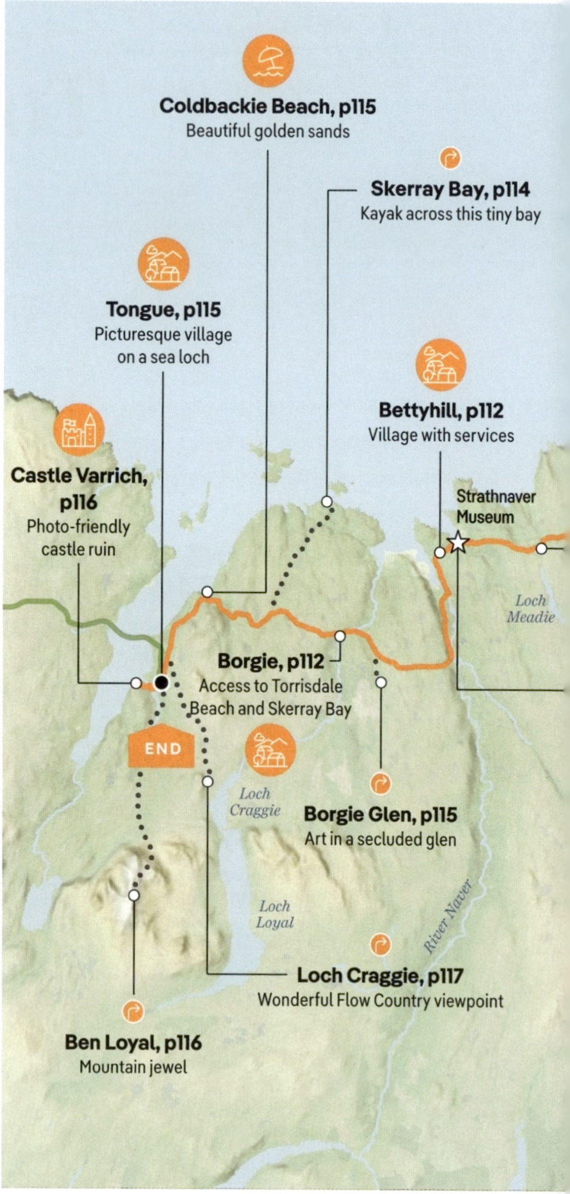

Coldbackie Beach, p115
Beautiful golden sands

Skerray Bay, p114
Kayak across this tiny bay

Tongue, p115
Picturesque village on a sea loch

Bettyhill, p112
Village with services

Castle Varrich, p116
Photo-friendly castle ruin

Strathnaver Museum

Loch Meadie

Borgie, p112
Access to Torrisdale Beach and Skerray Bay

END

Loch Craggie

Borgie Glen, p115
Art in a secluded glen

Loch Loyal

River Naver

Loch Craggie, p117
Wonderful Flow Country viewpoint

Ben Loyal, p116
Mountain jewel

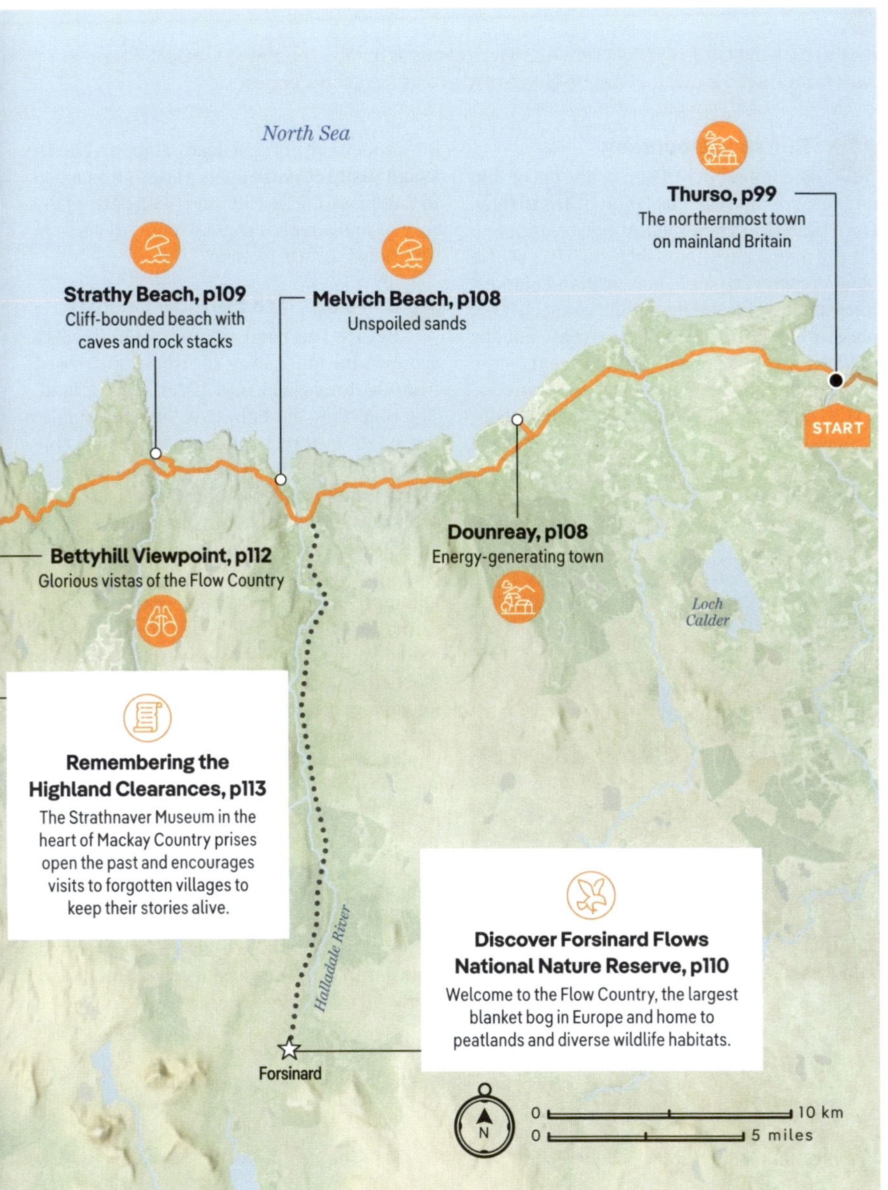
North Sea
Thurso, p99
The northernmost town on mainland Britain
Strathy Beach, p109
Cliff-bounded beach with caves and rock stacks
Melvich Beach, p108
Unspoiled sands
START
Bettyhill Viewpoint, p112
Glorious vistas of the Flow Country
Dounreay, p108
Energy-generating town
Loch Calder
Remembering the Highland Clearances, p113
The Strathnaver Museum in the heart of Mackay Country prises open the past and encourages visits to forgotten villages to keep their stories alive.
Halladale River
Discover Forsinard Flows National Nature Reserve, p110
Welcome to the Flow Country, the largest blanket bog in Europe and home to peatlands and diverse wildlife habitats.
Forsinard
N
0
10 km
0
5 miles

PREVIOUS STOP In the right light – and with cameras ready – the largely unspoilt drive west from Thurso is one that can be elevated to a road-trip showstopper.

PHIL JOHNSON/SHUTTERSTOCK

Thurso to Dounreay

Ten miles out of Thurso, one major blip on the landscape can't be ignored: **Dounreay**. Once the world's first nuclear power station to supply mains electricity, then the UK's centre of fast-reactor research, now Scotland's largest nuclear clean-up and demolition project, it is a massive eyesore on the Caithness coast, but one that provides much-needed employment for the surrounding towns. What you may also notice on this stretch is the propensity for wind farms. Renewable energy is big business here and new turbines are popping up at pace.

While guided tours were once offered by boffins in white coats, the power station is now off-limits to visitors. Instead, Thurso's **North Coast Visitor Centre** offers a brief introduction to Caithness' nuclear heritage, with parts of the reactor and a replica control room – Soviet-era Chernobyl springs to mind.

STEVE ALLEN/SHUTTERSTOCK

Dounreay power station

DETOUR: Into the Flow Country

Before the road reaches Melvich Bay around nine miles away, the route has crossed from Caithness back into historic Sutherland. The road then splits in two, with the single-track A897 cutting inland into the remarkable UNESCO-listed **Flow Country**. From the turn-off, it's around half an hour before you arrive in a landscape as wild and thrilling as it is empty and at peace. Enjoy your time exploring the blanket bogs that have been growing around Forsinard for 10,000 years, because the rest of the drive to Tongue lends itself more to roadside diversions than anything more full-blooded. In both directions, keep a watch out for wandering sheep and drive slowly – this is a route mostly used by farm traffic and goods lorries.

Melvich Beach

Back on the road heading west, **Melvich** is a tiny, blink-and-you'll-miss-it village, worth a stop for its lovely beach at the mouth of the River Halladale. It's reached by a short stretch of gravel track and the car park is signposted from the A836. It's unspoiled, smooth, sandy and lovely – if the weather cooperates.

Thurso
10.8 miles
Dounreay
8.7 miles
Melvich Beach
3.5 miles
Turn off here if you fancy the Flow Country

Strathy Beach

Strathy Beach

As you travel west, the isolated beauty of the NC500's beaches will become increasingly evident. More and more flash by to the right and the next one to pull over for is **Strathy Beach**. It merits a stroll, even in foul weather, and is sheltered by wave-whipped cliffs to the east and the River Strathy to the west, which is also a fine spot for sport fishing. Take the turn off just before the church, then it's a short drive northwards to a car park behind the cemetery. In summer, when the cowslips and wildflowers are out, you may be joined by a trickle of local surfers.

continued on p112

BEST PLACES TO EAT

Coastline Coffee Shop, Melvich £
A veritable Sutherland Starbucks, serving takeaway fresh coffee, teas, ice cream, milkshakes and cakes. *(10am-3pm Wed-Mon)*

The Store Cafe, Bettyhill £
Packed with history and characters, and an all-day menu of breakfast, sandwiches, double-patty burgers and loaded fries. *(storecafe.co.uk; 9am-7pm)*

Norse Bakehouse, Tongue £
Soups, cakes, pastas, wood-fired pizzas and focaccias overlooking the Kyle of Tongue. Family-run and friendly. *(norsebakehouse.wixsite.com/my-site; 11.30am-5.30pm)*

Varrich Restaurant, Tongue £££
Inside the Tongue Hotel, but open to non-residents and offering burgers, beef stews and puddings, plus Sunday roasts. *(highlandcoasthotels.com/tongue-hotel; noon-2pm & 5.30-8.30pm)*

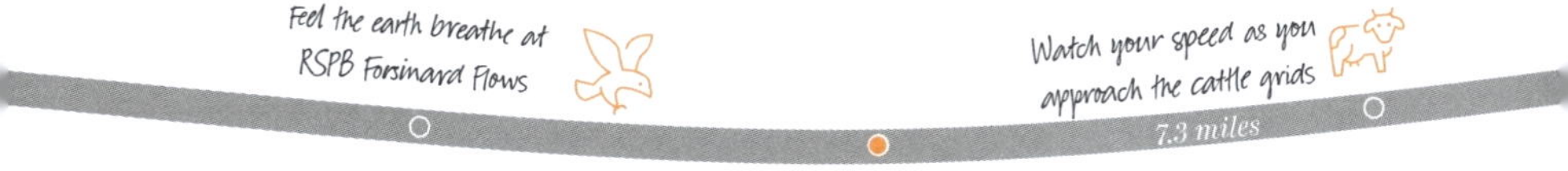

Feel the earth breathe at RSPB Forsinard Flows

Watch your speed as you approach the cattle grids

Strathy Beach

Discover Forsinard Flows National Nature Reserve

One of Europe's most important ecosystems, this vast blanket bog is lonely, yet rife with hidden riches.

Nearest stop: Melvich

Getting there: Forsinard Flows is 15 miles south of the NC500 on the A897.

Cost: Free

Tip: Arrive early or late in the day, when the insect, bird and wildlife are at their most active.

More info: *theflowcountry.org.uk;* visitor centre 10am to 5pm April to October, to 2pm November to March).

Mind-Boggling Bogs

An unrivalled strata of blanket bog, moorland and straths, the Flow Country is a bigger deal than it makes out to be. Its vast carpet of intact peatlands and intricate network of mottled bog pools means it was inscribed a World Heritage Site in July 2024, with UNESCO labelling it the most outstanding example of a blanket bog ecosystem in the world. And yet, despite such championing (and a mind-boggling 1500 sq miles to explore), its low-key subtlety means that outside of the summer peak all of it could be yours.

Stop, Look & Listen

The maxim here is the more you look, the more you see. Start at the visitor centre at RSPB Forsinard Flows National Nature Reserve, located at repurposed Forsinard train station. Inside, the permanent exhibition offers an insightful introduction to the area's natural history – one memorable line describes the peat as 'the memory of the land, the black pudding of time'. More rewarding still is the short wooden boardwalk trail above the sphagnum bog mosses to **Flows Lookout Tower** *(0.75 miles, 45-minute return)*. It's one of the few places where you can get out among the inky black pools (*dubh-lochain* in Gaelic) without getting your feet wet. Take time to look – carefully, slowly, silently – and you could see a rare world below your feet. A brief checklist includes insect-eating sundew,

ANDY HAY/RSPB-IMAGES.COM

SPOTTERS' GUIDE

Curlew
The Flow Country is an important breeding area for Europe's largest wader.

Golden Plover
Spotted from spring to autumn. Listen for their distinctive 'peep'.

Large Red Damselfly
The most common commuter on the Flows Lookout and Forsinain trails.

Left: Golden plover
Below: Insect-eating sundew

butterwort and bog myrtle, water boatmen and dragonfly, skylark, greenshank and wheatear.

A Long Hike

For a longer immersion into the Flow Country, the **Forsinain Trail** *(4 miles, 2 hours)* is an assault on the senses. Park four miles north of Forsinard on the A897, then cross the River Halladale and strike out across farmland into nesting grounds and open rolling hills. The silence may be eerie, but you'll have red-throated divers and dunlin for company. Maybe even buzzard and deer, both red and roe.

RSPB IMAGES

Strathy to Bettyhill

Ahead lies the blanket expanse of Sutherland's Flow Country, where isolated farmsteads pop up by the roadside and wide-ranging views of the flatlands fill the windscreen. After around 15 minutes (eight miles), a lay-by dubbed the **Bettyhill Viewpoint** comes into eyeshot, offering a chance to take in the first signs of the shadowy mountains and sea lochs to the west. It's picnic bench makes it a good spot for a break, but a better one to whet the appetite for what lies ahead. A set of binoculars are handy to have here.

Just before this, a gravel path peels off to **Loch Meadie**. If you're after more drama, albeit on the micro scale of the Flow Country, leave the car behind for a brisk two-mile walk for views of bog pools. Then, after a few more minutes further along the road from the Bettyhill Viewpoint, the road reaches the village of **Bettyhill** itself. It's a small crofting community that's emerged from tenant farming families resettled during the Highland Clearances.

Bettyhill to Borgie

Leaving Bettyhill, there's a gorgeous view of the **River Naver** and **Torrisdale Bay**, the sands curling out into the water to create the illusion of a lagoon. The road closely follows the river inland for around 1 mile, before crossing a narrow bridge and striking out over a rumpled swathe of bogs, lochans and peatlands.

Should the idea of beachcombing grab you, the golden sands of 1-mile-long **Torrisdale Beach** are hard to beat on a hot day – there are few places to park in Naver, so it's better to leave your vehicle north of **Borgie** on the minor road, then walk the 15 minutes to the beach.

ELI BOLYARSKA/SHUTTERSTOCK

Bettyhill

REWILDING SUTHERLAND

As one of Europe's emptiest quarters, you'd think Sutherland was wild enough already – but much of it has been depleted through centuries of mismanagement. A number of estate projects led by tourism pioneer Wildland are helping reverse the damage.

Eriboll
Deer numbers have been cut back from an unsustainable number and healthier tree life is returning.

Hope
Home to the UK's most northerly birch wood, as well as nesting golden eagles.

Strathmore
Location of the most northerly remnant of the Old Caledonian Pine Forest – plans are afoot to allow the forest to gain an ever stronger foothold in the landscape.

Bettyhill Viewpoint — 2.8 miles — Bettyhill — 6.7 miles — Borgie — 4.9 miles

Take a trip back through time at Strathnaver Museum

Torrisdale Beach is a lovely detour from Borgie

Remembering the Highland Clearances

Stories about the tragic Highland Clearances haunt the NC500 and come alive in Strathnaver.

HOW TO

Nearest stop: Bettyhill

Getting there: Follow the B871 south from Bettyhill, then continue onto the B873.

Cost: £5/under-18s free

Tip: The seasonal Clachan Cafe beside the museum car park has helpful tourist information.

More info: *strathnavermuseum.org.uk/strathnaver-trail;* 11am-3pm Wed-Fri Mar, 10am-5pm Mon-Fri Apr-Oct.

The unlikely place to find many of the answers to questions about the history of this stretch of the route is inside the former Parish Church of Farra, just outside Bettyhill. The church and cemetery – now the **Strathnaver Museum** – are often quiet, but are the custodians of a story that resonates throughout the centuries.

You'll learn about 8000 years of human history, from Clan Mackay to the brutal Highland Clearances (p156), which saw up to 15,000 people evicted to make way for sheep farming. As well as this, there are plenty of social history curios, including the St Kilda Mail Boat and a frightful fishing buoy made from dog skin.

To keep these stories and other memories alive, the **Strathnaver Trail Project** leads from the museum door, linking 29 archaeological sites, including brochs, chambered cairns, memorials and burial grounds between Bettyhill and Altnaharra.

At the furthest point, 20 miles to the south on the shores of **Loch Naver**, sits the ruined ghost village of Grummore Township, which was burned and cleared in 1819.

ROB FORD/ALAMY

Strathnaver Museum

At low tide, the rusting shipwreck of the SS *John Randolph* juts out at the west end of the beach like the fossilised bones of a beached plesiosaur.

By now, the soundtrack has turned to the rattle of cattlegrids and the gentle squeal of brakes as you move in and out of passing places. Here, the A836 exemplifies all that is terrific about the NC500: the road is meditative and it's a way of measuring the emptiness of this part of Scotland. This is your journey at its most isolated and far-flung.

DETOUR: Skerray Bay

3.5 miles north of Borgie

The B-road ends at Skerray, a tiny bay with limited parking. The lure here is what lies across the bay and the channel: **Neave Island** *(Eilean Nan Ron)* and its rock stacks and famous white-sand beach to the east. This is an adventurous trip for expert sea kayakers only – the island's north is on exposed coastline, offering no landings – but paddling to remote parts such as this is all part of the NC500's appeal.

BEST PLACES TO STAY

Forsinard Hotel, Forsinard £
Former hunting lodge turned B&B in the Flow Country. Only three rooms, plus a fine tearoom. *(forsinardlodge.com)*

Tongue SYHA, Tongue £
Stone lodge with plenty of history perfectly poised on the Kyle of Tongue. Private and family rooms, plus bike storage. *(hostellingscotland.org.uk)*

Tongue Hotel, Tongue ££
Once the Duke of Sutherland's home, now a lovely hotel: snug rooms, friendly service, a great restaurant and pub with log-stoked fire. *(tonguehotel.co.uk)*

Lundies House, Tongue £££
Scandi design meets Scottish heritage in this 19th-century house from rewilding pioneers Wildland. As swish as the NC500 gets. *(lundies.scot)*

Wreck of SS *John Randolph*, Torrisdale Beach

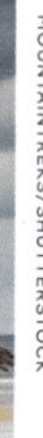
MOUNTAINTREKS/SHUTTERSTOCK

Along the Way We Met...

MARCEL WASSEN For me, Tongue offers world-class natural scenery and ultimate tranquillity. On our doorstep, you can discover the majestic Ben Loyal, Kyle of Tongue and Ben Hope. We're also situated at the gateway to the Flow Country World Heritage Site – that shouldn't be missed.

Marcel is the general manager of Tongue Hotel (tonguehotel.co.uk).

MARCEL'S TIP: *When travelling through Tongue, use the old road around the kyle for some superb scenery, instead of following the main road across the causeway. The old road was the main route until the causeway was constructed in the 1970s.*

DETOUR: Borgie Glen

1 mile east of Borgie village

The glen can be reached by turning south off the A836 and following the road for around three-quarters of a mile. It's a working forestry plantation on the edge of heathery moorland and empty hills that rise inland, and is also the location of *The Unknown* sculpture by Edinburgh-born artist Kenny Hunter. The enigmatic piece of art resembles an outcast, a giant skeleton looking for a home, its story echoing the area's traumatic clearances and disappearances from the land. As evocative as it is, the climb *(0.75 miles, 30 minutes)* through the pines to an outlook towards **Ben Loyal** and **Ben Hope** is equally worth it.

Coldbackie Beach

From Borgie, it's around five miles further until you get your first peekaboo glimpse of the Kyle of Tongue, a twisting sea loch with exceptional scenery and the three uninhabited Rabbit Islands offshore.

Slightly hidden from the roadside is **Coldbackie Beach**, an outstanding cove backed by red sandstone that pops with colour when reacting to the temperamental Scottish light and weather. Commonly, it's deserted apart from when the swell rises to tease out one or two cold-water surfers. Three miles further on through a thin band of forest and you'll arrive in Tongue.

Tongue

Of the few towns on the north coast, **Tongue** is arguably the loveliest of the lot. It certainly has the most attractive location, largely overlooking the brown-daubed ridges of Ben Loyal to the south and silvery blue waters of the **Kyle of Tongue** (contrary to what you may think, it doesn't look like the shape of a tongue). Many visitors are happy enough to rush through to the west coast, but it

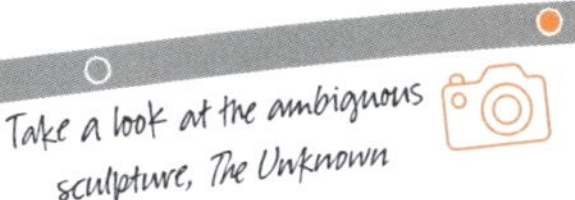

Coldbackie Beach

2.7 miles

Tongue

0.5 miles

merits an overnight stay, particularly because it has some of the most memorable hotels and restaurants since the road left Inverness.

Tongue all began as a crossroads. The surrounding land was controlled in various guises by Gaels, Picts and Vikings, with its harbour key for trade. As the Highland Clearances gripped the north centuries later, crofting families moved to the coast and the village grew. The Gaelic poet Ewen Robertson, known as the 'Bard of the Clearances', spent his life in Tongue and a memorial sits at the edge of the village. One stone is inscribed:

> *'In place of sheep, there will be people, cattle in the shieling in place of stags.'*

The story continues today in Tongue, with the arrival of **Wildland**, one of Europe's largest and most ambitious conservation projects, and its purposeful regeneration of several properties around the village. This includes a number of stylish Scandinavian-inspired homes, self-catering cottages and bothies, as well as the exclusive-use, five-star **Kinloch Lodge**.

Castle Varrich

All eyes in Tongue rest on this mysterious, ruined keep, which seems to float suspended atop a wooded hill above the kyle. While the true origins of **Castle Varrich** are hazy, it was once the seat of Clan Mackay and makes for a lovely ramble *(2 miles, around 1 hour)* from the village through thick forest, over a footbridge, then up a zigzagging path to the hill's exposed top.

The popularity of the NC500 means different things to locals, but its success has dramatically improved access to the castle; in 2017, a galvanised corkscrew staircase and viewing platform were added inside – and the landscape-scale vistas are epic. If you're not staying in the village, park opposite Ben Loyal Hotel and follow the signs through the trees.

WIRESTOCK/GETTY IMAGES

Castle Varrich

DETOUR: Ben Loyal

Ben Loyal, the Queen of Scottish Mountains, dominates the moorland south of the Kyle of Tongue and is dubbed so because seen from a distance, it wears a tiara-like crown of four spiked peaks.

It's not as famous as many Scottish hills, but that's largely because it's not a Munro (over 3000ft/914m), sitting at only 764m. And yet, its lonely position overlooking bog, moor and sea intensifies its appeal.

Castle Varrich

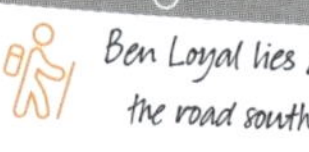

Ben Loyal lies at the end of the road south of Tongue

While the climb to the blocky granite tor that marks the summit of Ben Loyal summit isn't the hardest hike on the NC500, for walkers unaccustomed to Scotland's hill terrain it can be a gruelling slog: expect boggy and wet conditions underfoot, burn crossings and a rough path that frequently disappears (leaving you to forge your own route).

Set aside six to seven hours for the 8.5-mile round trip, and pack warm and wet-weather gear, regardless of the forecast. There's a car park near the start of the ascent at Ribigil.

DETOUR: Loch Craggie

Before continuing west, there's one more detour to consider: an old quarry viewpoint across the Flow Country from **Loch Craggie**, 3.5 miles to the south along the A836. On the expanse of peatland, best seen in the last rays of autumn light or with the road tapering into the mist, you'll be able to pull over for a low-lying panorama across the shallow loch. The gouges in the peaty landscape are an indicator of the landscape having been once harvested for fuel.

Ben Loyal

SARA WINTER/SHUTTERSTOCK

NEIL COWIE/RSPB

Beneath the Blanket: Explore the Flow Country

The Flow Country is the first peatland to be inscribed as a UNESCO World Heritage Site. This breathtaking landscape sweeps from the NC500, encompassing 187,000 hectares of rare blanket bog habitat. Explore the rugged yet delicate natural heritage with a visit to this important bog.

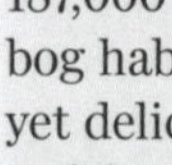

WORDS BY **MILLY REVILL HAYWARD**

The Flow Country

Looking inland from the NC500, you might be surprised to find you're gazing out towards a place that's quite remarkable – the Flow Country.

Named from the Norse word 'Floi' (meaning wet, boggy place), the Flow Country is a blanket bog – a rare habitat found in cool, wet climates. It's a peatland, where dead plant materials partially decompose to form peat soil. Peatlands are one of the best carbon stores found on Earth and provide a home for unique wildlife. The Flow Country stores over 400 million tonnes of carbon; more than double the amount stored in the UK's forests and woodlands.

Not only are blanket bogs themselves special, but the Flow Country is especially so. The peat here has been accumulating for around 9000 years and, in some places, is up to 10m deep. The bog here is the largest in Europe and the most outstanding example of a blanket bog worldwide. It was inscribed as a UNESCO World Heritage Site in 2024 – an accolade never before given to a peatland site – ranking it as a place of global importance amongst the likes of well-known natural sites, such as the Great Barrier Reef and the Serengeti.

Discover Forsinard Flows

In the heart of the Flow Country, the national nature reserve RSPB Forsinard Flows – managed by the RSPB – was established in 1995 to protect the peat-lands and wildlife, whilst restoring degraded terrain through the removal of non-native trees and rewetting.

Forsinard Flows Visitor Centre is housed within the old train station building. Spend time here with the interactive exhibit to gain a greater understanding of the natural and cultural heritage of the Flow Country, and learn about the ongoing work to protect, restore and research the peatlands.

The Dubh Lochain Trail begins across the road from the centre, the 1-mile walk follows a boardwalk towards the Flows Lookout Tower. Here, admire the intricate pool systems and blanket-bog landscape with a birds-eye view. You can spot many of the unique peatland species along this trail, from minute sphagnum mosses and hen harriers soaring overhead, to red deer roaming in the distance.

For a longer walk, head four miles north on the A897 to the Forsinain Trail, a circular four-mile route crossing farmland, peatland and forest.

Forsinard Flows is easily accessible from the NC500 route. From the north, turn off the A836 onto the A897 at Melvich and head south for 15 miles; from the west, turn off the A9 at Helmsdale and follow the A897 for 24 miles.

Flora & Fauna

Wherever you find yourself in the Flow Country, there is an abundance of peatland wildlife to discover.

Red deer are hard to miss – they roam in herds throughout the year, unhindered by fences or boundaries. In the warmer months, lizards or adders bask in the sunlight, damselflies dart along the surface of pool systems, and butterflies flutter by as you walk the trails.

For birdwatchers, the Flow Country is particularly exciting in the spring and summer months. Blanket bog is an important breeding habitat for ground-nesting waders such as golden plovers, greenshanks and dunlins. Red and black-throated divers and common scoters breed on the inland lochs, whilst golden eagles, merlins and short-eared owls soar in the sky.

Don't forget to look down and explore the flora too. Colourful and diverse bog-building sphagnum mosses, patches of carnivorous midge-eating sundews and beautiful bog bean flowers will have you discovering a whole new world on the surface of the bog.

Things to Do

There are many ways to explore the Flow Country: wind through the peatlands along the straths (river valleys) via car or bike, or for something different, go via rail. The Far North Railway Line is one of Britain's most impressive train journeys, providing spectacular views of the more remote sections of the Flow Country.

If you're looking for activities, hike the Ben Griams (Ben Griam Beg and Ben Griam Mòr) for magnificent summit views, or visit the Flows Lookout Tower for a night of stargazing. Local clubs offer salmon fishing in the rivers, and you can birdwatch from many spots throughout the area. Viewpoints can be found at Cnoc Craggie, Moine House, Loch Rangag and Crask, and are perfect spots to stop, look out and be inspired by the landscape. For more information, visit *theflowcountry.org.uk*

Tongue

The move from the vast expanse of the Flow Country to the cove-nibbled communities of northwestern Sutherland feels as if you're entering a whole new realm. By the time Loch Eriboll is in the rear-view mirror, the road ahead reveals a string of toffee-coloured beaches and terrific bays to enjoy, with rarely a bog in sight. Make the most of Durness village because, while the hills of Assynt get increasingly appealing to the south, the nearest town for services is Ullapool, 70 miles (two hours) away.

Mike MacEacheran

Durness

HEATHER GUNN/SHUTTERSTOCK

THIS LEG

- Tongue
- Tongue Causeway
- Moine House
- Hope
- Ard Neackie Lime Kilns
- Lotte Glob
- Ceannabeinne Beach
- Ceannabeanbe Township Trail
- Sangobeg
- Durness Beach
- Durness

Driving Notes

This is a section of two halves: first, the final curtain call of the sparsely populated Flow Country; then the road sweeps towards the beach-lined coast, as if it were in need of a holiday and dose of sun itself. Pay attention to wayward sheep, a few tight bends and keep your eyes on the road, not on bays like Ceannabeinne Beach and Durness Beach.

Breaking Up Your Journey

After the Kyle of Tongue, there are numerous places to park up are for photo opportunities, but none for services and fuel. Moine House, the last of the formal Flow Country viewpoints, is worth a leg-stretch, as is the viewpoint overlooking the Ard Neackie Lime Kilns on Loch Eriboll. If you like barefoot sand walks and coastal snoops, factor in plenty of time on the final push to Durness.

BEST MEAL World-class, if calorific, hot chocolate at **Cocoa Mountain** (p127).

FAVOURITE VIEW **Durness Beach** (p128) ranks as the most memorable beach because of its immediacy and easily accessible beauty.

ESSENTIAL STOP **Smoo Cave** (p131) is the big-ticket attraction – best explored out of season or with adventure-seeking kids.

ROAD-TRIP TIP Because of the oceanfront campsites, this section can get particularly busy with motorhomes. Use lay-bys and let people pass as necessary.

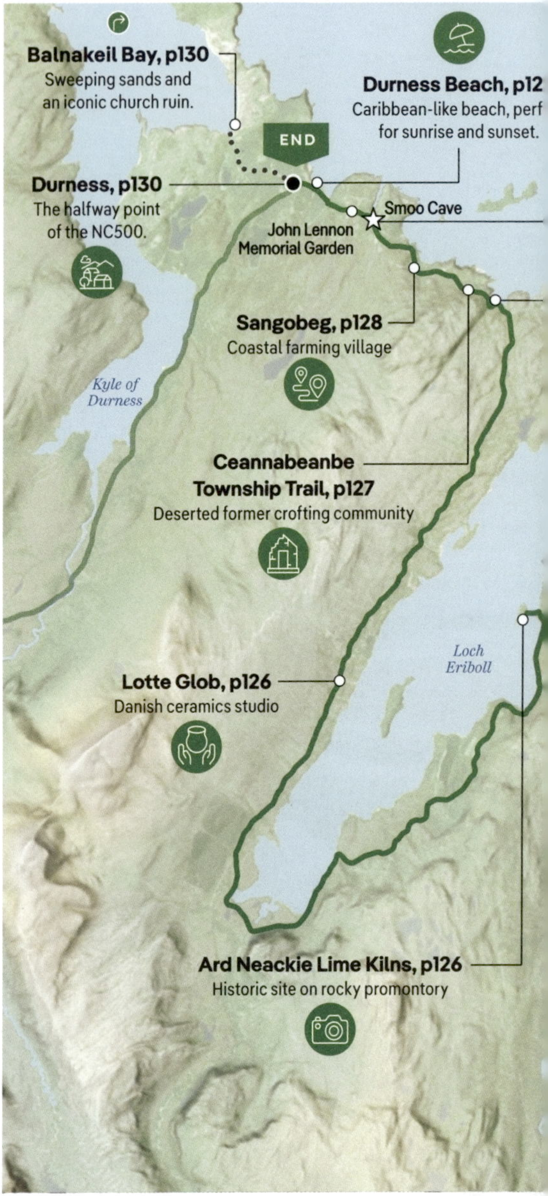

Balnakeil Bay, p130
Sweeping sands and an iconic church ruin.

Durness Beach, p12
Caribbean-like beach, perf for sunrise and sunset.

END

Durness, p130
The halfway point of the NC500.

Smoo Cave

John Lennon Memorial Garden

Sangobeg, p128
Coastal farming village

Kyle of Durness

Ceannabeanbe Township Trail, p127
Deserted former crofting community

Loch Eriboll

Lotte Glob, p126
Danish ceramics studio

Ard Neackie Lime Kilns, p126
Historic site on rocky promontory

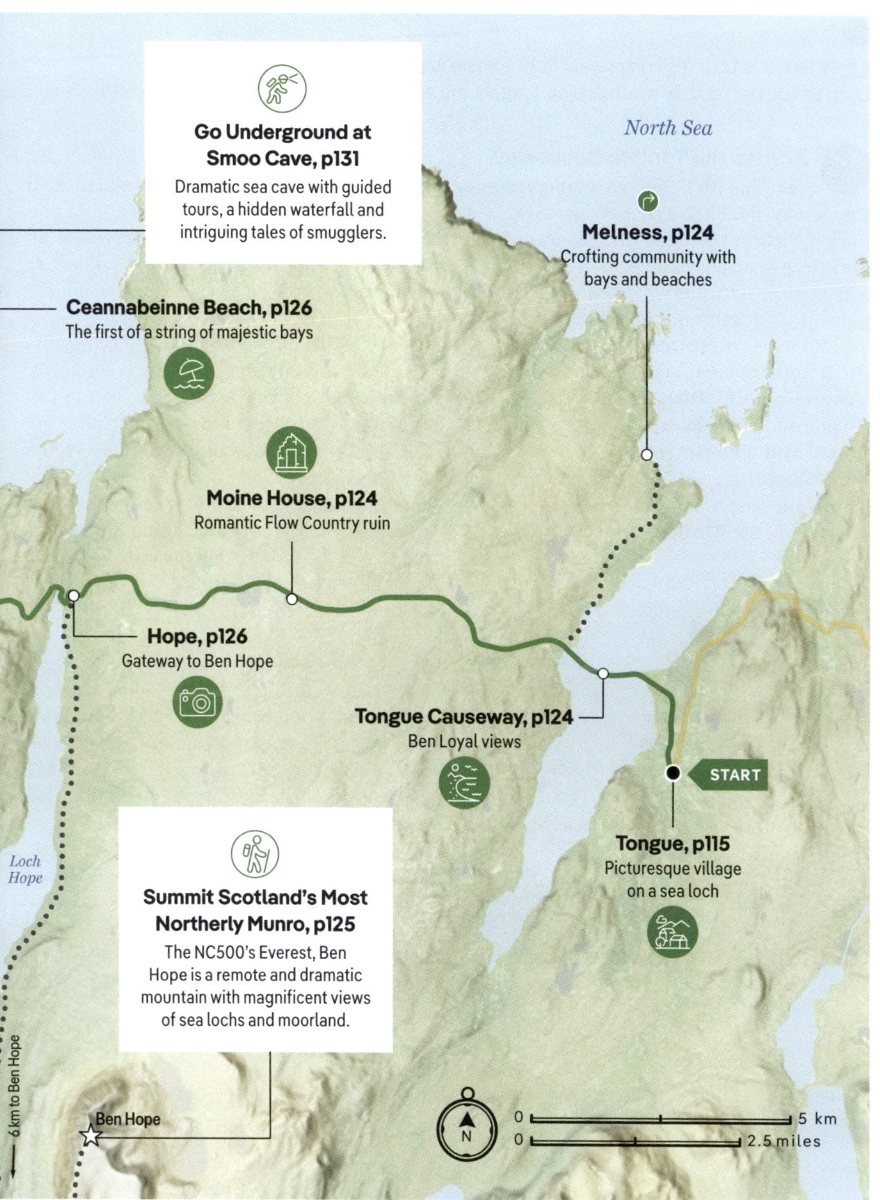

North Sea
Go Underground at Smoo Cave, p131
Dramatic sea cave with guided tours, a hidden waterfall and intriguing tales of smugglers.
Melness, p124
Crofting community with bays and beaches
Ceannabeinne Beach, p126
The first of a string of majestic bays
Moine House, p124
Romantic Flow Country ruin
Hope, p126
Gateway to Ben Hope
Tongue Causeway, p124
Ben Loyal views
START
Tongue, p115
Picturesque village on a sea loch
Loch Hope
Summit Scotland's Most Northerly Munro, p125
The NC500's Everest, Ben Hope is a remote and dramatic mountain with magnificent views of sea lochs and moorland.
6 km to Ben Hope
Ben Hope
N
0
5 km
0
2.5 miles

PREVIOUS STOP The drive west from Tongue is one of constant natural drama, with Loch Eriboll particularly eye-pleasing. Largely, the A838 is your constant companion.

Across the Tongue Causeway

Take the A838 and cross the **Tongue Causeway**, built half a century ago to prevent the long detour via the southernmost point of the kyle. After a few minutes' drive, you'll pass a geological information point and – if that grabs your attention – then the prospect of exploring deep time could see you add one or two impromptu detours to your route.

The west coast section of the NC500 between Tongue and Ullapool is home to six different **'Rock' and 'Pebble' routes**, created by the North West Highlands Geopark and each one brings the area's 'rock stars' to life (p176). From here, the **Moine Thrust Route** loops around the Kyle of Tongue via Altnaharra and Hope, focusing on landscapes studded with granite, syenite, Lewisian gneiss and Moine rocks. Who cares about boring old rocks? Well, these ones are some of the world's oldest at 3 billion years old.

TAKING IN THE SIGHTS/SHUTTERSTOCK

Moine House

DETOUR: Melness

The dead-end road crofting community of **Melness** is a worthwhile side trip in the right weather. Follow the first turn-off after the causeway for four miles, passing through yellow gorse and fields to Talmine Bay. There are a few holiday cottages, but the main reason to come are the sheltered bays and island beaches. If you have a sea kayak, then the crossing to the uninhabited **Rabbit Islands** is the stuff of blue-water daydreams.

Moine House

Continuing west, the landscape is a serenade of bogs, empty peat moors and little else: in shifting mist, horizontal rain or under storm-grey skies, it's not a destination for the faint-hearted. Bleak is the word that can sometimes spring to mind.

But in the right light, **Moine House**, which roughly marks the halfway point to Hope, is beautifully desolate. The moorland was a treacherous crossing place for travellers, so the shelter was built as a rest stop at the same time as the Duke of Sutherland ordered

Tongue — 1.8 miles — Tongue Causeway — 4.3 miles — Moine House — 3 miles

For a longer drive from Tongue, travel west via the old kyle road

Summit Scotland's Most Northerly Munro

Twenty minutes south of Hope, this lonely mountain offers a welcome break from the road amid a broad wilderness of lochans and steep escarpments

HOW TO

Nearest stop: Hope

Getting here: The car park for Ben Hope is 7 miles south of the NC500 and accessed from Hope along the Tongue–Lairg road.

More info: *historicenvironment.scot*

Follow the scenic minor road along Loch Hope and you'll find the Holy Grail of NC500 mountains: **Ben Hope**. The mountain's summit plateau sits in splendid isolation at 927m, with a craggy rock face facing west and a well-worn track leading first alongside a stream, then through a break in the cliffs to a grassy ridge that rises to the top. The five-mile walk takes around four to five hours to complete, with the best views of lochs Hope and Eriboll appearing slightly further north, beyond the summit cairn. Come in winter and you'll need to be prepared with crampons and an ice axe and, crucially for safety, know how to use them.

The etymology of the name is not, as many walkers would like to think, related to aspiration and yearning for the great outdoors. Instead, *hóp* is an Old Norse word for 'bay'.

For more history, three miles south of Ben Hope, 7m-high **Dun Dornaigil** near the roadside is an excellent example of a towering Iron Age broch.

OTHER LONELY PEAKS

Ben Klibreck
South of Altnaharra, Kilbreck is another isolated Munro in central Sutherland. As remote as Highland mountains get *(8.75 miles, six hours)*.

Conival & Ben More Assynt
Two sibling peaks and the only Munros in Assynt – in the next NC500 section.

NORRSCOTPRODUCTIONS/SHUTTERSTOCK

View from Ben Hope

construction of the peninsula's first road. Today, the photogenic relic marks the western extreme of the Flow Country and leads to viewpoints and two walks suitable for all ages and abilities.

Hope to Loch Eriboll

From Moine House, you'll tackle a few descending hairpin bends towards **Hope**, a tiny settlement at the northernmost point of Loch Hope. The road to the east of the water motors south for around seven miles of single track to **Ben Hope**, Scotland's most northerly Munro, with the main NC500 continuing west to a fine vantage above the **Ard Neikie Lime Kilns**.

Stop at the lay-by on the side of the road's descent towards Eriboll and take in the view: below is a lonely boathouse, a tombolo beach and four preserved furnaces that once produced large amounts of lime in the 1870s for surrounding farms. Seen together, it's the northwest Highlands in a nutshell.

Around Loch Eriboll

This is the last chance to savour Scotland's north coast at its most far-flung. The route curves around **Loch Eriboll**, with the single-lane A838 skirting moody peatlands and pockets of forestry. Other than views of mist-clad mountains and the silver-blue loch, the only stop is the **Sculpture Croft of Lotte Glob**, a Danish ceramicist who moved to the lochside 50 years ago. Visitors are welcome to visit her studio and landscaped sculpture garden, by appointment only, and it's not hard to miss: the entrance is marked by a very fancy set of gates.

KEEBLE1337/SHUTTERSTOCK

Ard Neikie Lime Kilns

Ceannabeinne Beach

Located five miles to the north, **Ceannabeinne Beach** is the start of what could be called the Costa del Sutherland: it's the first of many eye-popping curls of fudgy sand, with plenty of parking and steps leading right down onto the shore. In Gaelic, the beach was traditionally known as Traigh Allt Chailgeag, meaning 'the beach of the burn of bereavement and death'.

Golden Eagle Zip Line is the other reason to stop. Run by a Durness-based adventure tours operator, Britain's most northerly flying-fox is strung 30m above the beach between two spurs, giving you a bird's-eye-view of sparkling waves and Caribbean-blue tidelines. Should that be too tame, consider the controlled free-fall drop. Both experiences can hit speeds of 45mph, so you may well end up travelling faster than the

Hope — *6 miles* — ○ — *What a viewpoint at Loch Eriboll!* — Ard Neackie Lime Kilns — *9.8 miles* — Lotte Glob — *5.1 miles* — Ceannabeinne Beach — *0.4 miles*

rate you're tackling the NC500 *(£20, no booking required Apr-Oct, prebooking only Nov-Mar, durnesszipline.com).*

Ceannabeanbe Township Trail

Less than half a mile from the beach is another reminder of the Highland Clearances on the **Ceannabeanbe Township Trail** *(0.5 miles, 30 minutes)*. The story of inhumane eviction is one you'll likely be familiar with by now on the drive, but the signposted walk around this deserted crofting settlement is one that's accompanied by gorgeous beach views. Information panels placed along the walk tell the story of those who took a stand against the landed gentry until the bitter end.

In 1841, 50 people lived in the now-ruined cottages and longhouses that can still be seen here, but by the following year all their homes had been cleared. The crofters didn't go without

BEST PLACES TO EAT

Cocoa Mountain, Durness £
This chocolatier is the anchor tenant of the Balnakeil Craft Village. Sweet treats galore! *(cocoamountain.co.uk; 9am-6pm Mar-Oct)*

Cheese n Toasted, Durness Beach £
Street-food truck serving three-cheese sandwiches brimming with haggis, pastrami or pesto, in front of Durness Beach. *(10am-3pm Mon-Thu, to 4pm Fri, to 5pm Sat & Sun Apr-Oct)*

Sango Sands Oasis, Durness Beach £
Overlooking Durness Beach, the breakfast bar and low-key pub of Durness' most popular campsite serves breakfast rolls and pizzas. *(sangosands.com; 8-10am & 4-11pm Apr-Oct)*

Smoo Cave Hotel ££
Family-run hotel, restaurant and bar with the 'Smoo Crave' takeaway truck for non-residents. Serves soups, pastas and fish and chips. *(smoocavehotel.co.uk; hours vary)*

Golden Eagle Zip Line

DAVID FORSTER/ALAMY

a fight: in response to the unwelcome eviction notice, they burned it, disarmed, pursued and captured the special constables sent to drive them out, then marched the officers to the parish boundary. It triggered the **Durness Riots**, one of the most famous uprisings of the Clearances. The matter was finally settled when the Duke of Sutherland called in troops from the 53rd Regiment in Edinburgh. The one positive for the community was the chastised duke decided to spare the crofters of neighbouring Balnakeil.

Sangobeg

A few minutes from the lay-by for the Ceannabeanbe Township Trail is the small crofting community of **Sangobeg**, but before then is a wild, time-stood-still sandy bay. Like many of the beaches west of here, the vibrant colours of **Ceannabeinne Beach** can be an assault on the senses. There is no designated parking for the beach, only an extended lay-by, so use common sense if heading to the seaside for the day. Along the road, past a lot for overnight campervan parking, the road twists across a headland towards Smoo Cave.

A few minutes' drive west from the cave, the small service town of Durness has an edge-of-nowhere setting before the NC500 turns south towards Assynt and Ullapool. Happily, there are a number of attractions to see before leaving the north coast.

A Beatle & Durness Beach

After a stop in Sangobeg, it's on to Durness which has more than a few claims to fame – and they don't come greater than its ties to a former Beatle and one of the greatest singer-songwriters in history, John Lennon. As a

Along the Way We Met...

CHAZ POWELL It is an honour to help monitor, protect, and preserve the various iconic spots that are dotted along the North Sutherland coastline. My role as a Highland Council Access Ranger allows me to engage with the public about the Scottish Outdoor Access Code, encouraging people to play their part in travelling responsibly and respectfully, to both the environments they are passing through and to the local communities who live within this beautiful part of the world.

Chaz is a Seasonal Access Ranger for North Sutherland, Highland Council (highland.gov.uk).

CHAZ'S TIP: *Always leave places as you find them, or if opportunity allows, leave them even better than you find them!*

Ceannabeinne Township Trail

0.8 miles

Sangobeg

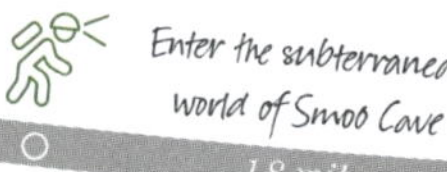

1.8 miles

Factor in time for a beach walk

Durness Beach

0.3 miles

BEST PLACES TO STAY

Sango Sands Oasis, Durness Beach £
Tents, campervans and motor homes are catered for at this beachfront stalwart with one of the NC500's best views. *(sangosands.com)*

Lazy Crofter Bunkhouse, Durness £
Lovely hostel with dorms, shared kitchen, laundry and terrace. *(visitdurness.com)*

Mackay's Rooms, Durness ££
Owners Robbie and Fiona Mackay (who also run the bunkhouse) are the brains behind the tastefully decorated rooms at this lovely B&B. *(visitdurness.com)*

Durness Smoo Youth Hostel, Smoo £
Simple, dog-friendly hostel 15-minutes' walk from Durness centre, with dorms and privates, plus breakfast and 'heat it and eat it' evening meals. *(hostellingscotland.org.uk)*

boy, from the age of nine to 14, Lennon summer holidayed in Durness at his aunt's croft, even returning post-Beatles fame in 1969 with Yoko Ono and son Julian. Durness isn't Liverpool or New York, but its size belies the impression it made on Lennon and his imagination – it's claimed by locals that his beloved Beatles' ballad 'In My Life' is, in part, an ode to the golden days he spent in the village. In tribute, the village created the small **John Lennon Memorial Garden** next to Durness Village Hall.

Continuing west from the village, **Durness Beach** is split by craggy black rock outcrops and is almost as brochure-perfect as those travellers fly halfway around the world to see in the Maldives: it's a strip of blue-on-gold brilliance. To get there, park at the beachfront car park off the A838, or walk the 400m from the village centre, marked by the Durness War Memorial.

Durness Beach

Along the Way We Met...

FRASER EADIE Durness has been my home for 20 years and the caves on the northwest coast are special because of the Durness Limestone, an ancient seabed dating back more than 500 million years. I'd recommend bringing a wetsuit and spending time in the sea – my favourite coastal spot is the cliffs at Smoo Cave where you can see whales, dolphins and otters. Durness is also memorable not just because of its beauty and wildlife, but also for its rich history.

Fraser is an enthusiastic caver and guide for Smoo Cave Tours (smoocavetours.com).

FRASER'S TIP: *On the NC500, I'd encourage people to visit Balnakeil Bay and walk to Faraid Head to see the puffins.*

Durness

Congratulations: you've made it to the halfway point of your journey. You're now around 250-miles from Inverness and attractive **Durness** is a fitting place to embrace the most memorable of the NC500's northern beaches, if you've haven't done so already.

In recent years, the popularity of the road trip has given rise to a number of B&Bs here, and because of its cluster of beaches and untamed landscapes, it's become a hub of summer activity. This is your best option for 24hr fuel and stocking up on supplies until you reach Scourie, 25 miles to the south.

DETOUR: Balnakeil Bay

Five minutes to the west of Durness, **Balnakeil Bay** represents the final frontier of northwest Scotland for the vast majority of NC500 travellers. Across the Kyle of Durness is Cape Wrath (p146), home to sheer cliffs and the most northwesterly point of Scotland, but it's also cut off from the main road network.

At Balnakeil, there is a fine crescent-shaped beach and a bewitching dune system that glows at sunset. In the tradition of cold-water NC500 swims, the sheltered bay is renowned as being one of the most sublime for stripping off and going for a dip. Next to the end-of-the-road car park is the photogenic ruin of 17th-century **Balnakeil Church** and its graveyard, where Elizabeth Parkes, the aunt of John Lennon, is buried. This metaphorical journey – from life to death, beauty to decay in only a few metres – is a sea change as pronounced as any in the Highlands.

The beach also marks the start of the **Faraid Head** peninsula, which provides excellent birdwatching opportunities – look for bright-lipped oystercatchers and ringed plovers. The headland is private farmland used for grazing, so take extra care during lambing season.

0.3 miles

Durness

The extra drive to Balnakeil Bay is worth it

The next stretch to Ullpool leaves the north coast behind once and for all

Go Underground at Smoo Cave

Hidden out of sight 1 mile to the east of Durness, this active sea cave is shrouded in mystery and tales of Vikings

HOW TO

Nearest stop: Durness

Getting here: Smoo Cave is a few minutes' drive from Durness or a 20-minute walk.

Entry: Free. Guided tours are extra.

Guided tours: £15/5 adult/child, cash only; 10am-5pm June-Aug; 11am-4pm Apr-May & Sept-Oct.

More info: *smoocavetours.com*

CAVE WILDLIFE

Fulmar
The limestone rocks are fertile ground for seabirds. Look for the fulmar nesting colony.

Otter
Herbs, grasses and fish provide sustenance for resident otters.

Grey seal
Try and spot seals swimming into the channel.

A deep waft of sea air creeps up the nostrils as the steps from the car park descend from the clifftop viewpoint a short distance from the A838 towards the vice-like chasm below. At the bottom, the grand reveal is the **Allt Smoo** river and a gaping 50ft-high limestone cave that ranks as having one of the largest entrances of any in Britain.

Legend says the name for **Smoo Cave** is derived from the Old Norse word *smuga*, meaning cave, and stories swirl that it has been in use for more than 6000 years. Excavations have found ship nails and rivets from the times of Viking occupation, as well as 12th- and 13th-century pieces of worked bone, antlers and knife handles. Archaeologists have established that the main chamber and three of the smaller adjacent caves were once used as workshops for boat building and repair.

Guided caving trips run from April to October into the smaller, flooded freshwater caverns, where a 20m-high waterfall plummets from the roof after heavy rains. Note, tours are weather and tide dependant – sensible footwear is a must.

ROBERT ORMEROD FOR LONELY PLANET

Ardveck Castle

CONNECT IMAGES/TIM E WHITE/GETTY IMAGES

INSIGHT

Mountains & Memories

In 1985, 40 years before the NC500 was launched, writer Mike MacEacheran took his first journey around the North Highlands in the company of his father, camping and hiking from Ullapool to Loch Broom to Durness, and being introduced to a incomparably beautiful part of the world that continues to haunt him to this day.

WORDS BY **MIKE MACEACHERAN**

The Landscape of Memory

Maybe my first memory of northern Scotland is seeing the hidden sea lochs and quartzite scree slopes of Sutherland's northwestern tip come into view, while standing proudly atop the rippling summit of Ben Hope, overlooking what is now the NC500. Or maybe it's the sight of Ardveck Castle and its tombolo beach on Loch Assynt, while setting up camp in the pink light of dusk.

With hazy recollections of my early childhood years hiking and camping through the Highlands, it's difficult to decide which one exactly came first. But what isn't up for debate is the effect the landscape had on me. These places possess the ability to inspire and thrill anyone in equal measure and, ever since my first journey along the minor roads of the NC500, I've felt a powerful desire to walk its ancient pathways and explore the freedoms of its hills as often I can.

The First & Last Journey

That first journey is all the more poignant now because my father Ian passed away, aged 80, almost a year to the day that I started researching and writing this book. In returning to many of the places we visited – Tongue, Lairg, Loch Eriboll, Loch Hope – I was reminded of the two of us exploring these nooks of the Highlands together. In inclement weather, the Kyle of Tongue is a haunting place for many reasons. It is even more so, when preoccupied by the ghost of youth. There are fading memories of us here, and for that I am grateful to be able to return to help keep them alive, before they vanish altogether.

> These places possess the ability to inspire and thrill anyone in equal measure.

I remember camping with my father near Altnaharra, before slogging up Ben Klibreck in thick mist to its isolated summit. Apart from the chocolate bar blackmail used as motivation to help me reach the top, I probably hated it at the time. But the moorland around the mountain now carries extra significance; in my father's last months, suffering from hard-hitting vascular dementia, he remembered very little. What he did recall were many of the hills he'd walked while completing his lifetime-long circuit of the Munros, a bucket-list achievement for so many Scots in the twilight years of their lives. Ben Klibreck, Conical and Ben More Assynt, all of which lie within the NC500's uppermost sphere, chiefly figure among them.

Centuries of Ache

What is it about this landscape that haunts travellers like me so much? Is it, perhaps, that it is synonymous with the barbarous tragedy of the Highland Clearances, which saw many thousands of crofters evicted from their homes and driven off the land? It's now a familiar suggestion that the landscape feels eerie, almost unearthly, because of the tumbledown settlements and ruined crofts that can be explored off the roadsides throughout Strathnaver and Mackay Country. This can feel like a place almost unlived in – though certainly not unloved – yet it is also one haunted by centuries of ache.

Moine House, overlooking the vast boglands of the Flow Country near Hope, is one particularly beautiful holy ground where travellers can reflect on the past. On my most recent visit, the cold touch of its stone reminded me of clambering over rocks decades before with my father. One time, a loose boulder was dislodged from above and it fell, landing on his right hand, crushing his index finger. So obsessed with the mountains was this tough-as-old-boots Scot that he didn't pay a visit to our doctor until we'd finished our camping trip two days later.

Stories of Stone

Another haunting spot is Knockan Crag, a geological haven between Durness and Ullapool. More than 3 billion years of history are preserved in the rocks here, but there is a bedrock of memories for me too. If the rocks could talk, the landscape would remind me how my father and I once walked here on a hot midsummer's day and were sunburned pink.

There are strata of impressions through this region and, like so many places along the NC500, there are whispers of past lives in the shadows of the rock. My father's story is only one of them, but it's likely that you will leave your own echoes too. And maybe one day you'll return to your own history, to listen and touch, and be moved by the passing of time.

PHOTO ESSAY

Northern Light

TO TAKE THESE photographs, I used a Canon R5 with a 70-200 and a Canon 5rs with a 50mm prime for exteriors, switching to 35mm prime and 80mm prime with a tripod for interiors. I was working in the depths of winter so if the sun was out, the light was usually soft and beautiful – the changing weather gave a gorgeous variety to conditions and light.

At the beginning and the end of each day, there would be the usual 'golden hour', but there would also be the most brilliant bursts of transcendent light that frequently left my jaw on the ground.

Living in Scotland I'm used to the landscape looking pretty good but something about the combination of the ends-of-the-earth feeling on this route and raw extremes of weather made this trip really special – and one of the best I've done in my home country.

Below left: The road around Loch Eriboll (p126)

Below: Castle Varrich, near Tongue, one of my favourite photographs from this trip (p116)

Right: Clachtoll Beach at sunset (p154)

PHOTOGRAPHS BY **ROBERT ORMEROD**

Right: Loch Kishorn (p223)

Below: Maiden Loch, on the road to Stoer Head Lighthouse (p154)

Left: Shorefront houses, Ullapool (p174)

Below: A view over the Kyle of Tongue (p115)

Above: The road looking back to Heilam on Loch Eriboll (p126)

Left: A viewing telescope near Stoer Head Lighthouse (p154)

Right: A beach on Loch Eriboll (p126)

Durness

I always feel a change in the air as the road turns south at Durness, near the ancient Viking landmark of Cape Wrath. Here the predominantly coastal scenery of the north coast gives way to dramatic vistas of mountain and moor as the route follows the line of early 19th-century roads into the heart of old hunting and fishing estates. It's also home to my favourite NC500 seafood stops at Scourie, Kylesku and Lochinver.

Neil Wilson

Lochinver

THIS LEG

- Durness
- Kyle of Durness
- Gualin House
- Rhiconich
- Laxford Bridge
- Scourie
- Kylesku
- Drumbeg
- Achmelvich
- Lochinver

STEVE ALLEN/SHUTTERSTOCK

Driving Notes

This is the time to pray for good weather – the views on this leg (and the next) are legendary. Be sure to make use of the strategically placed parking areas to stop for photos (do NOT stop in passing places). The Durness–Rhiconich and Drumbeg Loop sections are single track; watch out for sheep, and pull over to allow faster vehicles to overtake.

Breaking Up Your Journey

This is the least populated leg of the NC500, with only a handful of villages and two petrol stations en route (at Kinlochbervie and Scourie), so fill up at Durness before you set off. Kinlochbervie, Scourie and Kylesku are all possible lunch stops, with good places to eat. The Rock Stop near Kylesku is a good wet-weather break.

Neil's Tips

BEST MEAL Langoustine salad for lunch at **Shorehouse** (p148) in Tarbet.

FAVOURITE VIEW The iconic panorama of Suilven and the hills of Assynt and Coigach from **Strone Viewpoint** (p154).

ESSENTIAL STOP The elegant bridge set amid wild landscapes at **Kylesku** (p152).

ROAD-TRIP TIP For the best photo of **Kylesku Bridge** (p152), climb the rocky knoll across the road from the car park.

START

Durness, p130
The halfway point of the NC500.

Loch Eriboll

Gualin House, p144
Hunting lodge

North Sea

Kyle of Durness

Kyle of Durness, p144
Sand-fringed sea loch

Kinlochbervie & Oldshoremore, p148
Vibrant fish market and crofting settlements

Cape Wrath

Sandwood Bay

Oldshoremore

Kinlochbervie

Venture to Cape Wrath, p146
Scotland's northwest corner is a daunting and primal landscape of bleak moorland ringed by ferocious sea cliffs.

Hike to Sandwood Bay, p145
The coastal jewel of Sandwood Bay is often described as Scotland's most beautiful beach.

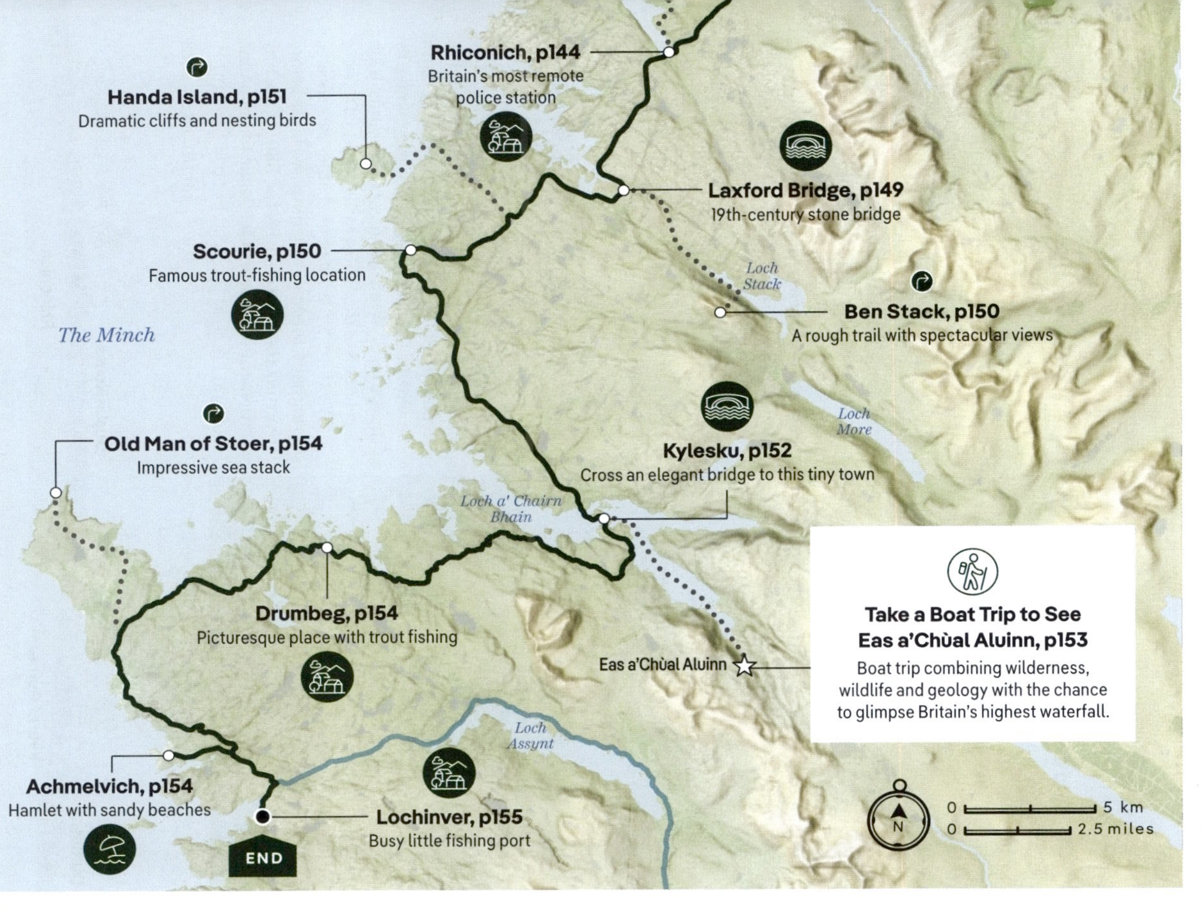
Rhiconich, p144
Britain's most remote police station
Handa Island, p151
Dramatic cliffs and nesting birds
Laxford Bridge, p149
19th-century stone bridge
Scourie, p150
Famous trout-fishing location
Loch Stack
Ben Stack, p150
A rough trail with spectacular views
The Minch
Loch More
Old Man of Stoer, p154
Impressive sea stack
Kylesku, p152
Cross an elegant bridge to this tiny town
Loch a' Chairn Bhain
Take a Boat Trip to See Eas a'Chùal Aluinn, p153
Boat trip combining wilderness, wildlife and geology with the chance to glimpse Britain's highest waterfall.
Drumbeg, p154
Picturesque place with trout fishing
Eas a'Chùal Aluinn
Loch Assynt
Achmelvich, p154
Hamlet with sandy beaches
Lochinver, p155
Busy little fishing port
END
N
0 5 km
0 2.5 miles

PREVIOUS STOP The village of Durness is where the North Coast 500 turns south and enters the most striking landscapes of the route.

Kyle of Durness

As you leave the north coast and begin to head south, a stretch of two-lane road leads through unexpectedly green and gentle countryside, a result of the fertile Durness limestone which underlies it (you can see the blue-grey limestone exposed in several roadside cuttings), before sweeping down to the shores of the **Kyle of Durness**, a sand-choked inlet of the sea.

A minor road on the right leads to a small ferry pier, the starting point for the adventurous trip to **Cape Wrath** (p146). A North West Highlands Geopark **'geopod'** (information booth) at the junction explains the local geology.

Strath Dionard

Gualin House

The 10 miles from Kyle of Durness to Rhiconich is one of the emptiest and bleakest stretches of the North Coast 500, almost all of it single track with passing places. As the road crosses **Drochaid Mhòr** (Big Bridge) and climbs away from the River Dionard, the vast expanse of **Strath Dionard** opens up to the south, a desolation of bog and heather where the only signs of habitation are the shepherds' cottages at **Carbreck** (now an Airbnb) and distant **Rhigolter**. A small plantation of conifers marks the location of **Gualin House**; completely hidden from the road, it was built by the Duke of Sutherland as a hotel in 1833 when the road was first made, and now serves as a hunting and fishing lodge.

Rhiconich

South of Gualin, across a scatter of lochs, rise the imposing mountains of **Foinaven** (from the Gaelic Fionne Bheinn, meaning 'white or shining mountain'), so named for its distinctive silvery-white quartzite scree slopes, and **Arkle** (from Airceal, meaning 'hiding place'). Both lie within the Reay Forest Estate, owned by the Duke of Westminster; two famous Irish racehorses of the 1960s, owned by the Duchess of Westminster, were named after these peaks. Eventually, the road widens to two lanes before reaching the junction with the B801 at the tiny settlement of **Rhiconich** (public toilet, phone box and hotel) at the head of Loch Inchard.

continued on p148

The way to Cape Wrath

Durness · 1.8 miles · Kyle of Durness · 8 miles · Gualin House · 4.4 miles · Rhiconich · 4.6 miles

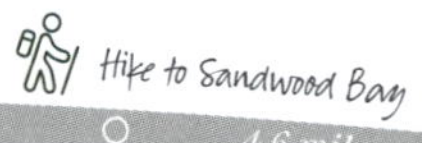

Hike to Sandwood Bay

The coastal jewel of Sandwood Bay is often described as Scotland's most beautiful beach, its allure only intensified by its remote and romantic setting.

HOW TO

Nearest stop: Rhiconich

Getting here: Drive to Blairmore car park, 3.5 miles northwest of Kinlochbervie; from here it's a 4-mile walk each way (allow 4 hours round trip).

More info: *johnmuirtrust.org*

From Blairmore car park, a good path (signposted) leads north across bleak moorland puddled with lochans. There is no view of the sea, and the landscape is desolate peat bog – it's part of Sandwood's charm that there is no hint of its existence until you are almost upon it. As freshwater Sandwood Loch comes into view, you will see the ruins of Sandwood Cottage, said to be haunted by the ghost of a drowned sailor and, far to the north, Cape Wrath Lighthouse just poking above the skyline.

The final stretch of path leads across sandy machair to the beach itself – almost two miles of glorious golden sand, heaped by Atlantic gales into huge marram-covered dunes.

The bay is bookended by outcrops of banded pink and grey Lewisian gneiss (among the oldest rocks in the world), and guarded at the southern end by Am Buachaille (The Herdsman), a sea stack of reddish-brown Torridonian sandstone. Few people walk all the way to the beach's northern end, so if you've packed a picnic, that's the spot to aim for.

FROM LEFT: PIXEL-SHOT/SHUTTERSTOCK, TOMMY LEE WALKER/SHUTTERSTOCK

EXPERIENCE ★

Venture to Cape Wrath

The northwest corner of the British mainland is a daunting and primal landscape of bleak moorland ringed by ferocious sea cliffs. The journey there and back by boat and minibus is a real adventure.

HOW TO

Nearest stop: Kyle of Durness

Getting here: Passenger ferry and minibus from Keoldale Pier.

When to go: The ferry only runs from May to September.

Cost: £25 (return trip)

Tip: There is no mobile phone signal or internet at Cape Wrath; prepare to go off-grid.

More info: *visitcapewrath.com*

The Journey

The way to Cape Wrath begins with a five-minute boat trip across the Kyle of Durness from Keoldale Pier, 2.5 miles south of Durness; there is parking on the left just short of the pier. The ferry runs twice daily from May to September, at around 9.15am and 12.15pm; exact times may vary because of tides and weather. Book ahead for the morning boat on 07534 591124 or email *info@visitcapewrath.com;* the midday boat is first-come, first-served.

When you're across the water, a minibus carries you the 11 miles across desolate moorland to Cape Wrath Lighthouse, but it takes an hour to do so – the road was built in the 1820s to serve the lighthouse and feels like it may not have been repaired since.

The Cape

The hazardous seas around the cape led to the building of the lighthouse here in 1828; the last keepers left in 1998, when automation replaced humans. Since 2009 the **lighthouse** complex has been lived in by John Ure and his family, who operate it as a hostel during the summer months and the basic **Ozone Cafe** (sandwiches, soup and toilet facilities) all year round.

LUCENTIUS/GETTY IMAGES

BOMBING RANGE

The vast expanse of uninhabited moorland on the way to Cape Wrath has served for decades as a Ministry of Defence training area and bombing range. **Garvie Island** (An Garbh-Eilean), 5 miles east of the cape, is around the same size as an aircraft carrier and is regularly ripped up by bombs and missiles during NATO military exercises. There is no public access when the range is in use; times are displayed at *gov.uk/government/publications/scotland-firing-times.*

Left: Cape Wrath Lighthouse
Below: Kearvaig Beach

From the lighthouse, you can walk the short distance uphill to the **old signal station**; from the rise beyond it there's a superb view back along the coast to **Clo Mor** (195m), the British mainland's highest vertical sea cliffs with their huge seabird colonies, and the sandy beach at **Kervaig**.

On a clear day you can see all the way to Dunnet Head and the Orkney Isles, 60 miles to the east, and the remote islets of Rona and Sule Skerry some 40 miles to the north.

MARKFERGUSON2/ALAMY

BEST PLACES TO EAT

Shorehouse, Tarbet ££
The definition of local produce – fresh langoustine and crab caught and landed within sight of your table. *(shorehousetarbet.co.uk; noon-7pm Mon-Fri Easter-Aug)*

Crofter's Kitchen, Scourie ££
Down by the beach, this outdoor kitchen serves top-notch local lobster, langoustine, scallop and crab. *(crofterskitchen.com; noon-6pm Mon-Sat Mar-Oct)*

Kylesku Hotel, Kylesku ££
Convivial, dog-friendly restaurant where you can toast your toes by the log fire or eat outdoors with a sea view. *(highlandcoasthotels.com/kylesku-hotel; noon-2pm & 6-8pm)*

Delilah's, Lochinver £££
Fine dining in the heart of the village, from lobster and steak to vegetarian including kids' and full vegan menus. *(delilahs.co.uk; noon-3pm & 6-9pm)*

Just 100m past the junction, on the right, you will see Britain's **most remote police station**, staffed by a single officer who covers an area of 900 sq miles. The station is housed in a former 19th-century travellers' inn, once known as the Stafford Arms, built by the Duke of Sutherland. The modern hotel is to the left, on the line of the old 1830s road with its original arched stone bridge.

DETOUR: Kinlochbervie & Oldshoremore

The B801 road leads west from Rhiconich to **Kinlochbervie**, one of Scotland's premier fishing ports, much used by east-coast boats to land their catch. The harbour was modernised in the late 1980s, when KLB (as it is known locally) was the third-busiest fish-landing port in Britain, close to the superb fishing grounds north and west of Cape Wrath. Although its

Police station, Rhiconich

Kinlochbervie (p145)

importance has since declined, it is still a hive of activity when the **fish market** is in full swing. Auctions are usually held at 4.30pm Monday to Thursday, and Fridays at 2pm; visitors are welcome to watch the action. A fleet of refrigerated trucks stands by to take the freshly landed catch away to grace the fishmongers' slabs and restaurant tables of France, Spain and Portugal.

A minor road continues beyond Kinlochbervie to the crofting settlement of **Oldshoremore**, which has a gorgeous stretch of golden sand backed by grassy dunes, and **Blairmore**, the starting point for the walk to gorgeous **Sandwood Bay** (p145).

Laxford Bridge

Continuing south from Rhiconich the A838 becomes a two-lane highway, built not for the benefit of visitors or locals but to accommodate the refrigerated trucks that export fresh Scottish seafood from Kinlochbervie.

There's a minor road on the right (signposted Skerricha) that leads to **Ridgway Adventure** *(ridgway-adventure.co.uk)*, run by Rebecca Ridgway, the first woman to kayak around Cape Horn and daughter of John Ridgway who was, with Chay Blyth, the first man to row across the Atlantic. The centre offers introductory **sea kayak days** *(adult/child £90/65)* for adults and children aged eight and over (must be booked in advance).

After crossing a short stretch of rough landscape hewn from pink and grey Lewisian gneiss, the road drops down to the sea again at the head of Loch Laxford, with the conical peak of Ben Stack (p150) rising in the background. It narrows briefly to single track to cross

SAVING SCOTTISH SALMON

Laxford comes from the Old Norse for 'salmon fjord', and the River Laxford was one of the most productive salmon rivers in the Highlands until recent decades, when numbers collapsed – possible causes include climate change and sea lice infestations from local fish farms. **Project Laxford** *(atlanticsalmontrust.org/project-laxford)* is a conservation project with the goal of restoring wild Atlantic salmon and sea trout populations. A million native trees will be planted across the river's catchment from source to sea – trees play an important part in keeping rivers cool and providing habitat for the insects that young fish feed on.

Learn how to kayak in the sea

FROM LEFT: VALERYEGOROV/GETTY IMAGES, MARISA ESTIVILL/SHUTTERSTOCK

Ben Stack

Laxford Bridge, built in the 1830s as part of the Duke of Sutherland's road-building programme.

DETOUR: Ben Stack

The single-track A838 leads from Laxford Bridge along the valley of the River Laxford, with the silvery grey scree slopes of Arkle rising to the north. It runs along the shore of scenic Loch Stack, famed for its sea trout (fishing can be arranged through the Scourie Hotel). About 400m beyond the end of the loch, a parking area on the left is the starting point for climbing **Ben Stack** (720m). The four-hour round trip over rough ground is rewarded by stunning views in all directions; for details check out the WalkHighlands website *(walkhighlands.co.uk)*.

Scourie

South of Laxford Bridge the road, now labelled the A894, continues across typical northwest Highlands 'cnoc-and-lochan' terrain – a landscape of craggy hillocks pockmarked with small lakes. As the road loops around the north side of Loch a'Bhagh Ghainmhich you'll pass a minor road on the right signposted Foindle, Tarbet and Handa Island (see Detour p151). After passing another pretty loch, 30mph speed limit road signs signal your arrival at the crofting village of **Scourie** (campsite, general store, post office, public toilets, 24-hour petrol station), famous worldwide for its trout fishing.

The **Scourie Angling Club** *(scourieangling.co.uk)* offers access to 47 hill lochs spread across 8100 hectares (20,000 acres) to the north of the village. Day permits *(£10)* are available online; no fishing on Sundays. The **Scourie Hotel** *(scouriehotel.com)* has been a famous destination for anglers since the 1850s and offers trout fishing on its 300 hill lochs (free to hotel residents), as well as salmon and sea trout fishing on Loch Stack and Loch More.

A site at the west end of the village, adjoining the road to the beach, has been earmarked for the new **Scourie Rocks Geocentre** *(scouriedevelopment.scot/scourie-rocks-project)*, a focal point for the North West Highlands Geopark. When completed, the centre will house an exhibition on the geology of Scotland along with a multimedia auditorium and a cafe with views across Scourie Bay to Handa Island. Most importantly, it will be home to the world-renowned **Shelley Collection** of rocks, minerals and fossils. Amassed by Don Shelley (1933–2002), the first warden of Knockan Crag National Nature Reserve (p167), the collection

Scourie

10 miles

consists of more than 2500 items and was purchased for the Geocentre by local landowner, the Duke of Westminster.

DETOUR: Handa Island

Just over halfway between Laxford Bridge and Scourie a minor road leads west for 3 miles to the tiny hamlet of **Tarbet** where you'll find the excellent **Shorehouse** restaurant (p000) and the little passenger ferry to **Handa Island Nature Reserve** *(scottishwildlifetrust.org.uk)*.

The island's western sea cliffs of stratified Torridonian sandstone rise to over 100m and provide nesting sites for important breeding populations of great skuas, arctic skuas, puffins, kittiwakes, razorbills and guillemots. There's a nice sandy beach near the ferry landing, from which a rough path leads for a mile or so across the centre of the island to the clifftops where you can admire the **Great Stack of Handa**, a

BEST PLACES TO STAY

Kylesku Lodges, Kylesku ££
If you feel like spending a few days around Kylesku, these gorgeous timber cabins have wood-burning stoves and balconies with stunning views of Quinag. *(kyleskulodges.co.uk)*

Scourie Lodge B&B, Scourie ££
Country house built by the Duke of Sutherland for his wife in 1835, now a luxury B&B with a wonderful old-fashioned atmosphere and superb outlook over the bay. Two-night minimum Apr-Sep. *(scourielodge.co.uk)*

Davar Guest House, Lochinver ££
Beautiful, welcoming B&B with a garden and fabulous panorama across the bay to Suilven and the Assynt mountainscape. *(davar-lochinver.co.uk)*

Razorbills, Handa Island

Kylesku Bridge

110m-tall sea stack, and enjoy fantastic views south to the Old Man of Stoer on the far side of Eddrachillis Bay. From here, follow a rough path westward around the coast to return to the ferry.

Kylesku

The road from Scourie to Kylesku continues as a good two-lane highway through a landscape softened by forestry plantations before bursting through a rocky cutting to reach a car park and **viewpoint** on the right. Here you can admire a panorama of Assynt peaks, from shapely Quinag directly across Loch a'Chàirn Bhàin (an arm of the sea) to the distinctive flat-topped Stack of Glencoul on the eastern horizon.

As the road descends to the coast, a large parking area on the right provides a view of **Kylesku Bridge**. Designed by Ove Arup, best known for their work on the Sydney Opera House, this elegantly curved bridge is often described as one of the most beautiful in the country. Opened in 1984, it was the final link in the North Coast 500 route, replacing a ferry that had until then been the only way to cross the narrow strait. On the far side of the bridge, the old road on the left leads down to the former ferry slip – starting point for scenic boat trips – and the excellent **Kylesku Hotel** (p148).

Kylesku

11 miles

Stop to look at Quinag's shapely peaks

Take a Boat Trip to See Eas a'Chùal Aluinn

A boat trip from Kylesku into lonely lochs Glendhu and Glencoul combines wilderness, wildlife and geology with the chance to glimpse Britain's highest waterfall.

HOW TO

Nearest stop: Kylesku

Getting here: Turn left off the main route 250m after crossing Kylesku Bridge to a car park opposite Kylesku Hotel.

Cost: £22

Useful tip: If the car park is full, head back to the large parking area immediately south of Kylesku Bridge and follow a footpath round the headland to the hotel (5-min walk).

LOCAL GEOLOGY

This area played an important part in the history of geology, its rocks revealing the secrets of thrust faulting where sheets of rock have slid one on top of another during a continental collision around 430 million years ago. You can see the layered structures on the headland between the two lochs.

Northwest Sea Tours *(northwestseatours.co.uk)* runs three boat trips a day from the old ferry slip beside Kylesku Hotel, each lasting 75 minutes. It's an open boat, so wrap up warm, take a waterproof jacket and be prepared to be on your feet for over an hour.

The tour takes you into the deep valleys of lochs Glendhu and Glencoul, whose roadless shores remain one of the remotest corners of the Highlands. At the head of **Loch Glencoul** is a deerstalker's house, abandoned in the 1950s; the smaller building next to it was once a school, and is now a bothy for hikers. In the wild country beyond you can see the 200m-tall white ribbon of **Eas a'Chùal Aluinn**, Britain's highest waterfall.

Bring your binoculars, these waters are rich in **wildlife**. Expect to see plenty of seals, both grey and common; possibly eagles, both golden and white-tailed; there's also a chance of spotting dolphins before the trip ends with a seal's-eye view of the graceful curve of Kylesku Bridge.

ALEXISAJ/ALAMY

Drumbeg

About a mile south of Kylesku Bridge at Unapool is the **Rock Stop** *(nwhgeopark.com)*, a cafe and geological exhibition devoted to the North West Highlands Geopark. Shortly after, the imposing, steep-sided northern peak of **Quinag** comes into view directly ahead, and the NC500 route turns right onto the B869 towards Drumbeg. This twisting single-track road is a proper roller-coaster of a ride, with lots of short, sharp ups and downs (cyclists beware) and expansive views across Eddrachillis Bay to the north.

Drumbeg itself is a picturesque place, famous for the superb **trout fishing** on neighbouring Loch Drumbeg and the 200 or so trout lochs managed by the **North Assynt Estate** *(theassyntcrofters.co.uk)*; permits can be purchased at Drumbeg Stores and the Drumbeg Hotel.

PIETFOTO/SHUTTERSTOCK

Old Man of Stoer

From the **viewpoint** at the far end of the village, you can look north across the bay to Handa Island (p151) and the mountains of Foinaven and Ben Stack.

DETOUR: Old Man of Stoer

Five miles west of Drumbeg the road passes the fine sandy bay of Clashnessie Beach before cutting across the headland to the hamlet of Stoer. Between Clashnessie and Stoer a minor road cuts north for 4 miles to **Stoer Head Lighthouse**. From the parking area below the lighthouse, a rough footpath (signposted; ignore the more obvious 4WD track heading inland) leads 2.5 miles along the clifftops to the **Old Man of Stoer**, a spectacular 60m-tall sea stack (allow three hours round trip). If you're lucky, there will be rock climbers scaling the stack; to get there they have to swim the chilly waters of the channel between the stack and the mainland before tackling the difficult climb.

Achmelvich

Beyond Stoer the road passes through the scattered crofting settlement of **Clachtoll** (sandy beach and campsite) then meanders inland for a few miles before reaching a parking area at **Strone Viewpoint**. The scenic panorama here takes in the distinctive sugarloaf peak of Suilven flanked to left and right by Canisp and Cul Mor, and provides a breathtaking impression of the wildness and isolation of the Assynt hills. A little further on, a side road leads to **Achmelvich**. It's no more than a hamlet with a campsite and youth hostel, but the fine sandy beaches here mean that it is mobbed with holidaymakers in July and August.

Drumbeg

13 miles

4.3 miles

Achmelvich

Along the Way We Met...

TIM HAMLET Suilven is an iconic mountain that dominates the skyline of Assynt. Personally, I feel that what this hill lacks in height it more than makes up for in personality. Mountaineer Sir Chris Bonington describes it as the mountain which most shaped his life, and it's easy to see why. While Assynt's hills could be described as remote and unforgiving, which is true, what that fails to capture is the sheer mystery of the place.

Tim is a mountain guide who runs Hamlet Mountaineering (hamletmountaineering.com), offering hillwalking, rock climbing and mountaineering experiences in the Northwest Highlands.

TIM'S TIP: *Stop and breathe. Take time to enjoy the little moments along the way.*

Lochinver

At last you reach **Lochinver**, the main village in the Assynt region; a busy little fishing port that's a popular port of call for visitors with its laid-back atmosphere, good facilities and striking scenery. It also enjoys a reputation as a foodie destination in miniature, with a couple of excellent places to eat including **Delilah's** (p148) and **Lochin-ver Larder** *(lochinverlarder.com; 10am-3pm Tue-Sat)*, whose gourmet pies are legendary – their venison and cranberry won Scotland's Best Meat Pie in the British Pie Awards 2022.

It's worth seeking out the **Highland Stone-ware Pottery** *(highlandstoneware.com)*, about 0.75 miles along the Badidarrach road northwest of Lochinver village. Established in 1974, this family-run operation turns out decorative stone-ware made by hand, with innovative glazes developed using local rocks such as Ledmore marble, Durness limestone and Lewisian gneiss. Visitors are welcome to watch the pottery being shaped and hand-painted. There's a factory shop here, and another in Ullapool; you'll also see Highland Stoneware items in use in restaurants across the country, including the Dipping Lugger in Ullapool.

Views of Suilven and the Assynt mountains

Lochinver

The Emigrants, memorial to the Highland Clearances, Helmsdale (p81)

DAVID LYONS/ALAMY; SCULPTOR: GERALD LAING

INSIGHT

The Legacy of the Clearances

As you travel the North Coast 500, reflect on the fact that the empty landscapes you see in the north and west weren't always so empty. All along the route you will find monuments, museums and relics of one of the most notorious episodes in Scottish history: the Highland Clearances.

WORDS BY **NEIL WILSON**

The Aftermath of Culloden

In the wake of the Jacobite rebellions, which culminated in defeat for Bonnie Prince Charlie and his army of Highland clansmen at Culloden (p34) in 1746, the British government outlawed the wearing of Highland dress and the playing of the bagpipes. The Highlands were put under military control and there was a concerted effort to wipe out traditional Gaelic language and culture, which were looked down on as barbaric.

The ties of kinship and duty that once marked the relationship between Highland laird and clansman gradually transformed into the merely economic relationship of landlord and tenant. Lands that had been confiscated after Culloden were returned to their owners in the 1780s, but by then the chiefs had tasted the aristocratic high life and were tempted by the easy profits to be made from sheep farming. The people who lived on the land were seen as a burden, with no economic utility.

The Clearances Begin

So began the Highland Clearances, when thousands of people were driven from their homes between 1750 and 1860. By no means all who left their townships in the late 18th and 19th centuries were forcibly evicted; in the Hebridean islands, for example, a combination of poverty, overcrowding and lack of suitable land led many to choose emigration. But some of the forced clearances, especially in Sutherland, were so brutal that newspaper reporting of the events caused a national scandal.

Although the Clearances took place two centuries ago, they remain an emotive subject in the region today.

Under the pretext of agricultural 'improve-ment', the peasant farmers, no longer of any use as soldiers and uneconomical as tenants, were evicted from their homes and farms to make way for flocks of hardy Cheviot sheep – in the Highlands the year 1792 (when Cheviots were first introduced) was known for decades afterwards as Bliadhna nan Caorach (the Year of the Sheep).

The Duke of Sutherland

George Granville Leveson-Gower (1758–1833), the 2nd Marquess of Stafford, became Britain's biggest landowner when he married Elizabeth, Countess of Sutherland in 1785. He was created 1st Duke of Sutherland in 1833, just six months before he died. Later known as 'the great improver', he opened up Sutherland by building roads, bridges and harbours, but became notorious for overseeing the eviction of thousands of tenant farmers to make way for sheep farms.

Some of the most notorious events of the Clearances took place on properties belonging to the duke, notably in the Strath of Kildonan in the east and Strathnaver (p000) on the north coast of Sutherland. Patrick Sellar – the duke's factor (land agent) – cleared people from their homes using dogs, and set fire to the roof timbers of the cottages while possessions were still inside, to prevent them from being reoccupied. In one case, it was claimed that an elderly woman was still in the house when it was torched; she died six days later. Sellar was afterwards charged with arson and culpable homicide, but was acquitted.

Relocation & Emigration

After the evictions, a few cottars (labourers or tenants) stayed behind to work the sheep farms, but most were relocated to desperate crofts on poor coastal land (as at Badbea, p82) or fled to the cities of central Scotland and northern England in search of work. Many thousands emigrated – some willingly, some under duress – to the developing colonies of North America, Australia and New Zealand. All over the Highlands today, only a ruckle of stones among the bracken marks where there was once a thriving township.

Although the Clearances took place two centuries ago, they remain an emotive subject in the region today. They marked the final nail in the coffin of the old clan system, and the beginning of the depopulation of the Highlands – between 1841 and 1951, the population of Caithness and Sutherland fell by 45%. But it was rarely a straightforward story, and recent scholarship has challenged the popular image of poor tenants versus greedy landlords, claiming that, in many cases, the population pressure on marginal land had become unsustainable – something had to give.

Lochinver

The leg between Lochinver and Ullapool crosses from the old county of Sutherland into the western part of the county of Ross & Cromarty, known as Wester Ross. This is the most dramatic stage of the NC500, where the mountains stand stark and isolated like colossal shipwrecks stranded on a sea of gneiss. It's my favourite part of the route – the temptation to pause here for a day or two and climb some of these otherworldly peaks is strong.

Neil Wilson

Ullapool

63 MILES

~2½ HOUR DRIVE~

THIS LEG

- Lochinver
- Leitir Easaidh Path
- Ardvreck Castle
- Inchnadamph
- Elphin
- Ardmair
- Ullapool

SCOTLAND BY JAN SMITH PHOTOGRAPHY/ALAMY

Driving Notes

The main NC500 route from Lochinver to Ullapool follows the A837 and A835 through wild mountain landscapes on a good two-lane highway. If you have time, take the opportunity to explore the winding single-track roads leading to the remote outpost of Achiltibuie. These backroads travel through some of the most spectacular scenery in Scotland; be prepared to pull over frequently for photo stops.

Breaking Up Your Journey

Ullapool is the biggest town in the region, and a fine place to overnight and restock; there's a large supermarket, plus restaurants, smaller groceries and delis. Elsewhere on this leg there are few places to stay and no food shops on the main NC500 route. Achiltibuie, a hefty detour from the main road, has a shop, campsite, restaurants and a hotel.

BEST MEAL Scallop salad at the **Seafood Shack** (p163), Ullapool.

FAVOURITE VIEW The hills of Assynt and Coigach from above **Achnahaird Beach** (p170).

ESSENTIAL STOP **Knockan Crag National Nature Reserve** (p167).

ROAD-TRIP TIP If you have a suitable vehicle, take the **Wee Mad Road detour** (p162) from the main NC500 route to visit Achiltibuie.

Ardvreck Castle, p163
Haunted ruins

Inchnadamph, p166
A geologist's heaven

Climb Suilven, p164
Suilven's sandstone tower looms on the horizon like a giant sugarloaf, the most iconic and alluring of Assynt's hills.

Leitir Easaidh Path, p162
All-abilities hiking trail

START

Lochinver, p155
Busy little fishing port

Wee Mad Road, p162
A detour for the daring

Loch Assynt
Suilven
Fionn Loch
Inverkirkaig
Enard Bay

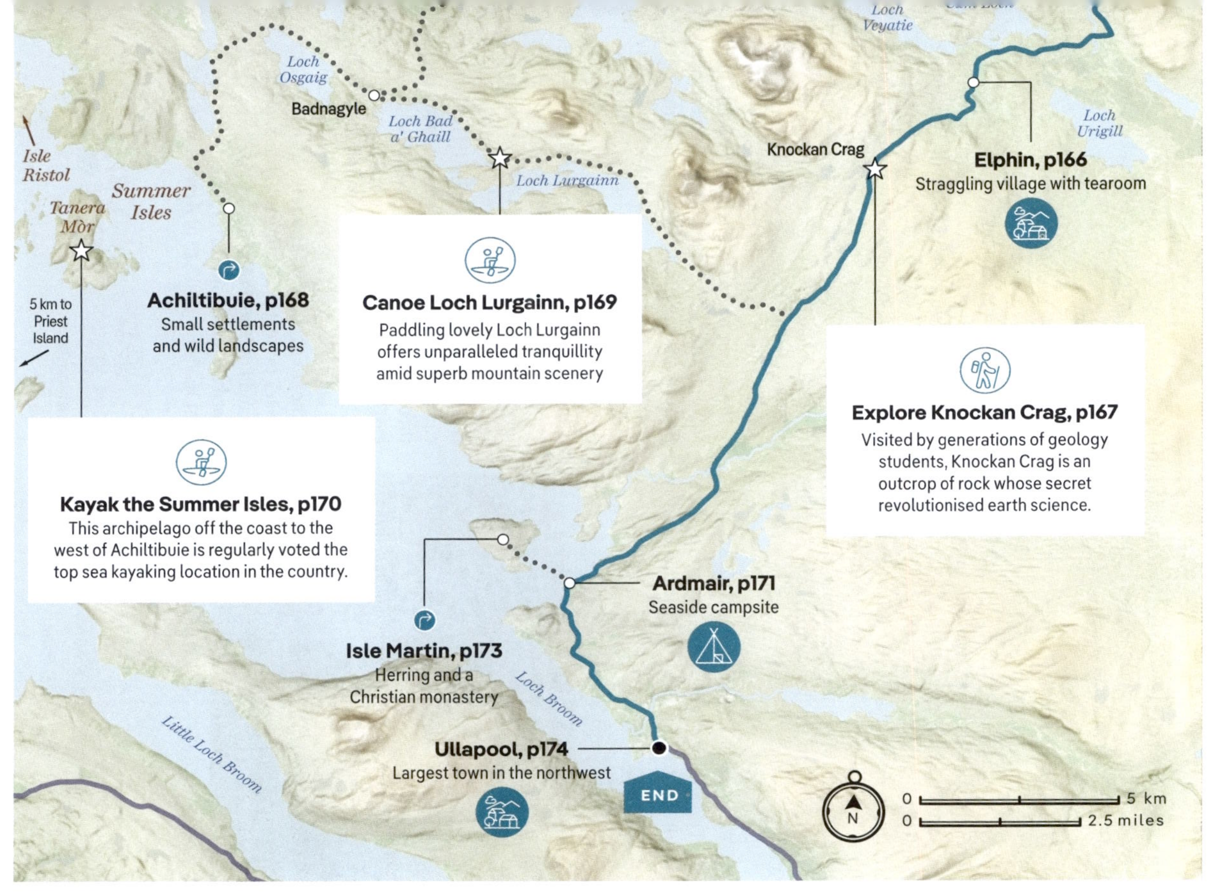
Loch Veyatie
Loch Osgaig
Badnagyle
Loch Bad a' Ghaill
Loch Lurgainn
Knockan Crag
Loch Urigill
Elphin, p166
Straggling village with tearoom
Isle Ristol
Summer Isles
Tanera Mòr
5 km to Priest Island
Achiltibuie, p168
Small settlements and wild landscapes
Canoe Loch Lurgainn, p169
Paddling lovely Loch Lurgainn offers unparalleled tranquillity amid superb mountain scenery
Explore Knockan Crag, p167
Visited by generations of geology students, Knockan Crag is an outcrop of rock whose secret revolutionised earth science.
Kayak the Summer Isles, p170
This archipelago off the coast to the west of Achiltibuie is regularly voted the top sea kayaking location in the country.
Ardmair, p171
Seaside campsite
Isle Martin, p173
Herring and a Christian monastery
Loch Broom
Little Loch Broom
Ullapool, p174
Largest town in the northwest
END
N
0
5 km
0
2.5 miles

PREVIOUS STOP Leaving Lochinver behind, the journey to Ullapool begins with a decision – head east on the main road via Inchnadamph and Knockan Crag, or detour south along the Wee Mad Road to Coigach.

JOE DUNCKLEY/SHUTTERSTOCK

Leitir Easaidh Path

The main NC500 route follows the A837 road northeast along the wooded valley of the River Inver. Soon after reaching the treeless landscape at the western end of Loch Assynt, you'll see a parking area on the left. This is the starting point of the **Leitir Easaidh Path**, a 1.5-mile all-abilities hiking trail that wanders past a couple of picturesque lochs with grand views north to the long mountain ridge of Quinag.

DETOUR: The Wee Mad Road

The minor road that leads south from Lochinver to join the Achiltibuie road at Badnagyle is a scenic single track so narrow and twisting that caravans, buses (and any vehicle more than 6m long) are prohibited. Built around the end of the 19th century by Inverpolly Estate to provide access to its hunting lodge, but not given a hard surface until the 1940s, it became known to locals as the **Wee Mad Road**. (Note –since the creation of the North Coast 500 some YouTube and social media accounts have referred to the B869 Drumbeg loop as the 'Wee Mad Road'. This is wrong – the Wee Mad Road is not part of the official route.)

Lochinver Primary School

MARKFERGUSON2/ALAMY

The detour begins by passing Scotland's most superbly situated school – **Lochinver Primary School** sits on a headland overlooking Loch Culag, with the distinctive sugarloaf peak of Suilven puncturing the horizon; a little further on at a cattle grid there's room to pull over for a photo. Four miles out of Lochinver, you reach **Inverkirkaig**, not far from the starting point for climbing **Suilven** (p164); if you're having second thoughts about the Wee Mad Road, this is your last chance to turn around. For the next eight miles the road meanders and switchbacks through heather, rock and lochan with views east to the rugged hills of **Coigach** – notably at Loch Buine Mòire where the panorama of peaks will take your breath away – before descending to the junction at **Badnagyle** (a single white house) beneath the improbable sandstone pyramid of **Stac Pollaidh** (p168).

Turn left here to return to the main road, or right to visit the village of **Achiltibuie** (p168).

Take a trip down the Wee Man Road

Lochinver

6.5 miles

5.5 miles

Leitir Easaidh Path

Climb Suilven

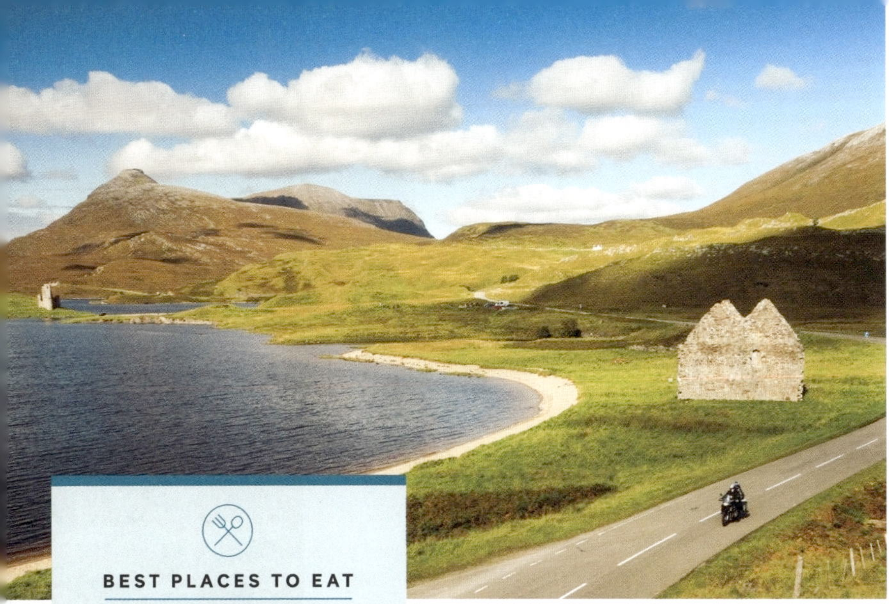

Loch Assynt

BEST PLACES TO EAT

Fuaran Bar, Altandhu ££
Snug little watering hole serving a selection of fresh local seafood, including plump langoustines, lobsters, scallops and crabs. *(amfuaran.co.uk; food served 12.30-2.30pm & 6-8pm)*

Cult Cafe, Ullapool £
New Zealand cafe culture in the heart of the Highlands – enjoy a flat white with typical kiwi treats such as lolly cake. *(check facebook.com/cult.cafe.ullapool for opening times)*

Seafood Shack, Ullapool £
This humble place, serving from a wooden shed, has local seafood (langoustines with garlic and thyme butter), as well as inventive takes on mac and cheese. *(seafoodshack.co.uk; noon-6pm Apr-Oct)*

Ardvreck Castle

The road hugs the northern shore of wild and moody **Loch Assynt** for another five miles to **Skiag Bridge**, where it is joined by the A894 (the direct route from Kylesku). About half a mile beyond the junction is a large car park, and perched on an island at the edge of the loch are the romantic ruins of **Ardvreck Castle**, built in 1597 by the Clan MacLeod of Assynt. There are rumoured to be several ghosts at Ardvreck, including the daughter of a MacLeod chieftain who was sold in marriage to the devil by her father. South of the car park are the ruins of **Calda House**, a mansion built in the 1720s to replace Ardvreck Castle, which had been sacked in the 1670s; the house burned down in the 1760s.

continued on p166

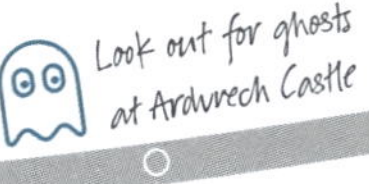

Ardvrech Castle

1.5 miles

Climb Suilven

Seen from Lochinver, Suilven's sandstone tower looms on the horizon like a giant sugarloaf, seemingly inaccessible, the most iconic and alluring of Assynt's hills.

HOW TO

Nearest stop: Lochinver

Getting here: Drive south on the Wee Mad Road towards Achiltibuie for 4 miles to the car park at Kirkaig Bridge. From here the hike to the summit is 14 miles round trip; allow 7-9 hours.

When to go: The best weather for hiking is usually in May, June or September.

Tip: You need to be fit and competent in navigation to attempt Suilven. If you are unsure, it's better to hire an experienced local mountain guide, like Tim Hamlet of Hamlet Mountaineering *(hamletmountaineering.com)*.

The Assynt Landscape

East from Lochinver spreads the uninhabited wilderness of Assynt, an awe-inspiring landscape of heather, rock and water. At its centre stands the shapely peak of **Suilven** (731m), one of the most distinctive of all Scottish mountains (the name is a Norse-Gaelic hybrid, *'súla bheinn'*, meaning 'pillar mountain'). No keen walker can resist its allure but, despite its modest height, the hill's remote setting makes it a challenging objective.

Reaching the Summit

There are various routes to the summit, but the approach from **Inverkirkaig**, four miles south of Lochinver, is the most scenic. Starting from the car park at Kirkaig Bridge, follow a good path southeast along the north side of the river. After 2.25 miles you reach the spectacular **Falls of Kirkaig**; a half-mile beyond that (at a cairn) fork left to cut across a neck of land to Fionn Loch. There are superb views of Suilven ahead as the path weaves around the head of the loch and along its boggy northern shore.

When almost level with the low point in the middle of Suilven's ridge, a fainter path strikes north across moorland towards the mountain itself.

JOHN BRACEGIRDLE/ALAMY

SUILVEN ON PAGE & SCREEN

Scottish poet Norman MacCaig (1910–96) famously spent every summer in Assynt, fly fishing, hiking and socialising. His poem 'Climbing Suilven' captures beautifully the feeling of plodding up a steep hillside ('down and down this treadmill hill must go') until the sudden revelation of magnificent summit views.

The mountain also featured in the 2017 film *Edie* starring Sheila Hancock as an octogenarian in search of a life-affirming challenge (she actually climbed Suilven during the making of the film).

Left: Suilven
Below: Falls of Kirkaig

The trail climbs steeply up boulders, turf and scree, becoming badly eroded in its upper part, to reach the saddle. Turn left for an airy ridge walk to the flat-topped summit, passing through a gap in a beautifully made drystane dyke – a so-called 'famine wall', commissioned by the landowner to provide work for local crofters during the potato famines of the 1840s and 1850s. At the top – and weather permitting – you will be rewarded with incredible panoramas of mountain, moorland, loch and sea. Return the way you came.

JAROSLAV SEKERES/SHUTTERSTOCK

Inchnadamph

A mile beyond Ardvreck Castle, at the eastern end of Loch Assynt, the tiny crofting hamlet of Inchnadamph sits amid a patchwork of fertile green fields. A favourite haunt of geology students and speleologists, it sits near the Moine Thrust (p167) and a large area of cave-riddled Durness limestone. The focal point is the **Inchnadamph Hotel** *(closed Nov–Feb)*, a 200-year-old coaching inn that feels as comfortable and lived-in as a pair of old hiking boots, a haven of peace (no TVs or mobile phone reception) in the middle of nowhere.

A car park about two miles south of Inchnadamph is the starting point for an enjoyable walk along the Allt nan Uamh (Stream of the Cave) to the so-called **Bone Caves** *(3 miles round trip, 2 hours)*. In 1889, geologists excavated the bones of various animals from these caves, and later digs in 1927 discovered remains of bears, wolves, Arctic foxes, reindeer and lynx. More recent explorations by cave divers revealed chambers 20m below the Bone Caves from where the almost complete skeleton of a brown bear, 18,000 years old, was recovered. The bones of four human beings, dating back to 4500 years ago, have also been found here; it's thought the caves were used as a burial site.

Elphin

As the road crests the watershed four miles south of Inchnadamph, the island-dotted waters of **Loch Awe** appear on your right, with the hills of Coigach peeking over the horizon to the southwest. In a mostly treeless landscape, the islands in the loch stand out with their abundant growth of Scots pine and birch; the trees are able to grow here because deer can't reach the islands to snack on the saplings. Two miles further on at **Ledmore Junction** take a right turn on the A835, signposted Ullapool.

Elphin Burial Ground

Here the view begins to open up to the west with vistas across the waters of Lochs Cam and Veyatie to the hills of Assynt. About a mile and half after the junction, to the right of the road, a couple of yew trees mark the drystone enclosure of **Elphin Burial Ground**, one of Scotland's smallest – a mere 22m by 10m – and most scenic cemeteries. The majority of the surviving gravestones date from the late 19th and early 20th centuries, and enjoy a wonderful panorama towards the conical summits of Cul Mor, the craggy twin peaks of Suilven and the wedge of Canisp.

Elphin's scattered cottages straggle along the road for more than a mile; keep an eye open for **Elphin Tearooms** *(elphintearooms.co.uk; closed Nov–Mar)*, a handy pit stop for coffee and cake.

Inchnadamph

8.6 miles

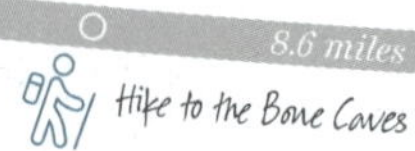

Hike to the Bone Caves

Canoe Loch Lurgainn and explore Knockan Crag National Nature Reserve

11.4 miles

Elphin

Explore Knockan Crag

First discovered by Victorian scientists, Knockan Crag is an outcrop of rock whose secret revolutionised earth science.

HOW TO

Nearest stop: Elphin

Getting here: The car park is beside the A835 road, 3 miles south of Elphin and 13 miles north of Ullapool.

Useful tip: Allow 20 minutes to visit the Rock Room, and another hour to hike the Crag Top Trail back to the car park.

More info: *nwhgeopark.com/knockan-crag*

THE MOINE THRUST

It was here that geologists first recognised the existence of thrust faults – low-angle shear zones where continental collisions have forced older rocks to slide up and over younger ones for distances of many miles. At Knockan Crag, the older Moine schist rests on top of the younger Durness limestone, a conundrum that puzzled geologists for almost a century.

From the car park an all-abilities trail leads 150m to an open-air **Rock Room** *(open 24 hours; unstaffed)* where information panels describe the geology of the local landscape and the fierce debate it inspired among Victorian scientists. Outside sit statues of the geologists **Ben Peach** and **John Horne**, whose meticulous fieldwork led to the publication of their 1907 memoir *The Geological Structure of the North-West Highlands of Scotland* which solved the riddle of Knockan Crag. On the far side, a sculpture of a young woman represents today's generation of geology students.

From here the **Thrust Trail** hiking path continues past carved stones and the remarkable drystone *Tilted Globe* (by sculptor Joe Smith) to an exposure of the Moine Thrust where you are encouraged to place your hands across a geological contact spanning 500 million years. The **Crag Top Trail** leads on up well-made stone steps to a viewpoint, then returns south along the top of the crag to another drystone sculpture, *Thrust*, with grand views over Coigach and Assynt, before descending back to the car park.

VINCENT LOWE/ALAMY

Rock Room

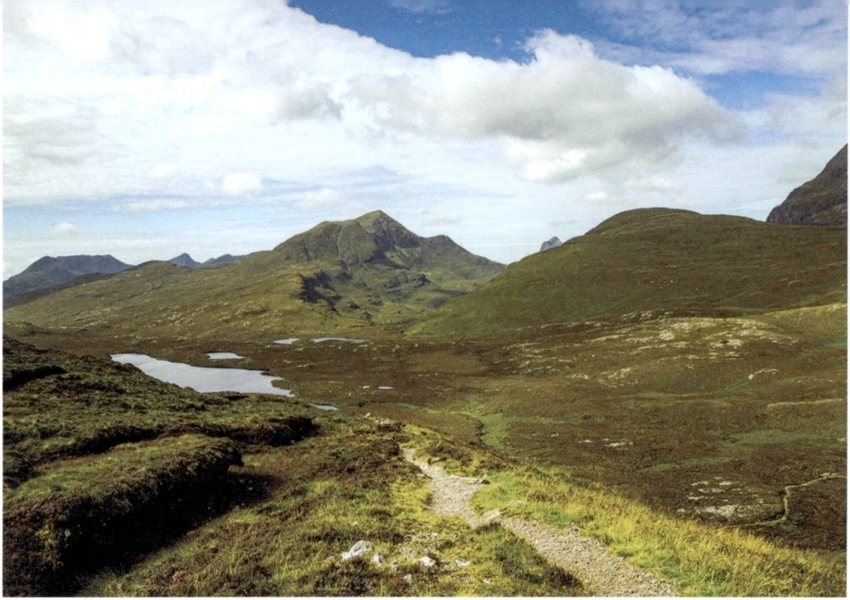

DAVID W BIRD/SHUTTERSTOCK

Coigach

DETOUR: Achiltibuie

At the junction five miles south of Elphin turn right on a minor road signposted Achiltibuie. This region, south of Assynt and west of the A835 road, is known as **Coigach** *(visitcoigach.com)*.

A lone, single-track road penetrates this wilderness (total population around 250, plus a hotel, shop and a petrol pump), leading through glorious scenery to the remote settlements of Achiltibuie, Altandhu and Achininver. Coigach is a wonderland for walkers and wildlife enthusiasts, with a patchwork of sinuous silver lochs dominated by the dramatic peaks of Cul Mor (849m), Cul Beag (769m), Ben More Coigach (743m) and Stac Pollaidh (613m).

The section hugs the northern shores of **Loch Lurgainn**, past the hikers car park at the foot

HIKE STAC POLLAIDH

Despite its diminutive size, **Stac Pollaidh** *(613m; 3 miles round trip, 2-4 hours)*) provides one of the most exciting hill walks in the Highlands with some good scrambling on its narrow sandstone crest. Begin at the car park overlooking Loch Lurgainn, five miles west of the A835, and follow a clearly marked and well-made footpath around the eastern end of the hill to ascend from the far side. The true summit is at the west end of the ridge, but requires some tricky and exposed scrambling; admire the view and then return by the same route.

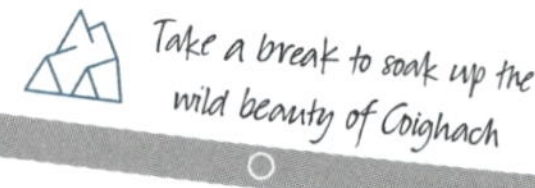

Canoe Loch Lurgainn

Cradled between the pinnacled ridge of Stac Pollaidh and the rocky wedge of Sgòrr Tuath, lovely Loch Lurgainn offers unparalleled tranquillity amid marvellous mountain scenery.

HOW TO

Nearest stop: Ardmair

Getting here: The usual starting point is the car park below Stac Pollaidh, 5 miles northwest of Drumrunie Junction on the A835.

Cost: £85/95 per person (half/full day)

Useful tip: Bring a packed lunch, waterproofs and warm clothing.

The convoluted Loch Sionascaig and its neighbours to the north, Loch Veyatie and Fionn Loch, provide some of the most spectacular wilderness canoeing in Scotland through remote and uninhabited country. But this is challenging terrain, involving portages and long paddling sessions, so for experienced canoeists only.

If you only have a day to spare and/or lack experience, **Kayak Summer Isles** *(kayaksummerisles.com)* run half- or full-day canoe trips on Loch Lurgainn with a professional guide. A gentle paddle of about two miles leads to the west end of the loch, where a gorgeous beach of golden sand enjoys one of the finest views in the northwest.

Your guide will likely rustle up a campfire here and brew up some tea, coffee or – if you're lucky – the best wilderness hot chocolate on the west coast.

The return trip makes its way along the southern shore of Lurgainn, pausing to explore hidden beaches, wooded coves and little waterfalls, while keeping an eye out for eagles, red deer and otters.

FROM LEFT: ANDREI KUZMIK/SHUTTERSTOCK, DANIEL ALFORD/LONELY PLANET

Kayak the Summer Isles

Scotland is famous for its superb sea kayaking, and the Summer Isles – an archipelago just off the coast to the west of Achiltibuie – are regularly voted the top location in the country.

HOW TO

Nearest stop: Ardmair

Getting here: Kayak trips usually depart from the beach at Badentarbat Bay, west of Achiltibuie; or Old Dornie harbour, south of Altandhu (p170).

Cost: £85/95 per person (half/full day)

Useful tip: If you don't feel up to kayaking, join a 2¼-hour boat trip to the Summer Isles from Ullapool with Shearwater Cruises *(summerqueen.co.uk; Apr-Oct)*.

Like a handful of jewels thrown carelessly across a blue velvet cloth, the 20 or so islands and reefs that make up the Summer Isles lie scattered on the sparkling seas to the south of Coigach. The largest, **Tanera Mòr**, is the only inhabited island; **Isle Ristol**, the closest to the mainland, and **Priest Island**, the furthest offshore, are both nature reserves, and the waters around the islands are part of the Wester Ross Marine Protected Area.

The guides at **Kayak Summer Isles** *(kayaksummerisles.com)* know these islands intimately and can tailor a half- or full-day trip to suit your level of experience and the weather and water conditions on your chosen day. Expect to explore hidden bays and uninhabited skerries, glide across emerald shallows and nose through natural arches and sea caves in the cliffs, before stopping for lunch on a deserted beach. Marine wildlife abounds – seals and sea eagles are common sightings; an otter if you're lucky – and all against the stunning backdrop of Coigach's dramatic skyline.

FROM LEFT: SERGEY URYADNIKOV/SHUTTERSTOCK, JAN HOLM/SHUTTERSTOCK

Along the Way We Met...

JEN MULLEN Slow and sustainable tourism is important for small towns like Ullapool, as it provides jobs and opportunities which help keep the community diverse and thriving. For me, kayaking in the Summer Isles gifts me the opportunity to slow down and linger in a truly magical place. Pausing on an island to practice yoga with the sound of nature all around is a special way to connect with the landscape – something we love to share with visitors.

Jen is a Wilderness Yoga instructor at Kayak Summer Isles, @kayak.summerisles.

JEN'S TIP: *Supporting local businesses and learning from local people will help you connect with the area at a deeper level.*

of Stac Pollaidh and the southern end of the Wee Mad Road (p162), to reach a T-junction over-looking a loch; turn right towards Achnaharid, and after a mile turn right again on a road signposted 'Beach'. The view from this road is one of the finest in Scotland, with all the peaks of Assynt and Coigach lined up on the horizon. From the car park at the end of the road a short walk leads to the pink-tinged sands of glorious **Achnahaird Beach**.

Continuing west, the road crests a rise revealing views south across the **Summer Isles** (p170) then loops through the settlements of **Altandhu** (campsite, small grocery store, restaurant and bar) and **Polbain** (home to Fisk Gallery, selling local arts and crafts).

At the next T-junction turn right to reach Achiltibuie, the main settlement in Coigach, which straggles for two miles along a dead-end road. With sheep nibbling the grassy verges, the gorgeous Summer Isles moored just off the coast and the silhouettes of mountains skirting the bay, this village epitomises idyllic Highland beauty.

Ardmair

South of Elphin you pass from Sutherland into Wester Ross as the road runs along the foot of a prominent cliff. This rocky escarpment marks the outcrop of an important geological feature known as the Moine Thrust; pause at Knockan Crag National Nature Reserve (p167) to learn more about this globally important site. Beyond Knockan the scenery level gets turned up to 11 again, with the shapely peaks of Coigach on your right joined by the rugged

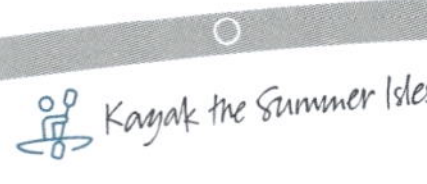

3.5 miles

TOM NEWLAND PHOTOGRAPHY/GETTY IMAGES

Ardmair Point

hills of Wester Ross on the far horizon. If you're planning to explore Coigach, look out for the minor road on the right signposted Achiltibuie.

Just over a mile south of the junction, a parking area on the right contains the Coigach Geopod (an information panel) and enjoys a superb view of the Coigach hills with the miniature pyramid of Stac Pollaidh (p168) prominent in the middle. The road descends into the broad valley of Strathkanaird then climbs over a hill and through a rocky defile before descending to the sea at Ardmair Point in Ardmair. A passenger ferry runs from the jetty here to Isle Martin.

Ardmair Point Holiday Park *(ardmair.com)* has a campsite *(open Apr-Oct)* and self-catering chalets *(open all year).*

Along the Way We Met...

MONICA SHAW I'm originally from America, but it was the NC500 that brought me to Assynt and made me feel truly at home. The solitude and fascinating nature – from the wild waves to the aurora's dance to the ever-present geological wonder – provide constant renewal and creative inspiration. This connection inspired my partner and me to open a holiday cottage and observatory, where we share this place's magic through dark-sky events, guided hikes and writing retreats.

Monica is a freelance writer and educator, who runs Eat Sleep Wild (eatsleepwild.com).

MONICA'S TIP: *Assynt boasts Europe's darkest skies, so remember to look up, or visit us for a closer view of the stars.*

Go birdwatching on Isle Martin

DETOUR: Isle Martin

Until WWII this island, just four miles northwest of Ullapool, had a population of 30. These days, it's deserted, but the local community run a nature reserve here, and visitors can go birdwatching, visit the tiny museum and explore the old herring curing station and the remains of an early Christian monastery, or just climb to the summit of the island for a view of the Summer Isles.

The **passenger ferry** *(11am-5pm Fri-Sun Apr-Oct)* leaves from the jetty just east of Ardmair Point; crossings are weather dependent so call or check their Facebook page *(facebook.com/IsleMartinTrust)* before deciding to visit.

Note: there's no parking beside the ferry; use the long lay-by 150m further on at the entrance to Ardmair Point Holiday Park.

BEST PLACES TO STAY

Inchnadamph Explorers Lodge, Inchnadamph £
Hostel dorms, private rooms, self-catering cottages and shepherds' huts based in and around a 19th-century lodge in the heart of Assynt. *inchnadamph.com*

Summer Isles Hotel, Achiltibuie £££
Once frequented by Charlie Chaplin, this has gorgeous sea views and an exceptional seafood restaurant. *summerisleshotel.com; closed Nov-Mar*

The Ceilidh Place, Ullapool ££
Rooms here go for character over modernity; no TVs, but a radio, books, eclectic artwork and cosy atmosphere. *theceilidhplace.com*

Westlea House, Ullapool ££
A comfy and quirky B&B with colourful decor, a plethora of unusual art and stylishly themed bedrooms. *westlea-ullapool.co.uk*

Isle Martin

KAREN APPLEYARD/ALAMY

Ullapool Museum

Ullapool

The appearance of a golf course on the shores of Loch Broom and a cluster of houses up ahead announce your arrival in the pretty port of Ullapool, the largest settlement in the northwest. With a row of whitewashed cottages along the harbour and views of the loch and its flanking hills, the town has a very distinctive appeal. There's a good range of places to stay, from a campsite and hostels to B&Bs and luxury hotels, but note that during summer Ullapool is very busy and finding a room for the night can be tricky – book ahead.

Housed in a Thomas Telford-built church, **Ullapool Museum** *(ullapoolmuseum.co.uk; 11am-4pm Mon-Sat, noon-4pm Sun Apr-Oct)* makes a good wet-weather retreat. It covers the prehistoric, natural and social history of the town and Lochbroom area, with a particular focus on crofting, fishing and Highland emigration to Nova Scotia.

Car ferries sail daily from Ullapool to Stornoway on the Isle of Lewis.

ULLAPOOL HISTORY

Ullapool takes its name from a Viking noble; its old Norse name, Ulla-Bolsadr, means 'Ulla's farmstead'. Today's tidy village was planned by the British Fisheries Society, which laid out the grid of streets in 1788. At the height of the herring boom, hundreds of 'dipping luggers' (sail-powered fishing boats) plied the waters around Loch Broom, but the 'silver darlings' eventually vanished from the loch after WWI (p178). The harbour also served as an emigration point during the Clearances, with thousands of Scots watching the loch recede behind them as the Highland diaspora cast them across the world.

Ullapool

Take the ferry to the Isle of Lewis

Lewisean gneiss

ASHLEY COOPER/ALAMY

Read the Riddle of the Rocks

The dramatic landscapes of northwest Scotland have attracted and inspired geologists for more than two centuries. The discoveries made here are of such importance that the region has been called the 'Cradle of Geology' and was designated by UNESCO as the North West Highlands Geopark in 2004.

WORDS BY **NEIL WILSON**

Geology and the NC500

It's impossible to follow the North Coast 500 through the Northwest Highlands without wondering about the subject of geology. There's a lot of naked rock exposed in this harsh but beautiful region, and since the 19th century geologists have learned a great deal about the history of the earth from mapping the area and attempting to understand its intricate details. Despite sections of great complexity, the geology of much of the region is fairly simple, and even a basic knowledge can add to your appreciation of the scenery.

Gneiss, Sandstone and Quartzite

The oldest and most fundamental rock type is **Lewisian gneiss** (up to 3 billion years old), a banded grey or pink crystalline rock that underlies much of Scotland's northwest coast and all of the outer Hebrides (it's named after the Isle of Lewis). Formed deep in the planet's crust, it creates poorly drained, acid soils that support meagre vegetation, and produces a distinctive 'cnoc-and-lochan' landscape (from the Gaelic for 'small hill' and 'small loch'), easily seen in Assynt and to the east of Scourie.

Overlying the gneiss is a great thickness of reddish-brown **Torridonian sandstone** (1 billion years old), which is itself topped by a layer of glittering white **Cambrian quartzite** (540 million years old). These rocks were carved and sculpted by the glaciers of the last Ice Age into the fantastically shaped hills of the northwest, with the sandstone forming steep, stratified cliffs and the quartzite shattering into silvery grey scree.

Mountains such as **Liathach** and **Beinn Eighe** in Torridon, and **Canisp** and **Quinag** in Assynt, display lower slopes of layered sandstone rising above foothills of hummocky gneiss, topped with summit caps of silvery quartzite. The photogenic sandstone hills of Suilven (p164) and Stac Pollaidh (p168) are what geologists call 'inselbergs' – meaning 'island mountains' – erosional remnants that have been left behind after the surrounding rock has been worn away by ice and water, rising stark and isolated above a rolling sea of gneiss.

Durness Limestone

The rock layers slope gently towards the east, so that as you travel from west to east you pass upwards through the geological succession. On top of the quartzite and outcropping along a narrow band that roughly follows a line between Ullapool and Loch Eriboll, lies the **Durness limestone** (500 million years old). This layered, grey rock – rare in the Highlands – produces a fertile, lime-rich soil that has created oases of lush green pasture among the more typical bog and heather of the region. Easily dissolved by rainwater, it is also responsible for the creation of subterranean rivers and caves such as Smoo Cave (p131) and the Bone Caves of Inchnadamph (p166).

The Moine Thrust

Finally, there are the **Moine schists**, which began life as siltstones and sandstones deposited far to the southeast around the same time as the Cambrian quartzite. Then, around 420 million years ago, a continental collision – of the type that created the Alps and the Himalayas – buried, folded and heated the Moine rocks (metamorphosing them into crystalline schists) and shunted them tens of miles to the northwest, sliding over the Cambrian, Torridonian and Lewisian rocks on a near-horizontal fault plane known as the **Moine Thrust**.

During this process, slices of the older rocks were caught up and shunted on top of younger ones, creating an enigma that puzzled geologists for decades until it was finally solved in a famous paper by Ben Peach and John Horne in 1907, commemorated at Knockan Crag National Nature Reserve (p167) on the NC500.

As you travel from west to east, the line of the Moine Thrust – which runs roughly from Achnashellach in the south via Kinlochewe and Inchnadamph to the eastern shore of Loch Eriboll on the north coast – marks a transition from the dramatic and varied landscapes of Assynt, Coigach and Wester Ross to the rounded, heather-clad hills typical of the Moine schists (which make up most of the eastern and central Highlands).

The Rock Stop

You can find out more about the geology of the region by visiting the Rock Stop (p154) near Kylesku, where you can browse their exhibition, pick up maps and leaflets, and buy geological guidebooks.

CYNTHIA SHIRK/SHUTTERSTOCK

INSIGHT

Ullapool's Silver Darlings

Tucked away in the a region of outstanding natural beauty is Ullapool, the largest town in Wester Ross. Buzzing and vibrant, Ullapool is like a metropolis in a place of soaring peaks, quiet glens and show-stopping wildlife. The harbour, even today, provides the real focal point, as fishing boats and ferries come and go, along with a steady stream of visitors.

WORDS BY **LAURIE GOODLAD**

Caught between Sea & Mountain

Strung out along the tranquil shores of Loch Broom with its picture-perfect rows of houses, caught between sea and mountain, Ullapool, home to around 1500 people, is more than just the gateway to the Hebrides or a fuel and supermarket stop on the NC500.

The town is synonymous with herring, but its history stretches beyond the drift nets that built it; Ullapool also served as a departure port for thousands of displaced Highlanders emigrating to new continents. Evicted from their homes during the 19th-century Clearances or driven away due to starvation, many of these Highlanders departed Ullapool on ships bound for a new world filled with promise.

The town's story is fascinating, and even today, this busy place depends on its traditional industry: fishing. Sheltered by the long arms and deep waters of Loch Broom, and with easy access to some of the most prolific fishing grounds within UK waters, both inshore and offshore, Ullapool continues to thrive on the sea's bounty.

It's not just a thriving fishing industry that makes Ullapool feel alive. The town also acts as a port for visiting yachts exploring Scotland's west coast and islands, as well as smaller expedition-style cruise ships and, of course, it serves as the main link between Stornoway in Lewis and the Scottish mainland. With fantastic walks and hikes and one of Scotland's best gastro highlights, the Seafood Shack (p163), Ullapool is an unmissable destination.

The Herring Port

Unlike so much of Scotland, Ullapool dates back not millennia but to 1788, when the British Fisheries Society commissioned the town as a herring port. This design town was created by renowned Scottish engineer Thomas Telford, who was also responsible for building many of the nation's roads, bridges, harbours, churches and manses.

Unlike so much of Scotland, Ullapool dates back not millennia but to 1788, when the British Fisheries Society commissioned the town as a herring port.

Herring – known lovingly as the 'silver darlings' – is a pelagic fish, rich in omega oils, and responsible for the greatest-ever boom in Scotland's fisheries. From the 18th century, fishermen used drift nets (hanging in the water like a curtain) to catch the fish. Herring was a popular delicacy throughout Europe and Russia, and by the late 19th and early 20th century, Scotland's catch was cured, barrelled and shipped to hungry European markets, creating a lucrative industry from Unst in the north, down the north and east coast of Scotland, and into the northeast of England.

Herring Girls

In addition to a ready market, government incentives offered generous payments to those who bought herring boats and for any fish sold abroad. For many, this was a golden opportunity to escape the relative poverty of the Highlands, particularly following the Clearances, which saw many thousands of people displaced and searching for work and homes.

Boats followed the fish as they migrated from north to south, and towns and villages would swell with incoming workers who would gut and pack the catch. Herring, an oily fish, spoiled quickly, so it had to be processed as soon as it was landed. While the men rested from their night's fishing, women, working in teams of three, did all the gutting and packing. These 'Herring Girls' worked with incredible speed and skill, with the best of them able to gut up to 60 fish a minute, and, at its peak in 1907, 2.5 million barrels of fish were cured for export. Listen to Bella Hardy's song 'The Herring Girl' for a poignant portrayal of the role of women in the industry.

Herring was the backbone of the economy throughout much of the Highlands and Islands before its eventual collapse after WWI. Although it has never fully recovered to its prewar levels, its legacy endures in the places and their culture, recorded in song, poetry and prose. Ullapool has carried this fishing heritage forward to the present day, and whiling away the afternoon at the harbour you'll discover a town that is alive and still thrives off the traditional industry that built it.

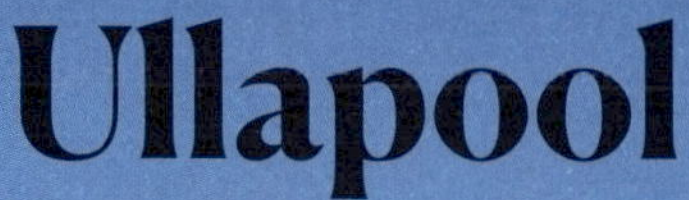

The drive from Ullapool to Gairloch skirts around the mountains of Fisherfield Forest, one of the largest wilderness areas in Scotland. It's a place that holds many fond memories for me of hillwalking, rock climbing and fly fishing spread across four decades. As with all the west coast sections of the NC500, the scenery is stupendous, with the added advantage of being able to end the day at Gairloch with the sun setting beyond the Hebrides.

Neil Wilson

Gairloch

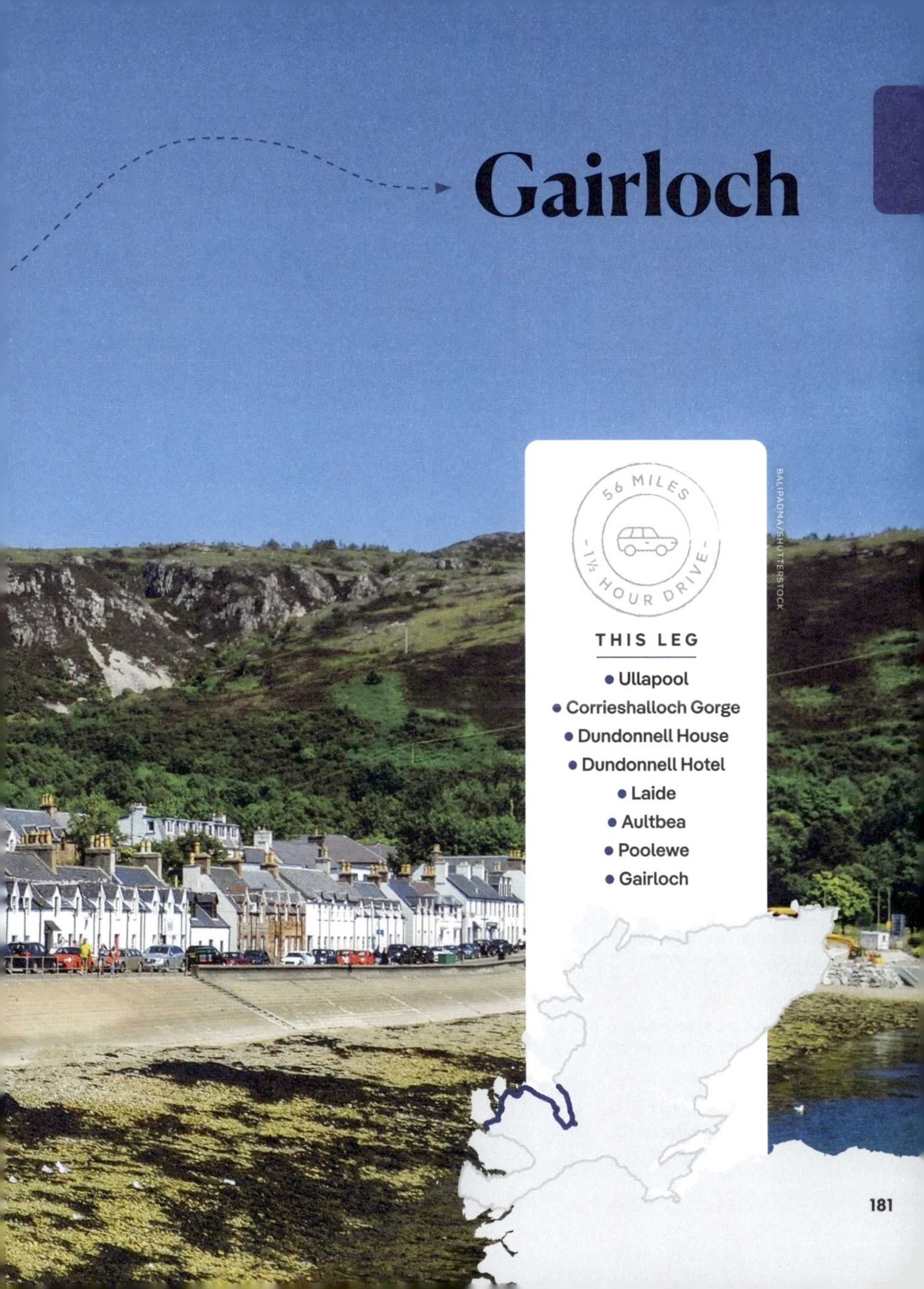

THIS LEG

- Ullapool
- Corrieshalloch Gorge
- Dundonnell House
- Dundonnell Hotel
- Laide
- Aultbea
- Poolewe
- Gairloch

BALIPADMA/SHUTTERSTOCK

Driving Notes

The route from Ullapool to Gairloch, which follows the A835 and A832, may not be a long one, but it winds its way along a chiselled, sometimes hilly coastline through widely scattered crofting settlements. You're best taking your time and enjoying the views of beaches, lochs and peaks, and watching for seals popping their heads out of the cold coastal waters.

Breaking Up Your Journey

There's not a lot in the way of shops and eateries along this leg. Badrallach has a good campsite, but there's no shop or cafe. Beyond here, Aultbea and Poolewe are well-stocked villages, while Gairloch is a larger coastal resort with a good range of accommodation options.

Neil's Tips

BEST MEAL Any seafood dish at the **Badachro Inn** (p188).

FAVOURITE VIEW From the lay-by above **Gruinard Bay** (p187).

ESSENTIAL STOP Hike into **Corrieshalloch Gorge** (p185).

ROAD-TRIP TIP Don't miss the tour of **Pool House** (p192); book in advance.

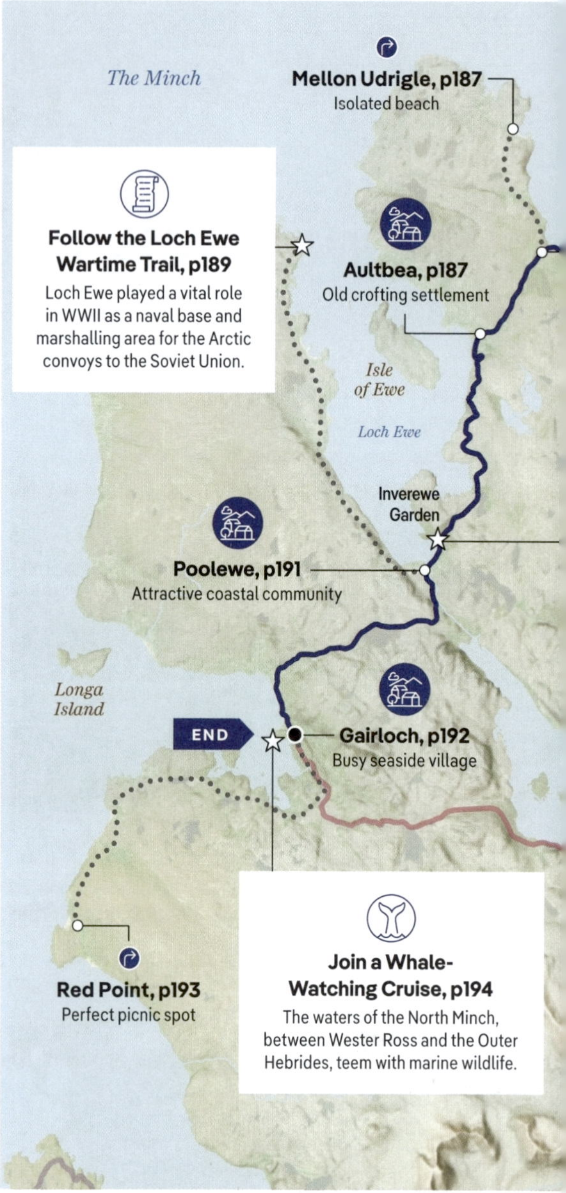

The Minch

Mellon Udrigle, p187
Isolated beach

Follow the Loch Ewe Wartime Trail, p189
Loch Ewe played a vital role in WWII as a naval base and marshalling area for the Arctic convoys to the Soviet Union.

Aultbea, p187
Old crofting settlement

Isle of Ewe

Loch Ewe

Inverewe Garden

Poolewe, p191
Attractive coastal community

Longa Island

END

Gairloch, p192
Busy seaside village

Red Point, p193
Perfect picnic spot

Join a Whale-Watching Cruise, p194
The waters of the North Minch, between Wester Ross and the Outer Hebrides, teem with marine wildlife.

Laide, p186
Village to pick up supplies
Badrallach, p184
Campsite and coastal walk
START
Ullapool, p174
Largest town in the northwest
Loch Broom
Little Loch Broom
Dundonnell Hotel, p186
19th-century coaching inn
Discover Inverewe Garden, p190
This splendid woodland garden provides a welcome splash of colour on an otherwise bleak stretch of coast.
Corrie-shalloch Gorge
Dundonell House, p184
Private estate with a lovely garden
Fionn Loch
Lochan Fada
Loch Maree
Explore Corrieshalloch Gorge, p185
This spectacular ravine is one of the most easily accessible natural wonders in the Scottish Highlands.
N
0 5 km
0 2.5 miles

PREVIOUS STOP As Ullapool recedes in the rear-view mirror, the mountains of Wester Ross rise up to fill your windscreen.

Corrieshalloch Gorge

Twelve miles southeast of Ullapool at Braemore, near the head of Loch Broom, a right turn on to the A832 doubles back towards the coast as you head in the direction of Gairloch (the A835 continues southeast across the wild Dirrie More pass and along Loch Glascarnoch to Garve and Inverness; it's sometimes closed by snow in winter). Immediately west of the junction, on the right, you'll see the car park for the **Corrieshalloch Gorge** (p185).

NEIL G PATERSON/ALAMY

Dundonnell House

Dundonnell House

The modern road to the west of Corrieshalloch Gorge follows the route of the **Destitution Road**, built during the potato famines of the late 1840s to provide work for destitute crofters. At the summit of the pass a grand view opens up ahead to the pinnacled peak of **An Teallach**, one of Wester Ross' most dramatic mountains. A little further on a lonesome derelict house marks the location of the Fain Inn (now demolished) which once served travellers on the Destitution Road.

After crossing **Fain Bridge**, where a bronze plaque commemorates the widening of the road to doubletrack in the 1960s, the route descends into the beautifully wooded valley of the Dundonnell River, a pleasant surprise following the bleakness of the moorland pass. Dundonnell is a private estate belonging to Sir Tim Rice (the lyricist of musicals such as *Evita*) and is now managed by his wife Lady Jane Rice; the garden of **Dundonnell House** *(scotlandsgardens.org)*, just off the main road on the way to Badrallach, is open to the public a couple of days a year.

DETOUR: Badrallach

The tiny village of Badrallach makes a fun detour or overnight from the NC500. Take the turn-off from the A832 just past Stepping Stones Cottage and follow the single-track road as it climbs high above the loch – until the opening of the Destitution Road in 1850 this was the main

Take a break to see the gardens at Dundonnell House

Ullapool — 12.4 miles — Corrieshalloch Gorge — 13.3 miles — Dundonnell House — 0.5 miles

Explore Corrieshalloch Gorge

One of the most easily accessible natural wonders in the Scottish Highlands, the Corrieshalloch Gorge cuts an improbably deep slash through beautifully wooded hillsides right beside the NC500 route.

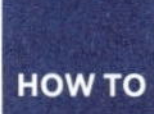

HOW TO

Nearest stop: Ullapool

Getting here: The car park and visitor centre are beside the A832 at Braemore Junction, 12 miles south of Ullapool.

Useful tip: A second car park, 800m past the visitor centre, is open at all times.

More info: *nts.org.uk/visit/places/corrieshalloch-gorge*

The **Corrieshalloch Gateway to Nature** visitor centre *(admission free)* opened in 2023, and has a cafe, toilets and EV charging points. It's open from 9.30am to 4pm daily April to October, and to 3pm Wednesday to Sunday November to March. There's a £5 charge for the car park, which is closed and locked one hour after the visitor centre.

Walking trails lead from the centre along the bank of the Abhainn Droma iver to the **Falls of Measach**, which thunder 45m into the spectacularly deep and narrow **Corrieshalloch Gorge**. You can cross to the far side of the gorge on a Victorian suspension bridge, built in 1874 by Sir John Fowler of Braemore (co-designer of the Forth Rail Bridge), and walk downstream for 250m to a viewing platform that juts out dizzyingly above a sheer drop. Walking the full trail from the visitor centre takes about 45 minutes; if you just want a quick photo op, you can reach the bridge from the second car park in five minutes.

ROBERT ORMEROD FOR LONELY PLANET

Corrieshalloch Gorge

Along the Way We Saw...

AN TEALLACH (from the Gaelic for 'the forge') is one of the most dramatic and complex mountains in Scotland, with no fewer than 13 peaks including two Munros and a spectacular leaning pinnacle known as Lord Berkeley's Seat, the favourite viewpoint of a 19th-century aristocrat. Along with a group of old university friends I made a memorable traverse of the mountain in 2019, finishing on the 1062m summit – my mate Paul's 282nd and final Munro. He is now ticking off the Corbetts (p8).

NEIL'S TIP: *Hamlet Mountaineering (hamletmountaineering.com) offers a guided scramble along An Teallach's spectacular summit ridge.*

Neil Wilson

route to Ullapool; the hairpin bend at the high point marks where the old road descended to Alltnaharrie where a ferry crossed to Ullapool (a passenger ferry continued to run until 2003). **Badrallach Campsite** *(badrallach.com)* lies at the foot of the hill, 0.75 miles before the public road ends at a parking area.

From here a delightful 5.5-mile coastal ramble *(allow 2 hours each way)* leads to the commune of **Scoraig** *(scoraig.com)*, where around 80 people live an alternative, off-grid lifestyle (visitors are welcome).

Dundonnell Hotel

The A832 reaches the sea at the head of Little Loch Broom, beside the **Dundonnell Hotel** *(dundonnellhotel.co.uk)*. Built around 1820 as a four-bedroom coaching inn, it has been rebuilt and extended into today's 32-bedroom hotel with bar and restaurant. This has long been a base for hillwalkers bound for the peaks of **An Teallach**, a magnificent Munro with rocky pinnacles soaring above a lochan-filled corrie. The summit can be reached by a path starting 500m southeast of the hotel *(allow 6 hours return)*.

Laide

The **waterfalls** at Ardessie, 2.5 miles west of Dundonnell, are worth a photo after heavy rain; you can see them from the bridge on the main road.

After passing through the hamlet of Badcaul you climb over a hill to reach a view across Gruinard Bay to uninhabited **Gruinard Island**. Gruinard is notorious as the site of a biological warfare experiment during WWII, when bombs containing anthrax spores were detonated. For decades afterwards the island was off-limits, with signs on the mainland warning the public

Dundonnell Hotel — 15.2 miles — Laide — 2.8 miles

Take time to hike An Teallach

ANDY BROW/SHUTTERSTOCK

Ardessie Falls

not to land on it. It was not decontaminated until 1990.

At the southern corner of the bay is **Gruinard Beach**, a beautiful expanse of pinkish-brown sand, easily reached from a large car park opposite. At the top of the next hill a lay-by on the right provides a **superb panorama** across Gruinard Bay and beach with the peaks of An Teallach in the background. You then pass through the quaintly named hamlets of Second Coast and First Coast to reach the village of **Laide**, with a petrol station, post office, general store and campsite.

DETOUR: Mellon Udrigle

Turn off the A832 at Laide petrol station and follow the minor road for three miles to the isolated crofting settlement of **Mellon Udrigle** (from *Meallan Ùdraigil*, Gaelic/Norse for 'little hill by the outer glen'). There's a small car park here with a path leading down to a gorgeous white-sand **beach** with views of the Summer Isles and the hills of Coigach. If you're tempted to stay overnight, there's a basic, all-year campsite next to the beach (the only facilities are fresh water and chemical toilet disposal; no showers or toilets).

For an even more isolated beach, you can hike or bike to **Slaggan Bay** along an unsurfaced road that begins halfway to Mellon Udrigle (look out for the green signpost). Allow three hours round trip on foot, or one hour by bike. Just north of this track lies **Loch na Bèiste**, meaning 'lake of the monster'. In the 1840s the locals believed the loch was inhabited by a mythical 'water-cow', so much so that they tried to drain the loch and then, on failing to do so, threw 14 sacks of quicklime into the water to poison the monster. It has never been seen since.

Aultbea

It's a short hop from Laide over to Aultbea, where the first building you reach on the right is the **Arctic Convoy Museum** (*arcticconvoymuseum.org; 10am-4pm Mon-Sat Apr-Oct*), dedicated to the important role played by the area during WWII. The deep, sheltered waters of Loch Ewe were used as a marshalling area for shipping convoys that carried vital supplies to Murmansk and Archangel in what was then the Soviet Union. The loch is still in use by the military – just

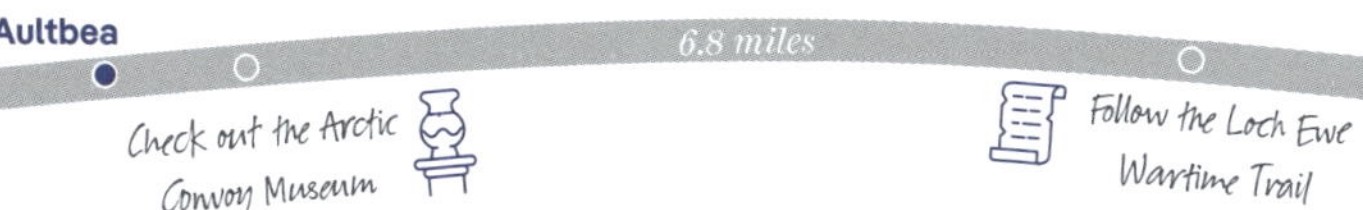

BASIL_01/SHUTTERSTOCK

Clapper bridge, Aultbea

south of Aultbea you will see a NATO refuelling jetty for naval warships.

The main part of **Aultbea** village lies just west of the main road, clustered around an 18th-century **clapper bridge** (supported by flat lintel stones rather than arches). There's a hotel, cafe and grocery store. Two miles west is the crofting settlement of **Mellon Charles**, where you can see old WWII gun emplacements on the headland beside **Boom Beach**, which marked one end of the anti-submarine boom that protected the loch from enemy attack.

In the middle of the water lies the **Isle of Ewe**, with a population of seven, all members of the Grant family who farm the island and run a traditional wooden boatbuilding yard. You can arrange a trip around the island by kayak with **Gairloch Kayak Centre** (p201) – it's a popular jaunt with honeymoon couples. Why? Say the island's name quickly!

continued on p191

BEST PLACES TO EAT

Bridge Cottage Art Café, Poolewe £
Enjoy homemade cakes, soups, toasted sandwiches and roasted coffee at this gorgeous little cafe with an art gallery and gift shop. *(10am-4pm Thu-Sun)*

Mountain Coffee, Gairloch £
This offbeat shrine to mountaineering and travel is a cafe-cum-bookshop serving tasty savoury bagels, home baking and sustainably sourced coffees. *(9am-5pm)*

Badachro Inn, Gairloch ££
Old Highland inn serving fresh local seafood landed at the pier beside the pub. Book a table in the conservatory for sunset views. *(badachroinn.com; noon-2.30pm & 5.30-8.30pm; closed Mon & Tue Oct-Mar)*

Walk across Aultbea's clapper bridge

Follow the Loch Ewe Wartime Trail

The sheltered deepwater anchorage of Loch Ewe played a vital role in WWII as a naval base and marshalling area for the Arctic convoys supplying the USSR.

HOW TO

Nearest stop: Aultbea

Getting here: The trail follows roads clockwise around the loch, from Mellon Charles on the east shore via Aultbea and Poolewe to Cove on the west side.

Useful tip: Pick up a leaflet on the Wartime Trail at the Arctic Convoy Museum in Aultbea.

More info: *arcticconvoymuseum.org/history-learning/loch-ewe-wartime-trail*

WHY LOCH EWE?

When Nazi Germany invaded the Soviet Union in 1941, Britain and its allies agreed to supply the Soviets with arms. Loch Ewe was chosen as an assembly area for convoys of merchant ships that braved foul weather and U-boat attack to ferry supplies to the ports of Murmansk and Archangel in Arctic Russia.

Begin at **Boom Beach** (p188) in Mellon Charles. The anti-submarine boom, made from a web of interlinked steel hoops that hung from buoys, stretched from here to Firemore Point on the far side of the loch. As you return through Aultbea look out for the community hall with its curved green roof, built in 1941 as a cinema to entertain the military personnel.

There are interpretation panels in Poolewe village, where **Pool House** (p192) once served as command headquarters for the convoys. Head along the minor road towards Cove; at the high point 1.8 miles from Poolewe a concrete gun emplacement provides a grand view of the loch. At **Firemore**, a minor road south leads to the point where the southern end of the anti-submarine boom came ashore.

Continue through Cove to the car park at **Rubha nan Sasan** at the road end. Here you can explore one of the most complete WWII coastal defence installations in the country; during wartime up to 200 artillery soldiers were stationed here to defend the entrance to Loch Ewe.

CLAUDINE VAN MASSENHOVE/SHUTTERSTOCK

Ruins of WWII bunkers, Cove

Discover Inverewe Garden

This splendid woodland garden provides a welcome splash of colour on an otherwise bleak stretch of coast, pulling in around 100,000 visitors each year.

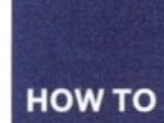

HOW TO

Nearest stop: Poolewe

Getting here: The garden is on the main A832 road, less than a mile north of Poolewe.

Cost: £5

Useful tip: Boat trips around Loch Ewe depart from the garden's jetty in summer.

More info: *nts.org.uk/visit/places/inverewe*

OSGOOD MACKENZIE

Osgood Mackenzie (1842–1922), third son of the 12th Laird of Gairloch, began his garden project at the age of 20 when he was gifted Inverewe and Kernsary estates by his mother. His memoir of a varied and fascinating life, *A Hundred Years in the Highlands* (1921), is worth seeking out.

A network of trails enables you to explore extraordinary **Inverewe Garden** at your leisure – it's 'calendar of colour' provides a display in every season, from the magnificent pale pink magnolia blooms of March to the blazing red maple leaves of October; and there's one rhododendron species or other in flower every day of the year.

Inverewe began life in 1862 when **Osgood Mackenzie** took up the challenge of creating a garden around his newly built house. What was once a barren headland overlooking Loch Ewe was transformed by digging out stones, bringing in new topsoil and planting shelter belts of hardy Corsican pine. The climate here is warmed by the waters of the Gulf Stream, which allowed trees and plants gathered from as far afield as Australia, South Africa, Chile and China to flourish. His daughter Mairi (1879–1953) continued his work, and gifted the garden to the National Trust for Scotland in 1952.

Inverewe House contains a small museum that tells the story of the garden and its creator.

IPLANTSMAN/SHUTTERSTOCK

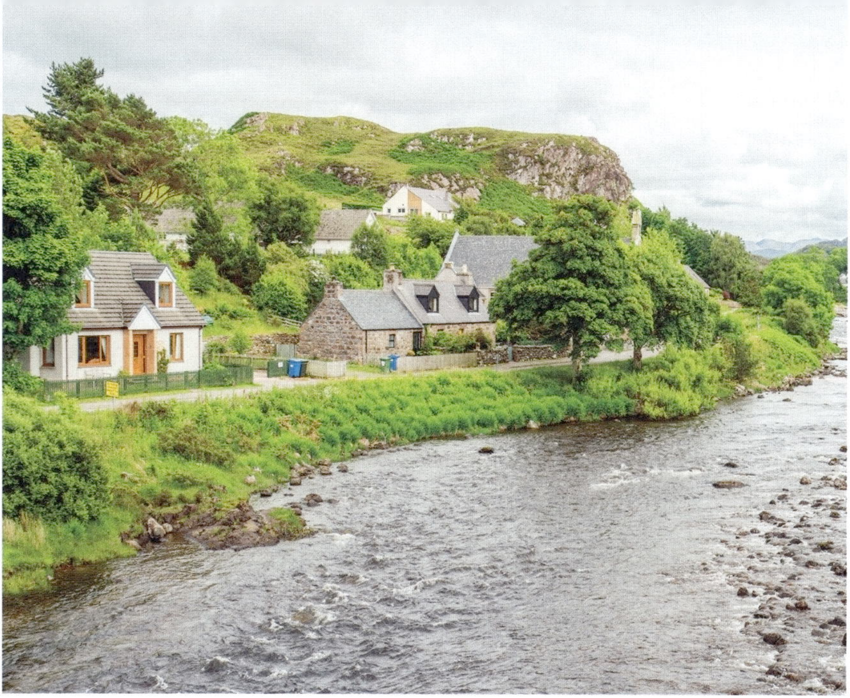

Poolewe

Poolewe

At the highpoint of the road about three miles south of Aultbea you'll find a **viewpoint indicator** where you get your first sight of the serried ranks of the Wester Ross mountains ranged along the southern horizon. Here the landscape begins to change from the barren grey gneiss and isolated hills of Assynt and Coigach, to the stratified slopes of closely packed mountains made mostly of reddish-brown Torridonian sandstone.

The southernmost corner of Loch Ewe is a sheltered nook where a far-sighted aristocrat created a magnificent wild garden in the latter half of the 19th century. **Inverewe Garden** (p190) is well worth a visit. Beyond the garden entrance, the attractive village of **Poolewe** spreads around the mouth of the River Ewe at the head of the loch. Here, you'll find **Pool House** (p192), a grocery store, a cafe, a well-equipped campsite and a couple of hotels; there's even an indoor swimming pool. The village hall comes alive for the **Tuesday Market** *(facebook.com/PooleweTuesdayMarket; late March to October)*, with stalls selling locally made arts and crafts.

KAY ROXBY/ALAMY

Pool House

POOL HOUSE

Pool House *(pool-house.co.uk; check Facebook for opening hours; closed Wed & Sun, and Nov-Mar)* in Poolewe began life as a 17th-century hunting lodge belonging to the Clan Mackenzie, and has since been used as an inn, a school, a post office, a family home, a WWII command headquarters and a luxury hotel. It's now open to the public as a museum celebrating its own fascinating history, with guided tours (book online) leading through rooms filled with antiques, furniture, toys and curiosities providing an insight into the lifestyle of the Victorian landed gentry. There's a decent cafe in the wood-panelled hall, with a full-size billiard table as a centrepiece.

Gairloch

The 5.5 miles from Poolewe to Gairloch offer glimpses of Loch Maree, the peaceful waters of Loch Tollaidh and finally the broad expanse of Loch Gairloch as you descend towards the sea. **Gairloch** is actually a group of villages comprising Auchtercairn, Strath, Smithstown and Charlestown scattered around the inner end of the loch. The surrounding area has beautiful sandy beaches, good trout-fishing and birdwatching.

As well as a good choice of accommodation, shops and places to eat, here you'll find the **Gairloch Museum** *(gairlochmuseum.org)*. Housed in a Cold War-era concrete bunker, the displays cover life in the West Highlands from Pictish times to the present, including a faithful recreation of a crofter's cottage.

Gairloch

Join a whale-watching cruise

DETOUR: Red Point

The B8056 runs along the southern shore of Loch Gairloch, past the cute little harbour of **Badachro**. The road passes through the crofting settlements of Erradale and Opinan to end at the gorgeous pink-sand beach of **Red Point** – a perfect picnic spot.

As the road crests the hill before reaching the parking area, there's a **viewpoint** with a magnificent panorama that ranges from the Trotternish Peninsula and the Cuillin Hills of Skye to the mountains of Torridon.

A little further on look out for a small, red **Victorian letter box** cut into the solid rock on the left side of the road – a rare survival, still in use after more than 120 years.

BEST PLACES TO STAY

Badrallach Campsite, Badrallach £
Rustic campsite with a range of accommodation, including a bothy and self-catering cottage, as well as boats and bikes for hire. *(badrallach.com; open all year)*

Cartmel B&B, Aultbea ££
Comfortable, homely B&B with a wonderful welcome. Breakfast is £10 extra but well worth it. *(cartmel-guest-house.highlandshotelspage.com)*

Shieldaig Lodge, Gairloch £££
Traditional hunting lodge with antique furnishings, grand chandeliers and tasteful bedrooms, the best of which have sea views. *(shieldaiglodge.com)*

Gairloch Sands Youth Hostel, Gairloch £
Stunning coastal position, close to beaches and well set up for walkers. *(hostellingscotland.org.uk)*

Red Point

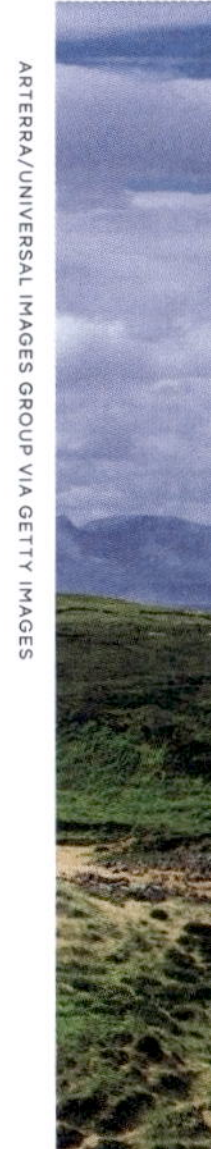

ARTERRA/UNIVERSAL IMAGES GROUP VIA GETTY IMAGES

Join a Whale-Watching Cruise

The waters of the North Minch, between Wester Ross and the Outer Hebrides, teem with marine life, from minke whales to dolphins; you might even spot orcas or basking sharks.

HOW TO

Nearest stop: Gairloch

Getting here: Cruises depart from Gairloch Harbour, at the south end of the village.

When to go: May to September is best for sightings.

Cost: from £65

Useful tip: check out *hwdt.org/species-index* for a list of whale and dolphin species you might see and how to identify them.

The seas off Gairloch, to the north of Skye, are acknowledged to be one of Scotland's hot spots for whale and dolphin spotting, with several operators offering wildlife-watching cruises. **Gairloch Marine Wildlife Centre** *(porpoise-gairloch.co.uk; Easter-Oct)* has a small visitor centre at the pier where you can browse interactive displays and chat with the knowledgable staff. During their two-hour boat trips you may see basking sharks, porpoises and minke whales. The crew collects data on water temperature and conditions, and monitors cetacean populations, so you'll be subsidising important research

The shed next door is the base for **Hebridean Whale Cruises** *(hebridean-whale-cruises.co.uk; Apr-Oct)* which runs 2½-hour boat trips to the waters around northern Skye and Raasay to look for minke whales, dolphins and porpoises, and also wider-ranging four-hour cruises to the far-flung feeding grounds around the spectacular, seabird-haunted Shiant Isles in search of orcas.

If you're pushed for time, the **Glass Bottomed Boat** *(glassbottomedboat.co.uk; £30 per person)* runs 90-minute tours to view the underwater world around the islands in Loch Gairloch.

FROM LEFT: CHRISTIAN MUSAT/SHUTTERSTOCK, KATIEHM/SHUTTERSTOCK

JL548
INS 111
Glass Bottom Boat

Gairloch

Groves of ancient Scots pine soften the Wester Ross landscape a little as the road loops east along lovely Loch Maree then back west through the jaw-dropping mountain scenery of Glen Torridon. This is a part of the North Coast 500 where I like to linger for a couple of days, exploring remote hill lochs with fly rod in hand, paddling a canoe around the islands on Loch Maree, or wandering the high ridges of the region's many Munros.

Neil Wilson

Shieldaig

37 MILES
1½ HOUR DRIVE
THIS LEG
Gairloch
Slattadale Car Park
Beinn Eighe Visitor Centre
Kinlochewe
Loch Clair Car Park
Coire Dubh Car Park
Torridon
Shieldaig
GAIL JOHNSON/SHUTTERSTOCK

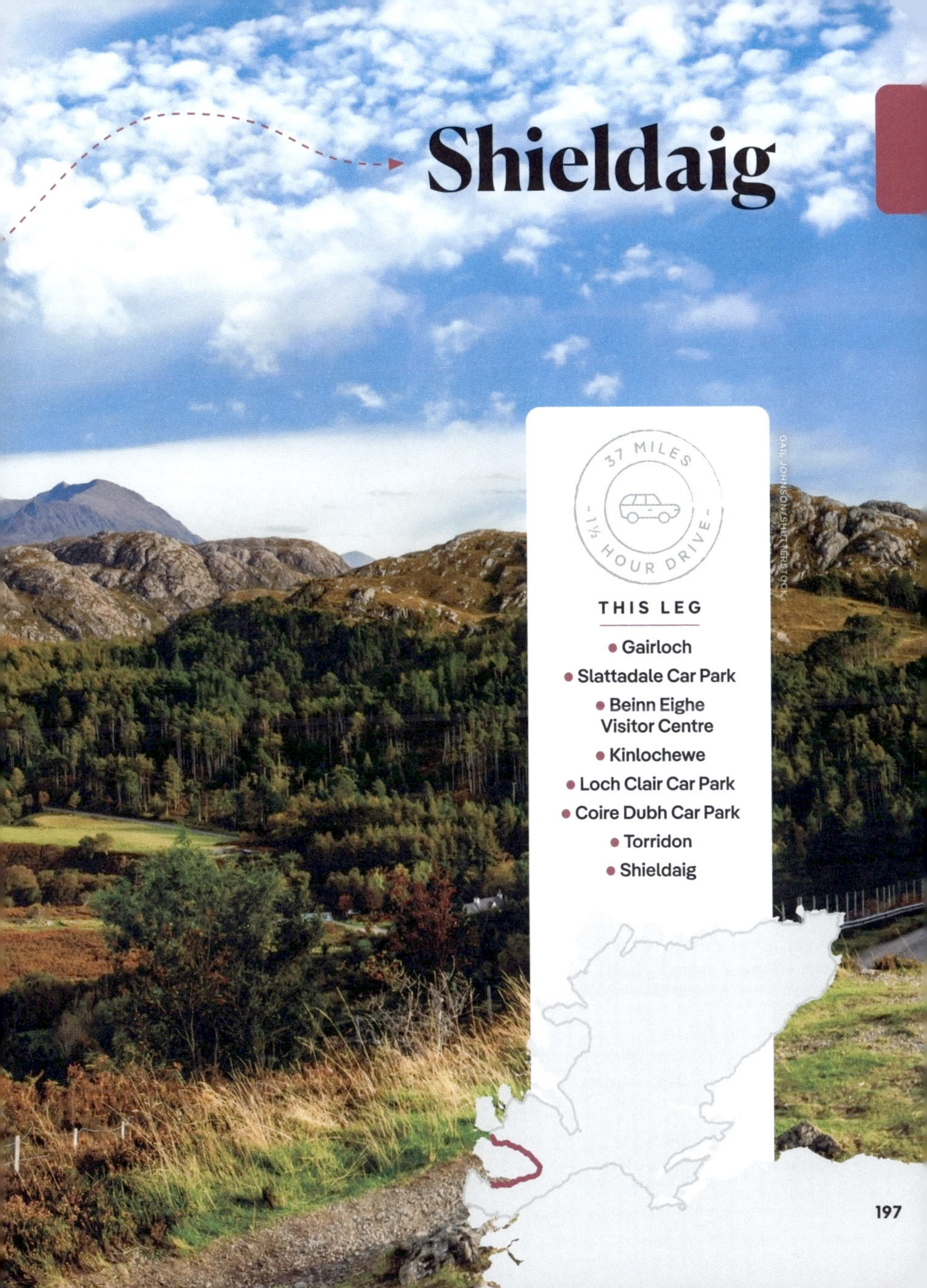

Driving Notes

This is a short leg and an easy drive; the road from Gairloch to Kinlochewe is a pleasure, and even the single-track section through Glen Torridon is easy going, with few tight bends and no real hills. Here Wester Ross turns the scenery up to 11, so take your time and try to keep your eyes on the road.

Breaking Up Your Journey

Shieldaig is an ideal overnight stop, with an excellent campsite and several B&Bs, as well as a hotel, cafe, pub and well-regarded seafood restaurant. However, Kinlochewe and Torridon are good alternative stopping places, whether for lunch or a longer pause. But the best way to break your trip is with one of the walks described here.

Neil's Tips

BEST MEAL The platter of local seafood at **Shieldaig Bar & Coastal Kitchen** (p202) is hard to beat.

FAVOURITE VIEW The classic mountain view of Liathach reflected in the still waters of **Loch Clair** (p205).

ESSENTIAL STOP Hard to pick a favourite on this leg – they're all good!

ROAD-TRIP TIP The **Beinn Eighe Mountain Trail** (p203) is a top spot for seeing golden eagles.

Gairloch, p192
Busy seaside village

START

Slattadale Car Park, p200
Views of Loch Maree

Discover a Remote Mountain Corrie, p207
Venture deep into the heart of the Torridon wilderness to experience the grandeur of Coire Mhic Fhearchair.

Loch Torridon

Diabaig, p208
Pastures, woodland and a scenic bay

Loch Shieldaig

Upper Loch Torridon

END

Shieldaig, p208
19th-century whitewashed fishing cottages

Loch Damh

N

0 5 km
0 2.5 miles

Kayak to the Loch Maree Islands, p201
Stretching for 12 miles between Poolewe and Kinlochewe, Loch Maree is one of the most beautiful in Scotland.
Loch Maree Islands
Victoria Falls
Lochan Fada
Loch Maree
Beinn Eighe Visitor Centre, p200
Information on the nature reserve
Hike the Beinn Eighe Mountain Trail, p203
This short but steep and challenging hike explores ancient Caledonian pine woodland and wild mountain terrain.
Kinlochewe, p202
Starting point to climb Slioch
Beinn Eighe
Coire Mhic Fhearchair
Loch Clair Car Park, p205
Starting point for walks
Glen Doherty, p205
Views down a U-shaped valley
Loch Clair
Loch Coulin
Coire Dubh Car Park, p205
Starting point for a mountain hike
Torridon, p206
Village with shop and cafes
Hike around Lochs Clair & Coulin, p204
This classic circuit of two scenic lakes enjoys some outstanding views of the Torridon mountains.

PREVIOUS STOP From Gairloch the route strikes inland to Kinlochewe before returning to the coast at Loch Torridon.

Slattadale Car Park

The road from Gairloch to Kinlochewe along the south side of Loch Maree is another 'Destitution Road', originally built in the late 1840s to provide work for crofters made destitute by the potato famines of that decade. It has been much improved since, of course, though it was only in 2022 that the last remaining stretch of narrow single track – two miles out of Gairloch where the road is hacked out of a rocky slope above the gorge of the River Kerry – was widened to two lanes.

Head for the **Slattadale** car park, just over eight miles from Gairloch – look out for the green Forestry sign just past a large lay-by on the left; the turn-off is 250m further on. Here there are lochside picnic tables with picture-postcard views along the loch to the majestic fortress-like mountain of Slioch (980m). A one-mile forest walk leads to a viewpoint looking out over the **Loch Maree Islands**, which can be explored by kayak from here (p201).

KAY ROXBY/ALAMY

Beinn Eighe Visitor Centre

Beinn Eighe Visitor Centre

It's a short hop – less than a mile – to another car park at the beginning of a short trail *(300m round trip)* leading to **Victoria Falls** – a scenic waterfall named after Queen Victoria, who visited here in 1877. The road continues along the shores of Loch Maree, one of the most beautiful stretches of the NC500, with ever-changing views across the loch and its islands, but dominated always by the towering presence of Slioch on the far bank.

Six miles from Slattadale you cross the **Bridge of Grudie**, built in 1972 to replace the Destitution Road bridge of 1849 which can still be seen to the left of the road. In another three miles, you pass the **Glas Leitir Trails** car park, the starting point for the Beinn Eighe Mountain Trail (p203) before reaching **Beinn Eighe Visitor Centre** *(nature.scot; 10am-5pm Apr-Oct)*. Here, you can learn all about the Beinn Eighe and Loch Maree Islands National Nature Reserve, and stretch your legs on the all-ability Pine Cone and Buzzard walking trails, which offer shorter and easier alternatives to the Mountain Trail.

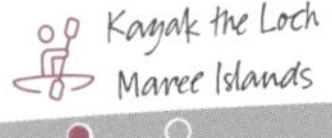

Kayak the Loch Maree Islands

Gairloch – 8.6 miles – Slattadale Car Park – 10.4 miles – Beinn Eighe Visitor Centre – 1 mile

Hike the Beinn Eighe Mountain Trail

Kayak to the Loch Maree Islands

Stretching for twelve miles between Poolewe and Kinlochewe, Loch Maree is one of the most beautiful lochs in Scotland. If you only kayak one loch on your trip, make it this one.

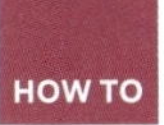

HOW TO

Nearest stop: Slattadale car park

Getting here: The only way to get to the islands is by canoe, kayak or private boat.

Cost: £120 per person

Useful tip: Bring a waterproof jacket and footwear that will survive getting wet, plus a towel and change of clothes.

More info: *gairlochkayakcentre.com*

LOCH MAREE WILDLIFE

The loch is noted for its dragonflies (more than 12 species) and birdlife – it is designated as a Special Protection Area for its breeding population of black-throated divers. Other bird species to look out for include red-throated divers, ospreys, white-tailed eagles and golden eagles.

The broad central part of the loch contains a scatter of beautiful wooded islands large and small – the **Loch Maree Islands** (part of the Beinn Eighe Nature Reserve, p203) – where some of Britain's last surviving untouched native woodland can be found. **Gairloch Kayak Centre** can arrange a full-day guided kayak trip on the loch for up to eight people; no previous experience needed.

Slattadale car park is the usual starting point, from where an 800m open-water crossing leads to **Eilean Ruairidh Mòr** (Big Rory's Island). From here you make your way along the chain of islands, exploring hidden bays and secret beaches as you go, to reach **Isle Maree** where the 7th-century Celtic missionary St Maelrubha built a monastic cell; the island and loch are named after him. There's an **ancient burial ground** here, a **sacred well** and a pagan **wishing tree** festooned with coins and rags – pilgrims would hammer a coin into its trunk or tie a scrap of clothing to a branch and make a wish.

GC STOCK/ALAMY

DUNCAN ANDISON/SHUTTERSTOCK

View of Loch Maree from Slioch

BEST PLACES TO EAT

Stag Highland Restaurant, Kinlochewe ££
Set in the Kinlochewe Hotel, an 18th-century coaching inn, serving Highland beef, venison and salmon dishes. *(kinlochewehotel.co.uk; 6-8pm)*

Wee Whistle Stop Cafe, Torridon £
Enjoy everything from a quick coffee to enticing bistro fare with views over Loch Torridon. *(9am-6pm mid-Feb–Nov)*

Nanny's, Shieldaig £
Coffee shop with a superb selection of hot lunch dishes, including smoked salmon chowder and squat lobster salad. *(nannysshieldaig.co.uk; 10am-5pm Tue-Fri, late Mar-Oct)*

Shieldaig Bar & Coastal Kitchen, Shieldaig ££
Attractive pub with waterside tables plus an upstairs dining room serving local seafood and wood-fired pizzas. *(noon-3pm & 5.30-9pm Feb-Dec)*

Kinlochewe

At the southern end of Loch Maree, you reach the tiny village of **Kinlochewe**. The name means 'head of Loch Ewe' – after the freshwater loch was changed to Maree, a few hundred years ago to distinguish it from Loch Ewe, the sea loch you passed at Poolewe. The village has a hotel, campsite, shop/post office, petrol station and cafe.

Kinlochewe is the starting point for any hill-walkers wanting to climb **Slioch** *(980m; (12 miles round trip, allow 9 hours)*, the imposing Munro that dominates the south end of Loch Maree. Although the ascent is fairly straight-forward, mostly following a good path, be warned that it is a long and tiring day, especially the return leg.

continued on p48

Kinlochewe

3.2 miles

Hike the Beinn Eighe Mountain Trail

This short but steep and challenging hike explores the ancient Caledonian pine woodland and wild mountain terrain of the Beinn Eighe National Nature Reserve.

HOW TO

Nearest stop: Kinlochewe

Getting here: Start at the Glas Leitir Trails car park beside the A832 road, 2.75 miles northwest of Kinlochewe.

Useful tip: The Mountain Trail is 4 miles long; allow three to four hours. You'll need walking boots and waterproofs – the weather can change quickly.

More info: *nature.scot/doc/beinn-eighe-nnr-visiting-reserve-leaflet*

The trail begins by passing under the road at the far end of the car park to a footbridge; don't cross it, but keep left instead (follow the marker posts and cairns with the mountain symbol). The trail climbs gradually at first, through open woodland of birch and Scots pine. After crossing a footbridge the trees thin out and soon you are climbing over bare slabs of blocky white quartzite; in places the terrain is steep and you will need to use your hands to steady yourself on occasional rocky sections.

Views of the Beinn Eighe massif open up ahead as the route reaches the Conservation Cairn, at 550m the high point of the trail. The 360-degree panorama takes in the precipitous Torridon peaks to the southwest, and the Letterewe mountains to the north. After threading its way among several beautiful lochans the path drops down below the tree line again, and joins the **Woodland Trail**, passing through ancient Caledonian pines – the oldest trees, known as 'granny' pines, are more than 350 years old – before returning to the car park.

FROM LEFT: IHOR HVOZDETSKYI/SHUTTERSTOCK, MAXBLACK/GETTY IMAGES

Hike around Lochs Clair & Coulin

If Munro-bagging is not to your taste, there are a couple of valley walks that should not be missed. This classic route enjoys some outstanding views of the Torridon mountains.

HOW TO

Nearest stop: Kinlochewe

Getting here: The walk begins at a small parking area on the right side of the A896, 3.2 miles south of Kinlochewe.

Useful tip: Do this walk in the morning to get the best light for photographing Liathach.

Beginning from the parking area on the A896, opposite the private the road to Coulin Estate (signposted 'Public Footpath to Glen Carron' by the Coulin Pass), follow the 4WD track over a bridge and along the eastern shore of **Loch Clair**. In good weather, this path provides one of the classic Scottish mountain views, reproduced countless times on postcards and paintings – the brooding hulk of **Liathach** reflected in the still waters of Loch Clair.

The route continues along the eastern side of **Loch Coulin**, following the green right-of-way signposts along an occasionally boggy footpath to rejoin a good 4WD track by the houses beyond the head of the loch. Turn right and cross the bridge over the River Coulin to the big white house, then right again (the public path to Achnashellach heads left here). The trail now follows the west side of Loch Coulin, with stunning views of **Beinn Eighe** up ahead, before rejoining the outward leg at Coulin Lodge. Total distance 5.5 miles; allow three hours.

FROM LEFT: GRESEI/SHUTTERSTOCK, DANIEL LANGE/SHUTTERSTOCK

Liathach and Loch Clair

Glen Docherty

DETOUR: Glen Docherty

In good weather it's worth making a detour three miles east of Kinlochewe on the A832 towards Inverness to the **Glen Docherty viewpoin**t. Here you get a splendid view back down the glen and along the full length of Loch Maree. It's a perfect example of what geologists call a U-shaped valley, eroded by a huge glacier 20,000 years ago rather than the tiny stream that flows here today.

Loch Clair Car Park

The mostly single-track road southwest from Kinlochewe passes through **Glen Torridon**, amid some of the most beautiful scenery in Britain.

Carved by ice from massive layers of the ancient, reddish-brown Torridonian sandstone that takes its name from the region, the mountains here are steep, shapely and imposing, whether flirting with autumn mists, draped in dazzling winter snows, or reflected in the calm blue waters of **Loch Clair** on a summer's day.

Even if you don't feel like doing the full hike around Lochs Clair and Coulin (p204), it's worth walking along the start of the route for 10 minutes to see the classic picture-postcard view of Liathach.

Coire Dubh Car Park

If you chose not to stop at Loch Clair, prepare to have your breath taken away as you crest the rise just 300m beyond the parking area. Here, as if a curtain has been drawn aside, the full majesty of Glen Torridon suddenly opens up ahead of you – the massive bulk of

THE BIG THREE

The hills on the north side of Glen Torridon – which are known as the **Big Three** – are **Liathach** (1054m; pronounced 'lee-ahakh', Gaelic for 'grey one'), **Beinn Eighe** (1010m; 'ben ay', 'file mountain') and **Beinn Alligin** (986m; 'jewelled mountain') and include six Munro summits, two on each massif.

These are big, serious mountains and the full traverse of each makes for a long and tiring but rewarding day. All three are for experienced hillwalkers only, though Beinn Alligin is arguably the easiest of the three. Hamlet Mountaineering *(hamletmountaineering.com)* and Climb Torridon *(climbtorridon.co.uk)* offer guided ascents of these summits.

4.2 miles

Loch Clair Car Park

Coire Dubh Car Park

Liathach looms ahead like a sleeping dinosaur, while to the right the quartzite screes and pointed peaks of Beinn Eighe shimmer in the sun. (If you want to take a photo, please don't stop in a passing place; continue for 800m to a short stretch of two-lane road.)

Another mile further on, a small cairn with a blue plaque on the right side of the road marks where you cross from Beinn Eighe National Nature Reserve into the National Trust for Scotland's **Torridon Estate**. Formerly a hunting estate, the 22-sq-mile property was accepted as part payment of inheritance tax on the death of its owner, the 4th Earl of Lovelace; ownership was transferred to the Trust in 1967.

Immediately after crossing a bridge, 800m beyond the cairn, you'll see the **Coire Dubh car park** occupying a raised area on the right. This is the starting point for one of the most dramatic hikes in Torridon.

Torridon

For the next four miles the road follows the River Torridon along the foot of mighty Liathach, its terraced sandstone slopes rising above in an unbroken sweep to the summit ridge almost a 1000m above. At the bottom of the glen a minor road on the right leads to **Torridon** village; it has a basic, tents-only campsite, a youth hostel, a shop and a couple of good cafes. There's an NTS visitor centre at the junction, but it's currently closed and its future is under review.

From the visitor centre a track leads west to the **Deer Enclosure** *(nts.org.uk; open 24 hours)* where you can see and photograph a small herd of red deer. The cottage across the road houses a tiny 'deer museum' which explains the history of deer management in the Highlands, alongside an impressive display of antlers.

Just east of the road junction, to the north of the road, a five-minute walk along a footpath leads to the **Celtic Jumble**. This cluster of giant sandstone blocks is one of Scotland's top hot spots for bouldering (a low-level variation of rock climbing), with hundreds of problems of all grades from easy to very difficult. If you fancy giving it a go, **Climb Torridon** *(climb torridon.co.uk)* runs half- or full-day taster sessions for complete beginners.

GILES WARHURST/ALAMY

Celtic Jumble

Torridon

7.5 miles

Go bouldering at Celtic Jumble

Discover a Remote Mountain Corrie

Beinn Eighe's most impressive feature can't be seen from the road; venture deep into the heart of the Torridon wilderness to experience the grandeur of Coire Mhic Fhearchair.

HOW TO

Nearest stop: Coire Dubh car park

Getting here: Begin at the Coire Dubh car park, 4.2 miles east of Torridon village.

Useful tip: This is a long and challenging hike; if in doubt about your abilities, hire a mountain guide.

The trek to **Coire Mhic Fhearchair** (pronounced 'corrie vik err-ekher', meaning 'the corrie of Farquhar's son') is a long one *(9 miles round trip, allow 5 hours)* but follows a well-made stalker's path all the way.

The path climbs up between the sandstone precipices of Liathach to your left and the silvery screes of Beinn Eighe to your right, before crossing a stream on stepping stones. After 2.5 miles, at a large cairn, the path forks; take the righthand branch which rises up around the flanks of Sail Mhor with fantastic views ahead to the Flowerdale hills and back towards the northern corries of Liathach.

The reward for your efforts comes into view as you approach **Loch Coire Mhic Fhearchair** – bare sandstone slabs dip beneath the crystal-clear waters, with the magnificent 300m-tall **Triple Buttresses** soaring above, three tapering towers of gleaming silver quartzite perched on a scree-skirted plinth of red-brown sandstone. In fine weather, the loch's edge is the ideal spot for a picnic lunch, perhaps followed by a wild swim, before returning via the same route.

GEOCOM/SHUTTERSTOCK

Coire Mhic Fhearchair

Along the Way We Met...

RUAIRIDH & HAZEL MACLENNAN The NC500 has been important for our business and family. We have three young children who go to the local primary school. We are grateful to each person who chooses to stay with us as it contributes to the local economy and makes continuing to live here possible. Nobody seems to do the route just once – we have so many guests who now choose to return each year. The first time round is very much a taster trip!

Ruairidh & Hazel are the owners of Shieldaig Camping & Cabins (shieldaigcampingandcabins.co.uk).

RUAIRIDH'S TIP: *If you like shellfish, we can get the fishermen to deliver that day's fresh catch direct to you when staying with us.*

DETOUR: Diabaig

West of Torridon village, a single-track road heads west along the north side of Upper Loch Torridon. Beyond Wester Alligin the road is unsuitable for caravans or large motorhomes as it climbs steeply through a landscape of knobbly crags to the Bealach na Gaoithe (meaning 'windy pass'), 250m above sea level. Towards the top of the hill, a **viewpoint** on the right commands a superb vista across Loch Torridon and its surrounding mountains.

After weaving across the summit of the pass, the road drops precipitously into the crofting hamlet of **Diabaig**, an unexpected oasis of green pastures and woodland amid rugged crags overlooking a picturesque bay. The motor road ends here, but a hiking trail continues along the coast for seven miles, past Craig bothy, to the beach at Red Point (p193). If you make it to Diabaig, the **Gille Brighde Restaurant** *(closed Mon & Tue, and Nov-Mar)* is a great spot for lunch.

Shieldaig

Although roads had been opened from Lochcarron to Shieldaig and from Kinlochewe to Torridon in the early 19th century, it wasn't until 1963 that the so-called **Balgy Gap** – the seven-mile stretch of road between Torridon and Shieldaig – was completed. The road runs along the south shore of Loch Torridon, with expansive views across the water to the peaks of Beinn Alligin and Liathach; there's a **viewpoint** with a large parking area halfway along.

Stop and take in the view over Loch Torridon

Shieldaig

Just as the main A896 road bends to the south, turn right to enter the village of **Shieldaig**, a pretty row of whitewashed cottages lining a sheltered anchorage. The village was a planned one, built at the beginning of the 19th century to provide trained sailors for the Royal Navy, then engaged in the Napoleonic Wars, although the bay had long been used as a harbour for the herring fishery (the name comes from the Old Norse 'sild vik', meaning 'herring bay'.

Shieldaig Island, just offshore, is almost entirely covered in Scots pine, thought to have been planted over 100 years ago to provide poles for drying the nets of local fishermen. The island is a haven for wildlife: herons use the trees for nesting platforms; a pair of white-tailed eagles are resident here; and seals can be seen along the rocky foreshore.

BEST PLACES TO STAY

Torridon Youth Hostel, Torridon £
Popular with backpackers, hill walkers and climbers, this great-value hostel is one of the area's best. *(hostellingscotland.org.uk)*

The Torridon, Torridon £££
A turreted castle-style former hunting lodge that's the region's most luxurious hotel – and a great spot for afternoon tea. *(thetorridon.com)*

Tigh an Eilean Hotel, Shieldaig £££
Cosy luxury with lovely sea views and an off-grid atmosphere – no TVs or phones in the bedrooms. *(tighaneilean.co.uk)*

Shieldaig Camping & Cabins, Shieldaig £
Superb campsite overlooking the bay, with great facilities (including a rustic outdoor shower) and unforgettable sunset views. *(shieldaigcampingandcabins.co.uk; closed mid-Nov–mid-Mar)*

Shieldaig

Golden eagle
SENECAS/SHUTTERSTOCK

INSIGHT

A Tale of Three Species

The wildlife of the Northern Highlands is one of the big attractions of the NC500. However, the fate of Scotland's three most iconic wild creatures is inextricably tied up with the history of the hunting, shooting and fishing estates that took over much of the Highlands during the 19th century, and with the demands of today's economy.

WORDS BY **NEIL WILSON**

Atlantic Salmon

One of Scotland's most thrilling wildlife spectacles is the sight of silver Atlantic salmon leaping the falls in a fast-flowing river, resolutely seeking a return to the same stream where they were born several years before. The salmon's life begins in early spring, hatching in the gravel bed of a burn in some Highland glen. They stay for a couple of years and then head out to sea. Their destination could be anywhere in the North Atlantic, but eventually, grown sleek and fat after several years feeding, they return home to reproduce.

It is these returning fish that have been the prized catch of salmon anglers since the early 19th century. Once the sole preserve of the wealthy owners of sporting estates, fishing for salmon on a Highland river is now open to all (though still not cheap). However, since the 1970s salmon farming has become big business, worth more than £1 billion annually to the Scottish economy and providing many jobs in remote areas. But these farmed fish are not like wild salmon. They are essentially domesticated animals, bred to grow quickly, kept in cramped cages and prone to infection with sea lice.

> The fate of Scotland's three most iconic wild creatures is inextricably tied up with the history of the Highlands' hunting, shooting and fishing estates

There has been a huge drop in the numbers of wild Atlantic salmon returning to Highland rivers in recent decades, and while climate change and competition for food sources at sea have probably played a part in this decline, many anglers and environmentalists believe that salmon farms are the main culprit. Not only do young wild fish get infected by the lice from salmon farms on their way out to sea, but every year farmed fish escape from their cages and interbreed with wild salmon, weakening the gene pool.

Along with concerns about pollution and animal welfare, this has led to the formation of Off The Table *(offthetable.org.uk)*, a campaign led by chefs and restaurants to discourage the use of farmed salmon.

Golden Eagle

Perhaps the most majestic wildlife sight that Scotland has to offer is the golden eagle, the apex predator of the Highlands. It uses its 2m wingspan to soar on rising thermals, searching for prey that consists primarily of mountain hares, rabbits and grouse. The Gaelic name for eagle is *iolaire* (pronounced yo-lehr-eh), and if you look at an Ordnance Survey map of the Highlands you'll notice plenty of place names like Creag na h-Iolaire (eagle's crag) and Cnoc na h-Iolaire (eagle's hill).

Seen as a threat to sheep, lambs and young deer, they were ruthlessly persecuted in the 19th and early 20th centuries by farmers and gamekeepers, so much so that they disappeared from most of Britain, hanging on only in the north of Scotland. Now a protected species, almost all of the 500 or so pairs known to nest in Scotland are to be found in the Highlands, preferring remote glens and open moorland well away from human habitation. It may be hard to believe, but the biggest threat they face today is still illegal shooting and poisoning, carried out by a tiny minority of gamekeepers on Scottish grouse moors.

Red Deer

The red deer, Britain's largest land animal, is present in large numbers in Scotland. You're bound to see them if you spend any time in the Highlands; in winter especially, harsh weather will force them down into the glens to crop the roadside verges. Since the early 19th century they have been managed as a sporting asset for hunting estates – visitors will pay large sums of money to stalk and shoot deer under the supervision of an experienced stalker.

The value of a sporting estate depends on good numbers of deer. But in the absence of natural predators, an unchecked deer population can damage the environment – in particular, they graze on young saplings, preventing the natural regeneration of native woodland. In lean years, food can be scarce and the animals can die from starvation in winter, so deer numbers are controlled by humane culling – upwards of 100,000 a year. It's little wonder that deer management remains a hot topic in the Highlands.

PHOTO ESSAY

Wildlife

THE NORTH COAST 500 weaves a winding trail through the least populated part of the UK, where vast expanses of moor, loch and mountain meet a spectacular storm-fretted coastline. This unspoiled landscape offers exceptional opportunities to spot wildlife rarely seen elsewhere in the country. Red deer, red squirrels and even eagles can often be glimpsed from the car, while nature reserves, such as Dunnet Head, Forsinard Flows, Handa Island, Beinn Eighe and the Loch Maree Islands, offer walking trails where patience – and a good pair of binoculars – can bring close encounters with an astonishing variety of wildlife.

Below left: The majestic golden eagle (p211) can be seen soaring above the hills in search of mountain hares.

Below: The abundant peat bogs below provide perfect habitat for the emerald damselfly.

Right: Monarch of the glen: the red deer (p211) is Scotland's largest land mammal.

FROM LEFT: ROBERT HOPE/ALAMY, TONY MILLS/ALAMY, SCOTIMAGE/ALAMY

Clockwise from left: Highland cattle offer many photo opportunities, their DNA shows that their ancestors interbred with now-extinct Ice-Age aurochs; Atlantic salmon (p210), the king of fish, can be seen leaping waterfalls in many Highland rivers; bottlenose dolphins (p43) frequent the Moray Firth near Inverness; and puffins (p98) nest on the sea cliffs around the north coast.

CLOCKWISE FROM LEFT: DOMINIC SAMPAULESI/ALAMY, DAVID CHAPMAN/ALAMY, CHARLIE PHILLIPS/ALAMY, DAVID CHAPMAN/ALAMY

Shieldaig

Applecross is one of those magical spots that lingers long in the memory, especially if you visit out of season when it's relatively quiet – the notoriety of the Bealach na Ba and the excellence of the Applecross Inn mean that the place draws lots of visitors in summer. But it's still a major highlight of the North Coast 500 at any time of year and a place I return to often. Take a last look at its hills as you leave – this is the final leg of your journey.

Neil Wilson

Inverness

GAIL JOHNSON/SHUTTERSTOCK

Driving Notes

The single-track road from Applecross village over the Bealach na Ba is the steepest and twistiest part of the NC500, with several hairpin bends and some awkward passing places – not recommended for nervous drivers! There's another short section of single track between Lochcarron and Achnashellach; after that, the rest of the way to Inverness is easy-going.

Breaking Up Your Journey

Shieldaig, Applecross and Lochcarron are all appealing overnight stops, with a range of accommodation and sleeping options. For a lunch break with local seafood consider Applecross or Kishorn. Rogie Falls is good for a final stroll before heading back to Inverness.

Neil's Tips

BEST MEAL Local langoustines served hot with garlic butter at the **Applecross Inn** (p221).

FAVOURITE VIEW Looking down the east side of the **Bealach na Ba** (p222), with the sandstone cliffs of Meall Gorm and Sgurr a'Chaorachain towering on either side of the switchback road.

ESSENTIAL STOP Applecross (p221) is the highlight of this stretch of the NC500 and not to be missed.

ROAD-TRIP TIP At the summit of the Bealach na Ba, walk along the 4WD track to the radio mast *(40 minutes round trip)* for even better views.

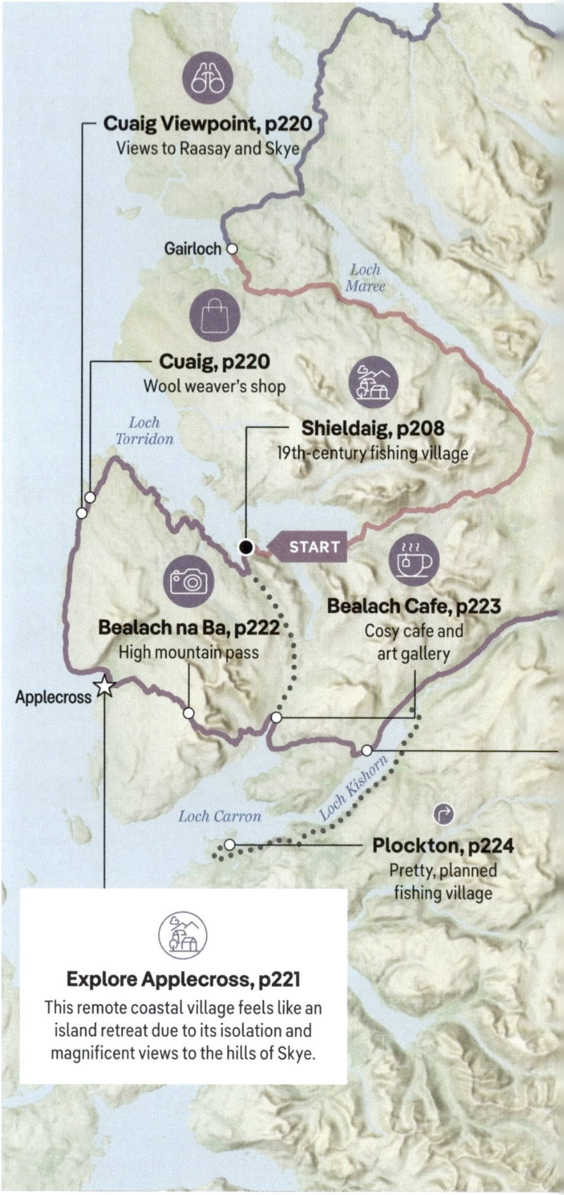

Cuaig Viewpoint, p220
Views to Raasay and Skye

Gairloch

Loch Maree

Cuaig, p220
Wool weaver's shop

Loch Torridon

Shieldaig, p208
19th-century fishing village

START

Bealach Cafe, p223
Cosy cafe and art gallery

Bealach na Ba, p222
High mountain pass

Applecross

Loch Kishorn

Loch Carron

Plockton, p224
Pretty, planned fishing village

Explore Applecross, p221
This remote coastal village feels like an island retreat due to its isolation and magnificent views to the hills of Skye.

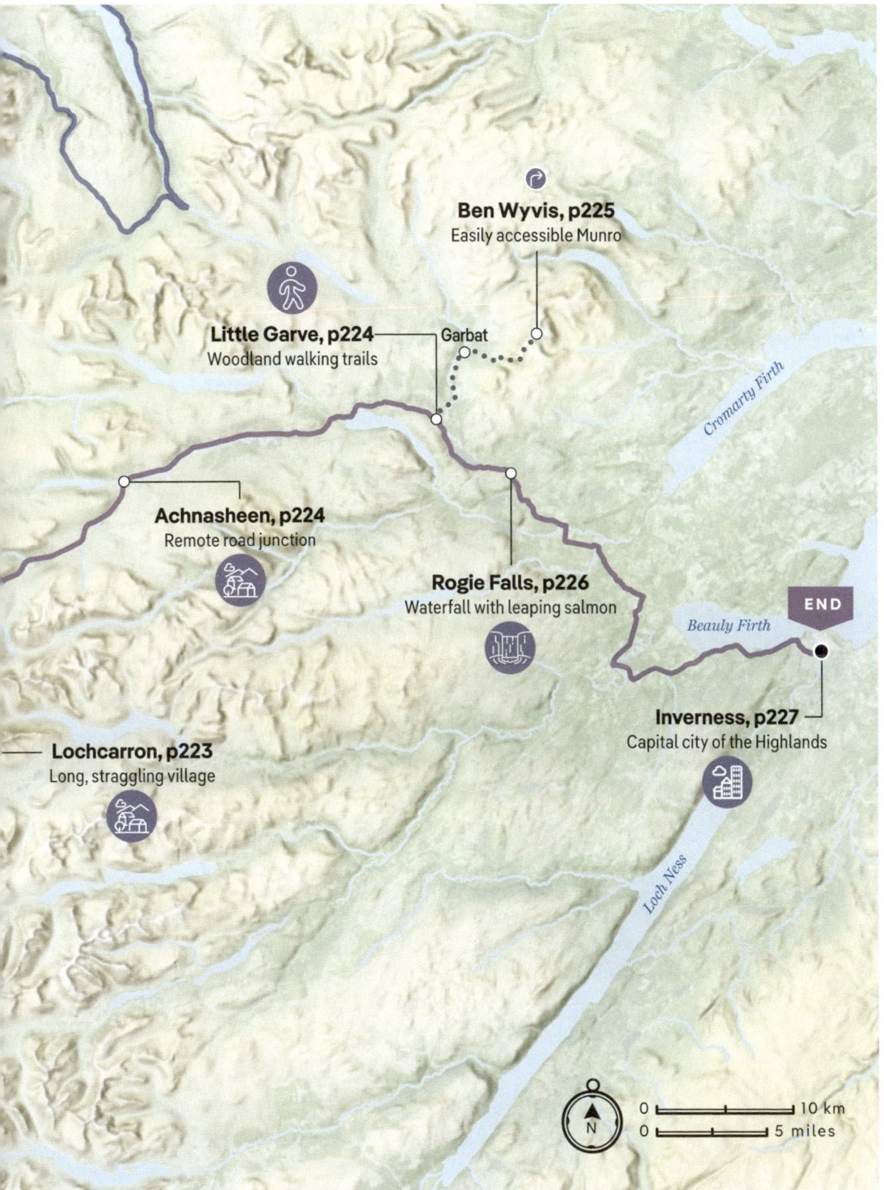

SHIELDAIG TO INVERNESS

PREVIOUS STOP The final leg of the North Coast 500 heads west from Shieldaig for a spectacular loop around the Applecross Peninsula, culminating in a drive over the notorious Bealach na Ba.

Cuaig

Decision time. If you are towing a caravan or trailer, driving a vehicle that is longer than 6m, or are of a nervous disposition, then avoid the tortuous drive across the Bealach na Ba by taking the direct route south from Shieldaig to Lochcarron along the A896.

Otherwise, buckle up and turn right a mile south of Shieldaig, signposted 'Lochcarron (Scenic Route)'. The signpost is not wrong. As the road wiggles its way along the coast, vistas across Loch Torridon to the humpbacked mountains of Flowerdale Forest give way to expansive views over the sea to the islands of Rona and Raasay and the hills of Skye beyond.

TIM GRAHAM/ALAMY

Croft Wool & Weavers, Cuaig

Keep an eye out for **Croft Wools & Weavers** *(spanglefish.com/croftwools; 10am-1pm & 2-5.30pm Tue-Sat May-Oct)*, a small wooden building with a red roof a half-mile north of the hamlet of **Cuaig**. Here you can shop for shawls, scarves and throws made from the wool of the owners' sheep, dyed using locally foraged plants and lichens.

Cuaig Viewpoint

At the roadside viewpoint a mile south of Cuaig pause to soak up one of the NC500's most breathtaking panoramas, stretching across the shimmering waters of the Inner Sound to the flat-topped cone of Dun Caan on Raasay and the serrated skyline of the Cuillin on Skye.

This section of road around the coast from the A896 to Applecross village was built to provide an alternative to the Bealach na Ba that was regularly blocked by snow in winter, cutting off the villagers for days at a time. It was completed in 1976, making it the youngest part of the NC500. If you're on a bike, cyclists generally agree that the 24 winding miles of coastal road, with its never-ending ups and downs, is harder work than the long but steady climb over the Bealach na Ba.

Applecross

Six miles south of Cuaig you pass the prominent sandy bay known appropriately as **Sand**, a good place to stretch your legs (there's a

Shieldaig — 14.4 miles — Cuaig — 1.1 miles — Cuaig Viewpoint — 9.8 miles — Hilly road that will test cyclists' thighs — Applecross — 5.3 miles

Explore Applecross

The coastal village of Applecross feels like an island retreat due to its isolation and the magnificent views of Raasay and the hills of Skye. On a clear day it's an unforgettable place.

HOW TO

Nearest stop: Applecross

Getting here: The village is 25 miles from Shieldaig via the coastal road, or 20 miles via the spectacular Bealach na Ba.

Useful tip: Book a table if you want to eat at the Applecross Inn; if you can't get one, there's a food truck opposite the inn that serves fresh seafood.

More info: *applecross.org.uk*

Applecross – not just the village but the whole peninsula – is a special place.

Since 1975 this former private estate has been run by the **Applecross Trust** whose stated mission is 'the preservation for the public benefit of the Applecross Estate, thereby maintaining its unique and historic character'.

The focus of the estate is 18th-century **Applecross House**, about a mile north of the village, a whitewashed hunting lodge built for the Mackenzies of Applecross. It's not open to the public, but you can visit the colourful **Walled Garden** and walk the nearby woodland trails. Across the river, near the old church, the **Heritage Centre** *(applecrossheritage.org.uk; noon-4pm Apr-Oct)* has all you need to know about local history.

Many travellers choose to make an overnight stop here to grab the opportunity of dinner at the **Applecross Inn** *(applecrossinn.co.uk; noon-8.30pm Thu-Mon, 3-8.30pm Wed)*. The inn is famous for its food, mostly daily blackboard specials that concentrate on local seafood and venison. It also has half a dozen snug bedrooms, all with a view of the Skye hills and the sea.

Applecross Inn

FROM LEFT: SHANE LOPES/SHUTTERSTOCK, ROBERT ORMEROD FOR LONELY PLANET

car park at the start of the private road that leads to the Ministry of Defence's BUTEC torpedo testing range). The prevailing westerly winds have blown the pale pinkish sand into a dune that stretches way up the hillside above the beach.

South of Sand the road rounds a point to reveal the broad inlet of Applecross Bay with the white houses of Applecross village (p221) visible on the far shore. At the back of the bay you cross the Applecross River, once known as the Crossan; the name of the village is an Anglicised version of the old Pictish *aber crossan*, 'mouth of the River Crossan'. In Gaelic, Applecross is known as *A'Chomraich*, or 'the sanctuary', because it was so hard to reach in the past.

D K GROVE/SHUTTERSTOCK

Bealach na Ba

APPLECROSS BY BIKE

The Bealach na Ba is the third-highest motor road in the UK (after Glenshee and the Lecht) and the longest continuous climb, rising from sea level to 626m in just six miles. As such, it's a popular challenge for road cyclists, and is the high point of the annual **Bealach na Ba Sportive** *(bealachsportive.com)*. The classic route starts and finishes in Shieldaig, and runs clockwise over the Bealach and down to Applecross village, finishing around the coastal road via Cuaig – a punishing and seemingly never-ending roller-coaster of a ride.

Bealach na Ba

The road between Applecross village and the A896 crosses the famous **Bealach na Ba** (the pass of the cattle), perhaps the most notorious part of the NC500. It started life as a footpath used by monks and pilgrims, but by the 17th century had become a drove road – a very rough track used to drive cattle from Applecross to market in Muir of Ord. In the 1820s it was made into a proper gravel road, with hairpin bends, stone bridges and culverts, to serve horse-drawn vehicles, but did not get a tarmac surface until the 1950s. It remains narrow single track, twisting and steep (20% in places) with big drops on one side, and is not for nervous drivers (caravans, large motorhomes and learner drivers should avoid it).

The climb from the Applecross side begins innocuously enough through green fields, but

White-knuckle ride down through the hairpins

6.1 miles

Pause to look backwards for the views over Skye

Bealach na Ba

Along the Way We Saw...

THE CIOCH: On the way down from the Bealach na Ba you can pause at the bridge over the Russel Burn and look up the glen to see the blunt tower of Torridonian sandstone known as the Cioch. A classic rock climb called the Cioch Nose, first ascended by Tom Patey and Chris Bonington in 1960, follows the near-vertical skyline and continues up the ridge above. I first climbed this route, graded Severe, as a teenager, and repeated the adventure in 2024 to celebrate my 65th birthday; an epic day out!

NEIL'S TIP: *Climb Torridon (climbtorridon.co.uk) offers guided ascents of the Nose for anyone with basic experience of rock climbing.*

Neil Wilson

soon enters desolate moorland; there are a couple of tight bends as the angle kicks up, but nothing extreme. Soon you reach a large parking area at the summit of the pass, 626m above sea level. The view back west towards Skye is superb, but ahead there's no inkling yet of the drop on the far side.

Bealach Cafe

A half mile past the summit car park the road bends to the right and suddenly the hillside falls away in front of you (there's space to park and gawp just before the first hairpin). From here the road descends sharply via three tight hairpin bends – stay in low gear, take the hairpins wide and try to ignore the drop. Keep an eye out for cars coming uphill (they have right of way); if necessary pull into a passing place and wait. Soon the angle eases a bit and you are coasting down the last few miles to the junction with the A896. Reward yourself with cake and coffee at the **Bealach Cafe & Gallery** *(thebealach.co.uk; check website for opening hours)*, and say hello to the friendly resident dogs.

Lochcarron

Turn right on to the A896 which sweeps around the head of **Loch Kishorn**, an inlet of the sea whose deepwater harbour is home to a fabrication yard for oil production platforms. Soon you pass the bright blue timber cabin that houses the Kishorn Seafood Bar (p225) before climbing through a narrow rocky defile and descending into the long, straggling village of **Lochcarron**. It's a veritable metropolis in these parts, with a supermarket, post office and two petrol stations. A long shoreline footpath at the loch's edge provides the perfect opportunity for a stroll.

DETOUR: Plockton

A 15-mile detour leads along the south shore of Loch Carron to the idyllic village of Plockton. The first eight miles of this single-track road were built in 1970 to replace the ferry across the loch at Stromeferry. It's squeezed between the railway and a steep slope plagued by rockfall; the most unstable part is protected by Britain's only road avalanche tunnel.

With perfect cottages lining a perfect bay, Plockton looks like it was designed as a film set, and in fact it *was* designed – planned around 1800 by Sir Hugh Innes as a fishing and crofting village, and has served as a film set – scenes from *The Wicker Man* (1973) were shot here. There's no denying its appeal, with 'palm trees' (actually hardy New Zealand cabbage trees) lining the waterfront, a thriving sailing scene, and several good places to stay, eat and drink.

BUCCHI FRANCESCO/SHUTTERSTOCK

Plockton

Achnasheen

After leaving Lochcarron you are on the 'home stretch', heading east back towards Inverness. The first 6.5 miles from Strathcarron Junction to Achnashellach is single track, but the rest of the route is a good two-lane road. After a rather dull drive through the thick woods of Glen Carron, you emerge into open moorland and reach the remote road junction at **Achnasheen**. The roundabout here dates only from 1998, replacing the road junction and bridge just to its west, which was built by Thomas Telford in 1815 as part of the road from Garve to Lochcarron; there's a **memorial plaque** by the bridge.

With a dozen houses, one hotel and a railway station, Achnasheen barely counts as a village, but is well worth a stop for a coffee break at the **Midge Bite Cafe** *(check facebook.com/midgebitecafe for opening hours)*.

Little Garve

If you have restless kids in the car, the forestry car park at **Little Garve** provides welcome respite. Turn left at the T-junction with the A835 (signposted Ullapool), then after 400m turn right on a minor road (signposted Little Garve); follow this for 800m (keep left at the fork) then turn right at the green forestry sign for Little Garve. From the car park you can walk across **Little Garve Bridge**, built around 1762 as part of a military road from Contin to Poolewe, to reach **Wyvis Natural Play Park** *(garve.org/wyvis-play-park; open 24hrs)*. This woodland adventure playground has climbing structures, swings and a zip wire, and is the starting point for a 2-mile round-trip hiking trail along the Black Water River to **Silver Bridge** (built in 1812), a scenic spot above a waterfall.

Achnasheen

Look out for the old bridge over the River Bran

16 miles

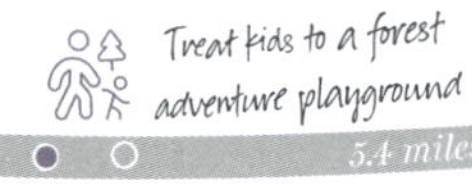

Treat kids to a forest adventure playground

5.4 miles

Little Garve

BEST PLACES TO EAT

Walled Garden Cafe & Restaurant, Applecross ££
Delicious menu of small bistro plates served in a colourful garden. *(noon-3pm Tue-Fri & Sun, to 8pm Sat mid-Mar–Oct)*

Kishorn Seafood Bar, Kishorn ££
Roadside cabin between Kishorn and Lochcarron, serving the freshest of local seafood simply and well. *(kishornseafoodbar.co.uk; noon-3pm & 6-8pm Mon-Fri, noon-3pm Sun Mar-Oct)*

The Bistro, Lochcarron ££
A fine-dining spot where you can watch the chefs at work from your table. Reservations required. *(tel: 07449-575509; 5-10.30pm Wed-Sat, 4-9.30pm Sun late Mar–late Dec)*

DETOUR: Ben Wyvis

The easily accessible Munro of **Ben Wyvis** (1046m) looms to the northwest of Strathpeffer (the name Wyvis derives from a Gaelic word meaning 'enormous'). The mountain's eastern corries hold snow for much of the year, fortunately for the ancient Munro clan of Foulis Castle – their lands were granted on the condition that they paid the king the annual rent of one snowball in midsummer.

The peak is usually climbed from **Garbat**, to the west of Strathpeffer on the A835 to Ullapool. The hike to the summit is straightforward in summer, about five hours' return from Garbat; use OS map No 20 and carry plenty of food and drinking water (there's no ground water on the hill). Stout footwear is essential as some of the tracks through the forest can be extremely wet.

Ben Wyvis

ANGUS ALEXANDER CHISHOLM/SHUTTERSTOCK

ZOONAR GMBH/ALAMY

BEST PLACES TO STAY

Hartfield House, Applecross £
Spacious hostel and bunkhouse accommodation in a former hunting lodge, with a boot room and drying room for hikers. *(hartfieldhouse.org.uk)*

Applecross Inn, Applecross £££
Seven snug bedrooms above the famous restaurant all have a view of the Skye hills and the sea. *(applecrossinn.co.uk)*

The Old Manse, Lochcarron ££
Elegant traditional guesthouse in a quiet lochside position; ask for a room overlooking the water. *(theoldmanse lochcarron.com)*

Rockvilla Hotel, Lochcarron ££
Twin and family rooms with sea views, and a restaurant that is renowned for its local scallops. *(therockvillalochcarron.com)*

Rogie Falls

The NC500 route continues southeast from the junction with the A835 (so retrace your steps if you visited Little Garve), passes through the scattered village of Garve and parallels the Inverness to Kyle of Lochalsh railway line along the shores of Loch Garve. About three miles out of Garve you'll pass **Tarvies Cafe** *(7am-3pm Mon-Fri, 9am-3pm Sat & Sun)*, a roadside pit stop serving hot breakfast and lunch (including vegan options), coffee and cake.

A mile further on look out for **RogieFalls car park** *(pay and display, £3/4 for up to*

Rogie Falls

24 miles

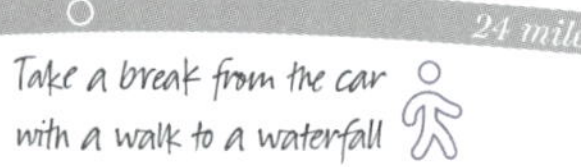

Glen Ord Distillery

2-4 hours; public toilets Apr-Oct) on the left. An easy hiking trail leads down to the Black Water River where a suspension footbridge provides a photo-worthy view of the waterfalls. From August to October, this is a good place to see salmon leaping on their way upstream to spawn in the headwaters.

Inverness

A mile or so beyond the falls car park, you pass through the village of **Contin** and emerge from the wild scenery of the west into the rounded hills and lush farmland of Easter Ross. A left turn at the far end of the village offers a two-mile detour to **Strathpeffer** (p49), if you missed it on the way north.

A right turn onto the A832 towards Muir of Ord, 1.5 miles past Contin, takes you across the River Conon via **Moy Bridge**, a single-lane iron structure dating from 1894.

After a few more miles, the industrial buildings and tall chimney stack of **Glen Ord Distillery** mark your arrival in Muir of Ord where, at the junction with the A862 on the other side of town, you rejoin the outward route for the final 15-mile run back to Inverness (p32).

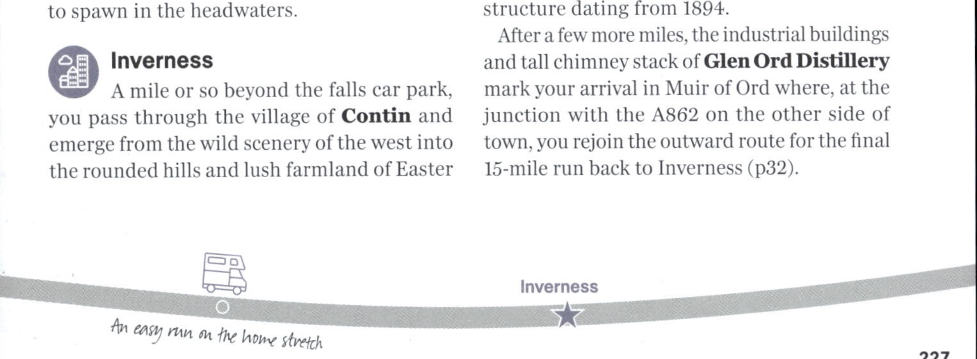

Inverness

An easy run on the home stretch

Toolkit

Applecross Inn (p221)
ROBERT ORMEROD FOR LONELY PLANET

First Time

For more information on arriving, see **Inverness** (p32)

PHOTO ID

Don't forget your ID (passport or driver's licence) when checking in to hotels and for buying alcohol – even if you're over 18.

SMOKE-FREE SCOTLAND

The Scottish government is working towards a smoke-free generation. Smoking in enclosed public places (such as bars and restaurants) is strictly prohibited.

TIME ZONE

The time zone in Scotland is GMT/UTC in winter, GMT/UTC+1 during daylight saving.

ETA Visa Waivers

Since April 2025, everyone wishing to travel to Scotland and the rest of the UK – except British and Irish citizens – requires an electronic travel authorisation (ETA) or visa. An ETA is a digital permission to travel and is quick and simple to apply for. It costs £10 and permits multiple journeys to the UK for stays of up to six months over a two-year period. Apply online or via the app: *apply-for-an-eta.homeoffice.gov.uk*.

Health Insurance

For necessary medical treatment, citizens of the EU, Switzerland, Iceland, Norway and Liechtenstein receive free or reduced-cost, state-provided healthcare coverage with a European Health Insurance Card (EHIC) issued by your home country. Each family member needs a separate card. Everyone else is advised to carry a valid health insurance policy.

Language

The Scottish Highlands is the traditional realm of Gaelic speakers, and while the language is seeing a resurgence at schools, and in art, literature and music, English is universally spoken. Learning the meanings of historical Gaelic place names will add to your understanding of the landscape – and they're a fixture on road signs and at many sights.

Phones & Wi-Fi

Scotland is firmly planted in the 21st-century, but telecommunications and wi-fi coverage in the far north of the country can, at times, feel stuck in a different era. Due to the rippling landscape of hills and heathlands, 5G and 4G phone service is intermittent on the road and it can often be hard to pick up any signal. Reliable wi-fi is best found at the NC500's hotels, guesthouses, hostels, cafes and restaurants.

TOUCHR/SHUTTERSTOCK

INSPIRATION

Find tips, branded NC500 merch and itineraries, from food and drink to history and archaeology, at *northcoast500.com*. There are also podcasts to inspire you, special offers and promos (if you sign up to its newsletter, of course).

ELECTRICITY 120V/60HZ

Type G 230V/50Hz

Money

Budget

The NC500's popularity has led to a surge in pricing in recent years, from an increase in motorhome hook-ups to more expensive meals at restaurants. There is still a range of options for all budgets, but factor in the remoteness of the destination, cost of transporting products and the limited availability of accommodation, and hotel stays and meals can cost more than in Edinburgh or Glasgow. A budget of about £300 per day for two people is a good estimate.

HOW MUCH IS a day on the NC500?

Coffee & snacks	£12
Museum/Castle entry	£30
Distillery tour	£50
Lunch at a cafe	£24
Hotel room	from £75
Dinner in a restaurant	£60
Drinks in a pub	£14
Parking	£0
Petrol per day	from £20
Car hire per day	from £20
Total (per day for two adults)	**from £305**

TIPPING

As a rule of thumb, tipping isn't expected in Scotland and is usually reserved for particularly good service. Around 15% is more than adequate.

Money-Saving Tips

Drive in the low season May to September: the busiest and most expensive months. November to February: more competitive accommodation rates, quieter roads and more space to explore.

Cheaper rentals Cut-price cars, camper vans and motorhomes can often be found outside of Inverness. Renting a car directly from the airport can also cost fractionally more. Shop around for the best price.

EV vs fuel The NC500 has a decent charging network and can save you 500-plus miles of expensive diesel or unleaded fuel.

THE NC500 ROUTE-DISCOUNT SCHEME

The official NC500 website *(northcoast500.com)* offers a variety of discounts around the route for all members for a £15 joining fee. Benefits include discounted car hire and 2-for-1 distillery tours.

Cards & ATMs

Outside of the NC500's major population centres (Inverness, Wick, Thurso, Ullapool), there are no banks; in this part of the world, drop-in, mobile branch services are the norm, not ATMs. Major credit cards are almost universally accepted and contactless is as common as cash. To be safe, take enough local currency to see you through all eventualities.

Free Attractions

The bulk of things to do along the NC500 are natural and (naturally) free. In fact, if outdoor adventures and landscapes are your primary motivation for coming, then you could well drive the whole loop without spending a penny. In some cases, the only charge will be for parking. Make sure to do so as the communities rely on every pound to help further invest in local services.

ALEXANDER V EVSTAFYEV/SHUTTERSTOCK

On The Road

GOOD TO KNOW

Drive on the left

Speed limit is 60mph on the majority of the NC500

Speed limit is 30mph in built-up areas and towns

Driver's Licence

Foreign visitors are allowed to drive any small type of vehicle, including cars, motorhomes and motorcycles in Scotland on a non-Great Britain licence. An International Driving Permit (IDP) is often necessary to hire a car in other countries, if rarely asked for, but this is not the case in Scotland. All you need is a full driver's licence and have been driving for at least 12 months.

Lay-By Etiquette

Much of the NC500 is on minor, single-track roads with lay-bys to let oncoming traffic pass. It takes a little getting used to, but the rules of the road are simple. Drive slower than you would on a two-lane road. Anticipate what is coming towards you in the opposite direction. Pull over at a safe distance to make space on the road. If you're in a motorhome or campervan, let any traffic building up behind you pass – nothing irritates locals more than being stuck behind slow-moving NC500 vehicles.

Drink Driving (or Cycling)

There is a zero-tolerance policy for driving a car or cycling while drunk in Scotland. The legal limit is 50mg of alcohol per 100mL of blood, or 22 micrograms of alcohol in 100mL of breath. This equates to around one drink. The best advice is to not drink anything.

HOW TO FUEL UP

Many petrol stations along the NC500 are self-contained community hubs, doubling as grocery stores. There are some, however, that are open 24hrs a day, with automated credit-card pay screens. To avoid anxiety, make sure to always fuel up in the major urban centres, as there are no options on the roads in-between.

Should I travel by car or motorhome? The hardest question to answer. A car will give you more freedom and speed, but at a cost (unless you're camping rather than staying in hotels or guesthouses). The NC500 roads were never built to handle motorhome traffic and, as a result, are often narrow, winding and hard to manoeuvre. If you're not used to driving a large vehicle, it can be daunting, especially with the mix of road users, from cyclists and buses to farm vehicles to heavy goods lorries. You'll also have to accept that you could be the cause of the traffic congestion, not the other way around.

How many miles can be covered each day? Always plan to drive less and see more. By placing deadlines on each day, you open yourself up to making up for lost time by taking risks on the road – and that's when accidents happen. The nature of the roads means it will almost always take longer than you think to reach your next stop. Remember that elective, unplanned breaks are part of the joy of the NC500 in the first place.

What hazards should I look out for on the road? Chiefly, wildlife. This is deer country, with estimates suggesting there are up to 1 million in total living wild throughout Scotland. They are a roadside hazard, particularly at dawn and dusk, and drivers should be extra vigilant if there are wildlife warning signs.

STEVE ALLEN/SHUTTERSTOCK

HOW TO

CYCLE THE NORTH COAST 500

The NC500 makes a great – if at times challenging – cycling route and enables you to take in the grandeur of the Highlands at a more leisurely pace. It's becoming increasingly more popular, especially from April to October, when there's plenty of daylight and the chance of some warmer temperatures.

Bike Rental

You'll find a range of rental options across the NC500 route, from Hi Bikes in Inverness that you can easily unlock using a smartphone app, to shops with a hire fleet and dedicated bike-hire centres.

Depending on what kind of ride you'd like to do, make sure you've got the right type of bike. For example, city rental bikes are excellent on flatter urban streets, but may be a slog on longer rural loops or if you're heading off-road.

A hybrid is generally good for most riding, as it can handle both on- and off-road cycling, as well as giving a comfortable position with flat handlebars.

SOLSTOCK/GETTY IMAGES

Cycling, Torridon (p206)

E-Bike Rental

Many bike-hire outlets will also offer e-bikes. The added electrical assistance can really take the sting out of steeper hills, especially in more undulating areas.

Modern e-bike technology means that you won't need to charge the bike during the ride, as battery range tends to be very good. If you're planning to hire an e-bike for multiple days, then you'll most likely be provided with a battery charger, which simply plugs into mains electricity.

Bear in mind that e-bikes are generally heavier than standard bikes, so you may need a specialist car rack to transport them.

OTHER GEAR

Acknowledging that most people don't travel with their own helmet or puncture-repair kits, these are usually on offer at bike-hire centres, either included in the price of bike rental or for a small supplement. Child trailers, tag-a-longs and child seats are also commonly available for family riding.

HOW MUCH TO HIRE...

a pedal bike **from £20**

an e-bike **from £45**

CYCLING TIMES

SECURITY

Whether you're using your own bike or hiring one, take sensible steps to reduce the risk of theft. Never leave your bike out of sight without a lock. If you do need to leave it somewhere, for example outside a cafe or museum, use a high-quality lock. Look for a Gold or even Diamond Sold Secure lock rating.

WEATHER

While Great Britain doesn't tend to have devastating natural disasters, bar localised flooding events, the day-to-day weather can be very unpredictable. Blue skies can quickly turn to downpours and winds can whip up out of nowhere. Be prepared by taking extra warm layers, gloves and waterproofs with you, just in case.

BREAKDOWN

If you suffer a mechanical issue with your bike, you have a number of options. Most bike-rental outlets will be able to help if you call. Alternatively, find your way to a local bike shop or flag down a fellow cyclist who may be able to assist. A taxi back to the nearest town is your last resort.

Where to Stay

Campsites

Once, the north coast of Scotland had limited campsites offering few facilities. Now, motorhome and caravan parks almost overwhelm parts of the region. Expect to pay anything between £12 and £30 per touring pitch, including water, electricity, waste and refuse disposal. For those with a tent, there's also a wide choice of campsites. Wild camping is permitted throughout the country – to be a respectful visitor, only cook using a stove and leave no trace behind.

Farm Stays & Glamping Pods

Often found in the unlikeliest of locations, the latest trend on the NC500 is for farm stays and farms offering pricey glamping cabins. Many are tagged as 'luxury' accommodations, but frequently the only luxury is the location, as most are straightforward 'hobbit' houses. The joy is the sense of tranquillity and many offer as little as two to three pods or cabins – so getting away from the crowds is almost guaranteed.

Hostels

Travel in the quietest season (November to February) and stay in the biggest towns for the largest selection of accommodation options and more competitive prices. Hostels are few and far between on the NC500, but those that do exist offer the best value accommodation on the coast. They're money-savers by nature, but they're also community-orientated and a great way to support the local area at a grassroots level.

Bothies

If hiking off the main NC500 route, particularly on the northwest coast, then lucky you if you stay in a bothy – it's a uniquely Scottish form of free, rustic, shelter-style accommodation. Many are off-grid, almost closely guarded secrets, requiring long walks or bike rides to reach their locations. The **Mountain Bothies Association** *(mountainbothies.org.uk)* manages nearly 20 on the NC500, all in the north and northwest between Thurso and Inverness.

FROM LEFT: NDSIGN/SHUTTERSTOCK, NEW AFRICA/SHUTTERSTOCK

Access, Attitudes & Safety

Travel with Children

Driving Every car-hire company will provide an appropriate child seat, as these are required by law. Costs vary from as little as £1 a day to £10+ for an entire trip. The main thing to consider before coming with children or even a baby is: how much driving can your children handle?

Eating out Children are welcome everywhere on the NC500. Bear in mind that special kids' menus are all too commonly uninspiring (fish and chips, chicken nuggets etc).

Child concessions often apply for museum and castle admission fees as well as tours. Don't forget to ask before booking.

The Case for Independence

The topic of nationalism in Scotland can be a divisive topic. Ever since the 2014 Scottish independence referendum, the country has largely been split 50/50 between wanting to remain part of the UK and leaving to take charge of its own affairs. It remains a political hot potato and, while most people will be happy to share their opinion with you, it can lead to furrowed brows and heated debate.

Travellers with Disabilities & Accessibility Needs

Attractions The main lure of the NC500 is the road itself, so, in the right vehicle, travellers with disabilities won't feel like they are missing out. However, the very nature of some attractions, like Duncansby Stacks, Smoo Cave and many of the west coast beaches, will be inaccessible.

Wheelchair access By law, all public buildings should to have made 'reasonable adjustments' for people with disabiities. However, this isn't always the case: veer on the side of caution and call ahead to confirm the accessibility situation.

Campsites There are campsites along the coast with tailor-made facilities for travellers with disabilities

Guides and tours Visit Scotland *(visitscotland.com)* and Euan's Guide *(euansguide.com)* are two great resources for travellers with disabilities.

Women & Solo Travellers

Women and solo travellers should not encounter any particular problems on the NC500. This is a sparsely populated area, where quiet roads and hiking trails are the norm, but there are also low crime rates, and communities are largely safe and trouble-free. Perhaps the only area of concern as a solo traveller should be the amount of driving to do – and lack of a fellow map-reader to blame if you take the wrong turn. Also, be sure to let others know if you are planning a potentially risky outdoor activity that will take you far from any of the roads – just in case you have an accident.

LGBTIQ+ TRAVELLERS

Scotland is one of the most gay-friendly and progressive countries in the world, and the large majority of travellers will encounter open-armed welcomes in every community, no matter how small. Like anywhere, however, prejudice and discrimination do still exist, so travel smartly. For more information on LGBTIQ+ rights and support services in Scotland, visit *lgbthealth.org.uk* and *lgbtyouth.org.uk*

PASTA DESIGN/SHUTTERSTOCK

Responsible Travel

Overtourism

Overtourism is the biggest issue facing the NC500. An increase in visitor numbers has led to a number of problems, from a rise in irresponsible wild camping to traffic congestion to a spike in accidents, as well as rubbish and waste discarded by the roadside. The problem is so acute, there is talk of some of the more popular sections being withdrawn from the official NC500 in a bid to discourage visitors. Thankfully, there are a number of ways in which you can help work towards a better solution for everyone...

WILD CAMP, THE RIGHT WAY

Wild camping is only permitted in Scotland when travelling by foot or bike. The law does not apply to vehicles such as campervans or motorhomes. If coming by motorhome, you must use designated sites along the route.

Sign the Pledge

To help combat overtourism, communities along the NC500 ask every traveller to sign a pledge *(northcoast500.com/visitor-pledge)* aimed at encouraging responsible behaviour. The idea is that by embarking on your NC500 journey you are not simply on the road for a memorable adventure, but are buying in to a long-term commitment to protect the region for the future.

Have a Positive Impact

Support local communities You'll have more memorable experiences and encounters if you shop from farm stores, not supermarkets, and take tours from insightful guides rather than heading out by yourself. Every community along the NC500 needs investment and this is the best way you can help. The Balnakeil Craft Village in Durness is open from April to October and there is no better place to meet local craftspeople.

Don't stick to the main route There are highlights at every turn, so consider detours and roads off the main coastal loop to see parts of the NC500 that the majority rarely see.

Dispose of waste wisely If there is no bin, take your rubbish with you. If bins are full, don't be tempted to leave it behind. As the marketing board behind the NC500 says: 'Give your litter a lift, take it home!'

Stick to the Scottish Outdoor Access Code The NC500 landscape is truly wonderful, begging you to spend as much time as possible in it – but only if you do so responsibly. Access rights include a host of activities like walking, cycling, climbing, horse riding, kayaking, swimming and watching wildlife. Recreations like shooting or fishing, however, aren't allowed and neither is access with motor vehicles. Find more info at *outdooraccess-scotland.scot.*

HEMIS/ALAMY

Balnakeil Craft Village, Durness (p130)

FROM LEFT: SERAPHP/SHUTTERSTOCK, JW.PHOTOGRAPHY31/SHUTTERSTOCK

Campervan, Bealach na Ba (p222)

RESPECT THE ROAD

The NC500 is only a decade old, but the communities on the route have been here for thousands of years. Often there is only a single-track road with no alternative, and this is used by school buses, post buses, ambulances, farmers and pedestrians – there is no pavement. These roads are lifelines for each community and should be used considerately – never as a race track.

Campervans: Dos & Don'ts

With limited accommodation and budget worries, the number of people driving the NC500 in a campervan has surged. There are crucial rules to follow when travelling responsibly.

- **Do** pull in to a passing place to allow traffic to safely pass if you are travelling below the speed limit.
- **Don't** travel in a convoy, especially on small roads, and always travel at least one passing place apart from the vehicle ahead of you.
- **Do** stay in the largest towns, not in remoter campsites, putting less strain on the NC500's fragile infrastructure.
- **Don't** be a dirty camper. Dispose of your black-water waste in the correct place.

Climate Change & Travel

It's impossible to ignore the impact we have when travelling; Lonely Planet urges all travellers to engage with their travel carbon footprint, which will mainly come from air travel. While there often isn't an alternative, travellers can look to minimise the number of flights they take, opt for newer aircrafts and use cleaner ground transport, such as trains. One proposed solution – purchasing carbon offsets – unfortunately does not cancel out the impact of individual flights. While most destinations will depend on air travel for the foreseeable future, for now, pursuing ground-based travel where possible is the best course of action.

The **UN Carbon Offset Calculator** shows how flying impacts a household's emissions

The **ICAO's carbon emissions calculator** enables visitors to analyse the CO_2 generated by point-to-point journeys

Index

Map pages **000**

Map pages **000**

Map pages **000**

Notes

Notes

Notes

Notes

THIS BOOK

Destination Editor
Amy Lynch

Production Editor
Claire Rourke

Assisting Editors
Mani Ramaswamy, Clifton Wilkinson

Book Designer
Gwen Cotter

Cartographer
Daniela Machová

Illustrated Map
James Gulliver Hancock

Cover Illustration
Matt Saunders

Product Development
Anne Mason, James Smart, Marc Backwell, Katerina Pavkova

Series Development Leadership
Darren O'Connell, Piers Pickard, Chris Zeiher

Thanks
Ronan Abayawickrema, Sofie Andersen, Melanie Dankel

Paper in this book is certified against the Forest Stewardship Council™ standards. FSC™ promotes environmentally responsible, socially beneficial and economically viable management of the world's forests.

Published by Lonely Planet Global Limited
CRN 554153
1st edition – Sep 2025
ISBN 978 1 83758 664 6

10 9 8 7 6 5 4 3 2 1
Printed in China

Mapping data sources:
©Lonely Planet, ©OpenStreetMap, ©Natural Earth, ©GEBCO, ©Esri, ©NASA Earth Observatory, ©USGS-ASTER and the GIS User Community

Acknowledgement:
North Coast 500 and NC500 are registered trademarks within UK and Europe of North Coast 500 Limited